Millwall FC Since 1987

Roars, Growls, Whimpers & Groans

Millwall FC Since 1987

Roars, Growls, Whimpers & Groans

**David Hall, Richard Lindsay
& Eddie Tarrant**

TEMPUS

Frontispiece: Millwall supporters flocking into the 2004 FA Cup final at Cardiff.

First published 2005

Tempus Publishing Limited
The Mill, Brimscombe Port,
Stroud, Gloucestershire, GL5 2QG
www.tempus-publishing.com

British Library Cataloguing in Publication Data.
A catalogue record for this book is available from the British Library.

ISBN 0 7524 3706 2

Typesetting and origination by Tempus Publishing Limited
Printed in Great Britain

Contents

The Authors

I was fourteen when I told my father I wanted to visit all the London football clubs and, living at The Borough, Millwall, being just a Number 21 bus ride away, was the obvious place to start. I cannot remember who the Lions were playing that day – it was either Hull or Watford – but they won and now, some forty years later, despite various distractions, I am still here, watching with my family in the Family Enclosure. I have written for the Millwall Matchday Programme for many years.

David Hall

I have supported the Lions since 1958 and have rarely missed a game since. I joined the Post Office on leaving Samuel Pepys School. I helped Jim Murray with *Lions of the South* and was encouraged by Jim to do further research of the club's statistics. This was accomplished while recovering from surgery, and resulted in *Millwall FC: A Complete Record*, published in 1991. Since the late 1980s I have supplied various information and statistical updates to the club's programmes.

Richard Lindsay

I was born in Lambeth in 1956, and have been a Millwall fan from the age of six. I lived in East Dulwich until I was ten when my parents moved to Downham, where I later met my wife Sally. We now live in Eastbourne with our three sons Daniel, Jonathan and Michael and still go to Millwall as often as we can. The stats shown in this book are from a database that I have compiled and Millwall currently use.

Eddie Tarrant

Acknowledgements

When you are sitting at a keyboard for endless hours there is always a need for refreshment and I would like to acknowledge the endless supply of drinks and food that my wife Winnie supplied for me as well as her proofreading over my shoulder. There were many times when she spotted a mistake or two.

For someone who could not understand the obsession that is watching men chase a ball around a football pitch and preferred watching old films from the comfort of her armchair, especially on those wet and cold afternoons, she certainly changed after her first match – away at Watford. Now a season ticket holder herself, wild horses could not drag her away from The Den. Thanks also go to my daughters Danielle (whose programme collection proved invaluable in remembering some of the games), Charlene and Eloise, my son Alex and son-in-law Scott, all of whom have spent many hours in all kinds of weather watching the Lions with Winnie and me, adding their own roars or groans, and to my grandson Arron and granddaughter Ciana, who have just started to join us and will soon understand what following the Lions is all about. Thanks also go Jeff Burnige for writing the foreword to this book.

David Hall

My very special thanks go to Maureen Neicho-Lindsay for her computer work. Sadly Maureen passed away before she could see the published work. Thank yous go to: Brian Tonks for the use of his photographs, Eddie Tarrant and the family for computerising my original research and making this update possible, David Hall for bravely taking on the considerable task of following in Jim Murray's footsteps, bringing *Lions of the South* roaring into the twenty-first century, Chris Bethell, David Webster, Graham Tonks, Tom Green, Mike Ford. John French, Jim Creasey, Adrian Wisson, Dave Sullivan, Melvin Smith, Ted Wilding, my family and friends for their support at this difficult time, Janet and Paul Williams, Vivien Lindsay, Mark Talbot, Danny, Alicia, Krystina, Daniella, Cameren and Kyle. We are still pursuing the Millwall FC museum project. If you can help visit www.millwallmuseum.co.uk or www.millwallmuseum.com.

Richard Lindsay

I would like to thank Richard Lindsay for his help over the years, but especially my wife Sally and sons Daniel, Jonathan and Michael for their help, patience and understanding.

Eddie Tarrant

Foreword

I am delighted to have the honour of welcoming the publication of this superb book. It was also my privilege to write a foreword to Jim Murray's classic club history *Lions of the South* in 1987, and it strikes me that this is the right time for the sequel.

Being a Millwall supporter is an intense and emotional experience for us, and while the highs are paradise, the lows seem like hell. I was absolutely sure in 1987 that great highs were coming, and they certainly did. Millwall had not long returned to the second tier of English professional football, which we had visited several times before. Now we feel we belong there and have realistic hopes of reaching the top flight as we did in 1988. We have been as close as the play-offs three times, and I am personally convinced that we will make the Premiership one day soon. I feel we have waited long enough.

There is no need for me to list the highs covered in this book. They are obvious to most of us. However, the FA Cup semi-final was the experience of a lifetime for my family and I feel the final was the well-deserved dream reward for all of our supporters, the most underrated and misrepresented group of people I can imagine.

I ask you to enjoy the memories in this book, and hang onto the dream.

Jeff Burnige

Introduction

When in future times, historians ask about the life of football supporters, their feelings of joy or despair, their pleasure or pain, their highlights and disappointments, then all they have to do is look at this book.

Supporters of Millwall FC have run the gamut of every emotion that can be found in a lifetime of following a football club. All the highs and lows from promotions and relegations to near extinction are covered in the last eighteen years.

Although we have included a potted history of the club from its inception, those details are well documented elsewhere. Here we are concentrating on seasons 1987/88 to 2004/05.

We have tried to include the viewpoints of the club, local and national newspapers and of course our own, but naturally we may not see things the way you do and you might feel that we should have highlighted events that only got a passing mention or were left out completely.

However, only so much can be included in an eighteen-year history of the club and inevitably some things will be left out, so we hope that you will read this book and consider it a reasonable record of what happened to the club during those years.

The authors have contributed in various ways in producing the book. Eddie Tarrant oversaw the statistics with Richard Lindsay, who also provided the milestones of players and managers and the club's early history, along with the various photographs. David Hall primarily provided the words.

David Hall, Richard Lindsay, Eddie Tarrant

In the Beginning
1885-1987

During the summer of 1885 a group of young men, mainly workers at Morton's Preserve factory in West Ferry Road (Isle of Dogs), decided to form a football club as a continuation of their social activities, already having a cricket and cycling section.

The new club was named Millwall Rovers FC and the club's headquarters was at The Islanders beerhouse in Tooke Street and the landlord's son, J.J. Sexton, was chosen as the secretary.

The club's colours were dark blue shirts and white shorts, mainly because of the Scottish connections of both Morton's and those workers who transferred south when the company opened their factory on the island. The first ground used was a patch of waste ground nearby.

Such was the enthusiasm of both players and supporters of the fledgling team that a ground was found near to the Lord Nelson. This pub stands at the junction of East Ferry Road and Manchester Road, and North Greenwich Station (Island Gardens) was nearby.

Having an enclosed ground enabled the Rovers to enter the prestigious FA Cup, London and Middlesex Senior Cups and the East End FA Senior Cup, which was won in three successive seasons and is now owned by the club.

Millwall Rovers were getting stronger and attracting better players with each passing season. However in 1889 the club received a year's notice to quit the ground and in the April of that year a meeting was convened where the club members resolved to continue and seek a new ground to play on.

The architect behind the club's survival was William Henderson, whose unstinting work behind the scenes as secretary of both the old Millwall Rovers and the new Millwall Athletic ensured survival. He contacted local businesses for donations, notably William Clark of The George who put up £100, a considerable amount of money in those days. Later he was instrumental in setting up the Southern League.

The new enclosure was also in East Ferry Road but more in the heart of the island, on land owned by the Millwall Dock Company. The area was enormous compared with the Lord Nelson ground. Tennis, cricket, cycling and athletics meetings were held there. Although The George was the new headquarters, dressing rooms were built as well as a grandstand, something that could not be done at the previous ground due to lack of space.

The new Millwall Athletic opened the Athletic Grounds with a friendly against fierce rivals London Caledonians on 6 September 1890, the result a 1-1 draw. With the board of directors and a perceived healthy income through improved facilities and attendances, rumours abounded in the press that Millwall Athletic were now a professional club, but the catalyst for turning professional came about three years later.

In 1891 the club had received a coveted invitation to be one of eight clubs to enter the London Charity Cup but, in the competition of 1893/94, a dispute arose as to the charitable distribution of the gate monies. Millwall felt that more should be allocated to the island, as they were the best-supported club in the competition but this was not forthcoming, so the club withdrew and turned professional on 4 December 1893, carrying on their fund-raising for local hospitals and charities through certain games each season.

Millwall Rovers with the East End Senior Cup. This cup was won three times between 1886 and 1889. From left to right, back row: Mr Hughes, T. Jessop, H. Gunn, H. Butler, J. Myerscough, Mr Henderson (Secretary). Middle row: J. Shave, J. Fenton, J. Musgrove, T. Pitt. Front row: H. Warner, J. Reeves, D. Hean.

Controversy was never far away from Millwall. They first used a substitute, Arthur Burton, in January 1892 when the unlucky Tom Horne broke his leg during a London Senior Cup game and at the end of the following season, during the game against West Bromwich Albion, the Military Police arrived to arrest Hyslop for being absent without leave from his army unit. Sensibly they waited until the end of the game.

In April 1894, during the last game of the season, Obed Caygill, the club's longest-serving player and captain, suffered a broken leg that ended his career. Caygill was the first of Millwall's exceptional goalkeepers; he was denied an England cap because of rumours about the club's amateur status.

The first attempts at forming a Southern League had failed; in those days the Football League comprised of clubs from the Midlands and the North of England only, but two years later the resourcefulness of William Henderson finally paid off and the new league commenced for the 1894/95 season.

The club's first game resulted in a 9-0 victory over Swindon Town on 29 September 1894. Willie Jones, a very talented and quick player, had the honour of scoring Millwall's first ever League goal and, when scoring the winning goal in the Isle of Wight Cup final in March 1899, he paid the ultimate price. Trying to beat the advancing goalkeeper they collided, and Willie died later that night of internal injuries.

Having won the inaugural Southern League title it was retained the following season with a solitary defeat after going 32 games in the Southern League unbeaten.

The club also entered the United League for the 1896/97 season, during which the record win for any league game was achieved, 12-0 over Wolverton, the railway works team. John Calvey scored five times in that match and he held the club's goalscoring record until Teddy Sheringham took the total in all competitions to 111 goals in 1991.

The first substitute in a league game was used when Archie McKenzie came on for the injured Joe Davies in the 6-5 win over Tottenham Hotspur. Davies later became Millwall's first international, playing for Wales in March 1897.

The championship of the United League was won on the last game: a 2-0 away victory at Loughborough enabled Luton Town to be overtaken.

During 1898/99 the club's most prolific goalscorer, John Calvey, created a number of club records. He reached 50 Southern League goals at Spurs in April 1899 and against the same club, in a United League fixture, he notched up his ninetieth goal in all competitions. The 3-1 win was Millwall's last game in that league, and also secured the championship for that season.

During the 1899/1900 season the nickname of the Dockers was about to be replaced by the much more inspiring title of the Lions.

FA Cup success had so far eluded Millwall. Not once had they passed the first round after battling through the qualifying rounds. But 1899/1900 was about to change all that as they progressed to the first round by beating Clapton, Chatham and Thames Ironworks in the qualifying rounds.

The first round draw gave Millwall the worst possible tie; a trip to Jarrow in the North-East. But this was overcome with a 2-0 victory. The second round produced the same result at Queens Park Rangers and next came a match against the Football League champions, Aston Villa, for a place in the semi-final. After two drawn games the tie was settled 2-1 in Millwall's favour at the neutral venue of Reading.

The newspapers had given Millwall the title 'Lions of the South' because of their FA Cup exploits and so the Lions were born. Unfortunately Southampton put an end to the cup run by winning 0-3 in the semi-final replay.

Also in 1899/1900 the club had entered the Southern District Combination and achieved a unique hat-trick of success. They had won the championship of each new league they entered at the first attempt.

However this ended when they finished runners-up in the Western League in 1900/01. As this season was ending the Lions received notice from the Millwall Dock Company that they must leave the Athletic Ground. The company needed the land to build timber storage sheds. So again Millwall found themselves homeless, and again players left the club thinking the adventure had ended. By July a new, somewhat cramped, venue was acquired and somehow, in the next two months, a potato field was turned into a football ground. It was organised by Elijah Moore, who found many helping hands from the local population and those players still being signed who thought Millwall Football Club had a future.

This ground was still on East Ferry Road, back towards the Lord Nelson, and behind the railway viaduct, through the arches of which supporters entered the ground. The ground was referred to as North Greenwich, as the station of that name was the nearest to the club, although in the club's first two official handbooks the address is given as simply East Ferry Road. It was also around this time that the 'Athletic' had been dropped from the club's title, although the press continued to use it, as did Obed Caygill's 'Krect Kard', which was sold on match days.

Aston Villa were invited to play the opening game on 18 September 1901, a game that resulted in a 2-0 victory for the Lions.

1902/03 saw the resurrected club reach the FA Cup semi-final again. This time they played three games against Bristol Rovers, who were finally beaten 2-0 at Villa Park. Luton Town were defeated 3-0 and then Preston North End 4-1 and Everton 1-0, all at North Greenwich. This meant a return to Birmingham for the semi-final against Derby County. History repeated itself, however, as the players were below par and succumbed to another 0-3 semi-final defeat.

The following season the Lions won the London League without losing a single game but the cupboard was then bare of silverware until the Western League was won in February 1908 with the championship retained the following season.

The FA Cup replay against Woolwich Arsenal in 1910 brought home to the directors the shortcomings of the tight enclosure and the difficulty of the supporters in getting onto the island.

The two main roads had swing bridges, which would hold up travellers to allow shipping into the docks. The trains would be crowded as far as Poplar Junction station and then, with smaller-sized carriages, the dock trains were described as 'cattle trucks'. The decision to move south of the river Thames came as no surprise but brought about heated debate in the local papers. The last game on the island was a 1-0 victory over Woolwich Arsenal in the London FA Challenge Cup.

This competition had been introduced in the 1908/09 season when the London professional clubs were readmitted as members of the London Football Association. Millwall were the first winners of this trophy, beating Leyton in the final.

In those bygone days it was unusual for players to stay more than a couple of seasons at any club and only eight players made over 200 competitive appearances for Millwall. Topping the list was goalkeeper Tiny Joyce (385) as the era north of the river Thames ended.

Also at the end of this period in the club's history, Billy Hunter, Dick Jones and Alf Twigg all made valiant attempts to match Calvey's goal-scoring achievements. Jones reached 85 in all competitions and Twigg got to 88, but he did manage to beat Calvey's Southern League goals tally by two.

Although the move to The Den, Cold Blow Lane, New Cross, was a financial success, the playing side was at times woeful, which led to the Lions having to win the last game of the 1910/11 season to avoid a first ever relegation. Thankfully, they breezed past Southampton 4-0.

The directors appointed Bert Lipsham as Millwall's first professional manager; since 1890 various directors had been given the title honorary team manager: Fred Kidd, Edward Stopher and George Saunders.

The Kent FA Senior Shield was won in 1912/13 and 1913/14 followed by the London Challenge Cup in 1914/15. Joe Wilson had established a club record of 123 consecutive Southern League appearances between 1911 and 1915 and Millwall's Welsh international star, Wally Davis, had improved Alf Twigg's Southern League goal tally to 67, but fell seven goals short of the all-competition total of 98.

The First World War brought an end to Southern League Football until 1919 and the London clubs formed the London Combination in 1915 for the duration of the war.

Millwall's players gave five per cent of their wages to the Prince of Wales' War Relief Fund and the unmarried men enlisted, as The Den became a recruiting centre on match days, allowing servicemen in for free.

The Lions had two runners-up spots during this time, mainly due to the scoring power of Wally Davis with 70 goals in 62 games. His career was ended by a wartime injury; he tried a comeback but was forced to retire in January 1919.

Four players were killed in action: C. Green, G. Porter, J. Williams and J. Dines, who had won an Olympic gold medal in 1912. Bill Voisey returned a hero, his bravery having gained him a Military Medal, a Distinguished Conduct Medal and the Croix de Guerre. He played for England against Wales in a 1919 Victory International.

The return to peacetime football in 1919/20 was Millwall's last in the Southern League, and a new signing, Jim Broad, became the first player to score over thirty goals in a Southern League season, although only Wilson managed to get onto the list of over 200 appearances and Davis to the top ten goalscorers chart.

In 1920 Southern League First Division clubs were elected to the Football League in the Third Division (South). This was an amazing turn of events as the top half of the Southern League was equal to, if not better than, the Northern and Midland-dominated Football League Second Division.

A gradual improvement in league form occurred during the 1920s. During the 1926/27 season, Alf Moule notched the club's Football League goalscoring record of 66 goals.

The season started with Richard Parker netting five times in the 6-1 win over Norwich City and he finished with a hat-trick in a match with the same scoreline at Crystal Palace. It was the Lions' record Football League away win.

Parker became the first Millwall player to score over thirty goals in a Football League season – reaching 37 in total – a record that still stands today, as does his total of 38 in all competitions. John Landells came close with 33 the following term as the Lions scored a record-breaking 127 goals in winning the Third Division (South) title.

This revival was based on Robert Hunter's ability to keep a good nucleus of players together who, until the early 1930s, formed the backbone of the team. Unfortunately as these players gradually left, not enough talent was sufficiently nurtured to keep the Lions in the Second Division.

During this time both Richard Hill and Len Graham achieved over 300 Football League appearances and Jack Cock extended the Football League record to 77 goals for the club, although he too fell short of Calvey's record of 98 goals in all competitions.

Robert Hunter died in office at The Den on 29 March 1933 and relegation occurred the following season. Bill McCracken, who took over in April 1933, found Hunter a hard act to follow and left in 1936 to make way for Charlie Hewitt, who also became secretary, until he left under a cloud in the summer of 1940.

Hewitt was responsible for the Lions' resurgence of the late 1930s. He put Reg Smith in charge of installing electricity at the ground and Millwall also erected a huge clock, which was the largest at any football ground in the country.

Captain and England international Len Graham, one of the club's great players, pictured in 1927.

Under Hewitt, Millwall were the first Third Division side to reach an FA Cup semi-final, beating Aldershot 6-1 away from home, which was a club record. They also beat Gateshead 7-0 at home, which equalled another club record. Fulham, Chelsea, Derby County and Manchester City were all beaten at The Den along the way.

Nevertheless it was not to be third time lucky. Despite Millwall scoring first and playing well, Sunderland won the semi-final 1-2. Before the game there was some controversy when the Football Association announced the venue for the game was to be Huddersfield, much nearer Sunderland than London, and needless to say Millwall's protest failed.

Hewitt followed this up by clinching the Third Division (South) championship by winning the last game, at Exeter, 5-1, after being a goal down.

The 1939/40 season was three games old when the Second World War broke out and these games were made void. Jimmy Forsyth had become the third player to go over the 300 Football League appearance mark, eventually extending the figure to 321, and Bill Voisey took over as manager in June 1940 as well as being the club's trainer.

He invited numerous youngsters to The Den for training sessions in the search for young footballing talent from the area. Even so, he had to play in at least one League fixture himself at the age of fifty.

The various wartime leagues were now on a regional basis and stayed that way until 1946. Owing to the new threat of air raids, limitations were put on the size of crowds and the games at The Den against Crystal Palace and Luton Town were both unfinished even though the results stood. Guest players often became a necessity to fulfil fixtures.

All of Millwall's players were involved in some sort of war work. They were either ARP, firewatchers, auxiliary police or physical training instructors with the armed forces.

In 1941 a dispute arose over the distance of travelling to some fixtures so the eleven London clubs, plus Aldershot, Reading, Brighton, Portsmouth and Watford resigned from the Football League. Happily the differences between the rebel clubs were settled in time for the start of the 1942/43 season.

This season brought more heartache for the club and fans. During April, The Den was bombed and then, a week later, after a hasty clear-up operation had enabled the London FA Senior Cup final to go ahead, the grandstand was completely destroyed by fire. This forced the Lions to share premises at The Valley, Selhurst Park and Upton Park.

Millwall celebrated their homecoming with a 5-0 victory over Portsmouth in March 1944 and later that year Voisey reverted to trainer with Jack Cock installed as manager.

Just over a year later the club were celebrating a War Cup semi-final win over Arsenal. A goal by Jimmy Jinks won a game in which Arsenal missed two penalties, but the club's first visit to Wembley saw a disappointing game and a 0-2 defeat by Chelsea.

The Illderton Road end floodlight offers a very precarious vantage point to watch the Lions knock Newcastle United out of the FA Cup.

Wartime football had many problems. For instance, on a trip to Spurs at around this time, the players' coach broke down and they had to finish the journey in the back of a sand lorry. Reg Smith, George Williams and Fred Fisher all made wartime international appearances but Fred Fisher was killed in action when the Lancaster bomber, in which he was the rear gunner, was shot down over France in July 1944.

Millwall resumed peacetime football for 1946/47 under manager Jack Cock in a devastated ground, with no grandstand, the grand old clock in ruins, and no roofing over the terraces. This all had an effect on attendances and of course the gate money.

In 1948 Charlie Hewitt returned as manager after a major boardroom upheaval brought an end to the Thorne family's rule, but the next season saw the Lions finish at the bottom of the Third Division (South) and, although there was a small revival in the early 1950s and promotion was narrowly missed in 1952/53 with the Lions in second place, from then on it was downhill to the Fourth Division, which had been formed in the 1958/59 season.

There was some excitement to be had in the FA Cup. The Lions unluckily lost at home to both Fulham and Manchester United by the only goal and achieved a major giant-killing feat by beating Newcastle United 2-1 in a fourth round tie at The Den in 1957. Unfortunately Birmingham City ran out 1-4 fifth round winners in the February.

John Shepherd also broke Alf Geddes' club record by scoring 15 FA Cup goals, a record that had stood for over fifty years.

Ex-player Reg Smith was brought in as manager in 1959 and his shrewd tactics saw the Lions off to a tremendous start to the campaign, creating a Fourth Division record of nineteen games unbeaten from the start of the season. However, with eleven of the games as draws, Millwall were only in second place by November and dropped to fifth by the end of the season.

The following season new signing Peter Burridge equalled Richard Parker's club record of 38 goals in all competitions in a single season, but defensive frailties saw the Lions again just miss out on a promotion spot.

Due to financial problems at the club Reg Smith left and Ron Gray took over and led Millwall to the Fourth Division championship of 1961/62. During this season Accrington Stanley had to resign and had their playing record deleted. Millwall's top scorer, Burridge, was sold to Crystal Palace, due to the same money worries that had led Reg Smith to leave. It was to produce many irate letters to both the local and London newspapers.

Ron Gray was released in November 1964 after the Lions had got off to an abysmal start and were glued to the bottom of the Third Division. Billy Gray took over and revamped the club from youth level upwards, setting the scene for a productive conveyor belt of young talent. Unfortunately the Lions suffered relegation when Barnsley secured the point they needed with a 2-2 draw at Queens Park Rangers, after being two goals down.

The 1964/65 season saw a startling reversal of form: Millwall were defensively sound, conceding only 45 goals while scoring 78. Gray had introduced a healthy blend of experience and youth, which continued throughout the next season and culminated in another runners-up place, this time in the Third Division.

Millwall also were unbeaten at home in the League for two seasons, and created a new Football League record of 59 undefeated matches. Unfortunately Billy Gray resigned after being criticised by a director and, though the players persuaded him to carry on, he left when promotion was assured. Goalkeeper Alex Stepney joined Chelsea and then Manchester United, winning most of the game's top honours.

Benny Fenton, who replaced Gray, had the same managerial talent and continued the renaissance, consistently keeping the Lions in the top half of the Second Division. His signings of Burnett, Possee and Weller in the summer of 1967 made Millwall a potent attacking team.

Brian King also joined at this time from Chelmsford City and became recognised as probably Millwall's best ever goalkeeper. He also broke Stepney's club record of 137 consecutive Football League appearances for a goalkeeper, extending it to 168 games.

Derek Possee went on to break Jack Cock's long-standing club record of Football League career goals with the Lions, taking his total to 79.

There was more heartbreak at the end of 1971/72 as Millwall were pipped for second place in the Second Division when Birmingham City won their last game. Unbeaten at home, the inability to win away had cost the Lions dearly. During this period Harry Cripps broke all previous appearance records for both Football League and all competitions.

After a wonderful nine years in charge, Benny Fenton left in October 1974 after a poor start. Gordon Jago was unable to stop the decline and the Lions found themselves playing back in the Third Division in 1975/76. But promotion was quickly gained when Crystal Palace failed to win any of their games in hand. For the first time in many years Millwall also had some success in the cup competitions, reaching the quarter-final of the League Cup before losing 2-0 at Villa Park in 1976/77.

In the last game of this season Dave Mehmet, at the age of sixteen, became the club's youngest Football League player, coming on as a substitute in the 2-0 victory over Burnley.

The following season the same stage was reached in the FA Cup when Millwall lost to Ipswich Town. Crowd troubles marred the match when late-arriving Town fans were escorted to an already packed part of The Den. This resulted in the ground being closed and the League game with Bristol Rovers taking place at Portsmouth.

After a poor league campaign, in which George Petchey had taken over from Jago, it all came down to the last home game in May 1978, which had to be won to avoid relegation. This was achieved with a 1-0 win over Mansfield Town.

The same disastrous situation occurred the following season when just seven wins after Christmas meant relegation. Millwall's youth side won the FA Youth Cup for the first time by defeating Manchester City in May 1979 and many of those players appeared at first-team level in the coming seasons.

Then, in the late 1970s and early 1980s, the closing of the docks and affiliated industries tore the main supporter base out of the club as families moved from the area amid redevelopment. Asda and the club sought permission for a ground development and supermarket on the site of The Den. This was quietly shelved and Asda then developed a site in East Ferry Road. The irony was that the new superstore was built on Millwall Athletic's old ground on the island.

After the end of Jago's three-year reign as manager, he resigned and went to America. George Petchey and then Peter Anderson managed the club and both lasted less than two years in charge.

Barry Kitchener became the first player to make over 500 Football League appearances; he also passed the 600-appearance milestone in all competitions by the time he retired from playing in 1982.

George Graham took over in December 1982 with Millwall deep in a relegation mire that once again hinged on the last game of the season. A penalty by Dave Cusack at Chesterfield saved the club from the drop to the Fourth Division. Millwall did, however, win their first national cup competition, the newly created Football League Trophy, which was open to all league clubs.

Most of the club's poor league positions were due to a lack of away victories; only 16 came in the last 115 games since demotion in 1979 so in 1984/85 it was nice to see that there were eight wins on the road allied to another campaign unbeaten at home. This saw the Lions climb into the runners-up slot in the league behind Bradford City and reach the FA Cup quarter-finals with splendid victories over Crystal Palace, Chelsea and Leicester City before unluckily bowing out to Luton Town amid appalling crowd scenes.

Top scorer was Steve Lovell with 21 League goals to his credit, who became the first player to top twenty goals in a season since Alf Wood in 1973/74.

In the aftermath of the Luton cup tie crowd restrictions and all-ticket games in 1985/86 nearly achieved what the authorities seemed to have wanted: the demise of Millwall Football Club. But a new company was formed to save the club from extinction once again. This season was one of consolidation and, at the end of it, George Graham left to join Arsenal and fellow Scot John Docherty took over.

The 1986/87 season was poor on the goalscoring front. Twelve away goals was a record low for a Football League season but it also saw the arrival of Teddy Sheringham, who was top scorer with 13 out of a total of 39. Things could only get better!

In Search of the Holy Grail
1987/88

Having finished the previous season sixteenth in the division it was now time to make that extra push for promotion to the First Division. Manager John Docherty and his assistant Frank McLintock, who Docherty had persuaded back into football, were determined to use the money provided by chairman Reg Burr and his fellow directors to buy the players to make that push.

In came forwards Tony Cascarino (a £200,000 buy from Gillingham), George Lawrence, who cost £160,000 from Southampton and Kevin O'Callaghan, whose return to The Den saw £80,000 move to the South Coast at Portsmouth.

Defender Steve Wood was bought from Reading for £85,000 and midfield player Wesley Reid joined the club on a free from Arsenal. Only Micky Nutton had left the club and Docherty felt sure that this was the squad who would finally make the break out of the Second Division.

Pre-season friendly matches, where the Lions lost only one of the eight played, 1-3 away to Chelsea, boded well for the club.

It was also a season that would see a football first, the first sponsorship deal between a football club and their local council when Lewisham put their name, and money, on the players' shirts.

Only Cascarino and Lawrence of the new signings found themselves in the team for the opening match of the season, when the Lions travelled to Middlesbrough on 15 August. The surprise in the team was the inclusion of eighteen-year-old defender Sean Sparham, thrown in at the deep end because of injuries. An equaliser to Teddy Sheringham's twenty-eighth minute goal with just fifteen minutes left in the match foiled a deserved win and perhaps it was inevitable that Terry Hurlock became the first Millwall player to be shown the newly installed yellow cards. This also proved to be Dave Mehmet's last game for the club as Les Briley replaced him because of injury after just twenty-seven minutes.

Three days later a Darren Morgan goal in a 1-1 draw away at Leyton Orient in the League Cup was the base for a move into the next round. The advance was secured with a 1-0 win in the return match a week later. The goal, scored in the bottom corner after a fifty-yard run by Lawrence, was the beginning of 'Chicken George' establishing himself as a favourite with the fans.

Sandwiched between these games was the first home match of the campaign against Barnsley. This match saw the Millwall debut of summer signing Steve Wood, replacing injured captain Alan McCleary, and although the Lions ran out 3-1 winners they were made to wait until ten minutes into the second half before Cascarino scored his first goal for his new club. Goals from Sheringham and Lawrence completed the scoring.

This match also gave the fans their first sighting of the new floodlights and blue seats that had been installed in part of the stand, neither of which helped to protect them from the torrential rain that accompanied the match.

A 0-1 defeat away at Leicester failed to curtail the aspirations of the team. In fact only the outstanding display of Leicester goalkeeper Ian Andrews stopped the Lions taking something from the game.

A home match against Birmingham – a game billed as the first big test of Millwall's promotion potential – brought August to a close. Despite conceding a fourth-minute goal, the Lions won the match 3-1 with what the newspapers called 'an enthralling brand of soccer', although it was only in the last ten minutes that the points were finally made safe.

'We all had to catch our breaths as we left the scene,' wrote sports reporter Peter Cordwell. 'Millwall could make it to the First Division and there could be a lot of excitement on the way.'

However September started with the team at exactly mid-table in the league and a 1-3 defeat away to Bradford did nothing to enhance their promotion credentials.

They moved into eighth position after the next game, a 2-1 home win against Ipswich, the points secured with a penalty scored by ex-Ipswich player Kevin O'Callaghan, making his long-awaited debut after returning to The Den, delayed because of injury.

Brought down to earth by being beaten 0-4 away by Manchester City, they bounced back with a 2-1 away win over Sheffield United, O'Callaghan again scoring a late winner.

This win got the fans buzzing with excitement again but manager Docherty was more cautious. 'I am pleased,' he said, 'but not satisfied.' However the wheels nearly came off the promotion wagon just four days later and not because of a league defeat. Five thousand fans travelled across London to watch the Lions play Queens Park Rangers at Loftus Road in the first leg of the second round League Cup game, but the match ended in a 1-2 defeat for Millwall. Alan Walker gave the side a lifeline by scoring late in the game, in what had been a delayed second half, and it was the reason for the delay that brought concern to the club.

Half-time in the match saw some of the Lions' fans force their way into the main stand. It was really no more than a skirmish with a few items thrown onto the pitch, including a firework, but the reputation of the fans once more came to the fore and the newspapers were quick to quote QPR manager Jim Smith when he joked, 'I'd better get in touch with Michael Caine to help combat the Zulus when we go there.'

Fortunately the calls to ban the club came to nothing and the league campaign continued with a 2-0 win against West Bromwich Albion at The Den in what was virtually one-way traffic.

A boring 0-0 draw against Oldham brought the month to a close and the Lions went into October looking to put a little more effort into their promotion push.

A hotly disputed penalty, given for handball against Terry Hurlock, brought an end to the Lions' 100 per cent home record in a 2-2 home draw with Swindon, a match that once again brought the fans into the limelight for the wrong reasons after one had to be hauled from the pitch after taking a swing at referee Vic Callow, who had given some bizarre decisions throughout the match. The game itself had everything that you could ask for in a battle between two teams fighting for a position at the top of the table and Swindon had perhaps given the Lions their strongest test yet as to their promotion credentials.

The League Cup adventure came to an end when QPR came for and got, a very cynical 0-0 draw, so it was off to Selhurst Park and a match against local rivals Crystal Palace. The game saw referee Michael Brown limp off with a calf strain and the Lions drop to tenth in the table after losing 0-1. They only had themselves to blame, having wasted enough chances to have comfortably won the match by half-time.

So the 4-1 home victory over Shrewsbury came as relief, although the match itself was not as easy as the scoreline suggests. Having gone a goal down after fifteen minutes, the Lions only got back into the match with a Kevin O'Callaghan penalty on the half-hour and, although both Sheringham and Cascarino scored, it was an own goal from Shrewsbury defender Colin Griffin, sandwiched between them, which eased the nerves.

A trip to the West Country came next and goals from Sheringham and Cascarino provided the Lions with a 2-1 win over Plymouth Argyle. This game saw the debut of Steve Anthrobus, in for the injured O'Callaghan who needed an operation on both calf muscles.

The final game of the month saw the Lions dominate the away match at Huddersfield. But they contrived to miss a hatful of chances and lost 1-2 with skipper Les Briley saying after the game,

'We were in control for long periods of the game... but you don't get anything if you can't put the ball in the net.'

So with the first three months of the season gone, the Lions found themselves in ninth place, with the top of the table looking like this:

	P	W	D	L	F	A	Pts
Bradford City	16	12	3	2	30	14	36
Middlesbrough	16	9	3	4	26	13	30
Hull City	16	8	6	2	26	17	30
Aston Villa	17	7	7	3	23	14	28
Ipswich Town	16	7	5	4	18	9	26
Birmingham City	16	7	5	4	19	21	26
Swindon Town	15	7	3	5	26	19	24
Crystal Palace	15	7	3	5	29	23	24
MILLWALL	15	7	3	5	23	20	24

November started with another dent in the Millwall promotion push with a 1-2 home defeat against Bournemouth. Although the winning goal had more than a touch of fortune about it, it was Millwall who shot themselves in the foot again with their poor finishing, and perhaps a lack of confidence was now creeping through the side.

These fears were dispelled however when four days later a trip to the Midlands produced a 2-1 win against Aston Villa. This was possibly the best Millwall away performance to date with Les Briley scoring the winner, his first of the season, to add to Cascarino's fifth-minute opener.

A well-practiced offside trap ensured the win for a side that had Lawrence, Wood, Hurlock and O'Callaghan all missing through injury, although the return of Jimmy Carter after a four-month fitness battle was welcome. In fact it was Carter's trickery that set up goals for Cascarino and Sheringham in the midweek 2-1 away win over First Division opponents West Ham in the first round of the Simod Cup.

And the wins just kept on coming. Cascarino brought his season's goal tally to ten when he scored a hat-trick in seventeen minutes – two of the strikes were penalties – in the 3-1 home demolition of Leeds United, including the 6,500th goal scored for the club, and he scored another brace in the Lions' 2-1 away win at Stoke. 'Tony had a poor game,' said manager John Docherty after the match, 'he looked sluggish and lethargic but I cannot really complain.'

The fifth win in a row duly came with a 2-0 scoreline over Hull. This time a spectacular goal from Sheringham and another from David Byrne saw the Lions end the month in seventh place in the table.

December began in the same vein with a 3-0 home win against Reading, in a match rescheduled from the beginning of the season and one that saw three different match balls used. Two more goals from Cascarino and another from Lawrence, who came on after just four minutes to replace the injured David Byrne, saw the Lions move into the top three for the first time in the season.

Jubilant Millwall fans now headed north expecting Blackburn to be their next victims. It was not to be. The Lions went down 1-2 and lost goalscorer Cascarino with a broken rib into the bargain.

A 2-0 home win against Leeds in the second round of the Simod Cup did not help matters as Lawrence injured himself in the match and needed a cartilage operation.

Now short on strikers, Docherty signed Robbie Cooke from Brentford, who made his debut in the 0-1 home defeat against Manchester City.

Worse was to follow the following week in a match described by Docherty as, 'a comedy of errors', with the Lions going down 1-4 away to Barnsley. Paul Sansome replaced goalkeeper Brian Horne in this match for what Docherty said were 'disciplinary reasons' and defender David Thompson made his Lions' league debut.

Three league defeats in a row certainly did not help the Lions' cause but if there was any truth in the saying that championships could be won or lost over the Christmas and Easter games then we were about to find out.

West Bromwich Albion at The Hawthorns on Boxing Day is perhaps not the best place to go with the home side struggling at the wrong end of the table and your own form looking decidedly dodgy. But the return of Horne in goal, a hat-trick from Sheringham, the first of his career, and a goal from Briley made the 4-1 win the perfect response to suggestions that the Lions had blown it.

Two days later it was the turn of Sheffield United to suffer at the hands, or should that be feet, of the same goalscorers, when they were beaten 3-1 at The Den. Both players scored one each, along with Robbie Cook who scored his only goal for the club.

The Lions ended the year in fifth place in the table, just four points behind leaders Middlesbrough.

	P	W	D	L	F	A	Pts
Middlesbrough	26	14	7	5	36	17	49
Bradford City	26	14	6	6	41	29	48
Aston Villa	26	12	10	4	37	23	46
Crystal Palace	25	14	3	8	53	37	45
MILLWALL	26	14	3	9	45	34	45

Two games in two days is a daunting challenge for any side. However, Leicester were beaten 1-0 at The Den in a game that saw the return of Cascarino from injury, and a creditable 1-1 draw away at Ipswich – Cascarino grabbing the equaliser in the dying seconds – kept promotion hopes alive. January had started well. On then to the FA Cup match against Arsenal at Highbury.

The newspapers were full of assistant manager Frank McLintock's return to his old club and the Lions putting one over their old manager, George Graham. There was also the rather silly talk of Millwall fans stealing the famous clock and of bets being taken as to when and how it would be done.

A poor display by the Lions demanded answers. Whether it was because the team froze on the day with all the hype, or their opponents overawed them, or because the players returning from injury were still match rusty was impossible to say. Arsenal ran out easy 2-0 winners but the papers focused their attention on the crowd trouble rather than the game.

Officially 5,000 fans – although there were probably nearer 8,000 – were crammed into a stand that should have held just 4,000. With hindsight the match should have been an all-ticket affair with Lions fans given the whole end rather than just half of it: Arsenal supporters occupied the other half.

Heavy-handed police tactics did not help the situation and once again the actions of a small element of so-called Millwall fans tainted the experience for the rest. FA chairman Bert Millichip called for the club to be banned from every cup competition and relegated from the Second Division. Fortunately common sense prevailed in the end.

So it was back to league action and a clash with Middlesbrough, who were one place above the Lions, in what proved to be an exciting game at The Den. It looked like it would be one of those days. The score was 1-1, the bar had been hit twice and there was only a minute left, when Sheringham grabbed the winner and the Lions moved back into third spot in the division.

Three days later, against Norwich, the Lions could not find a way past their opponents' stand-in goalkeeper Robert Rosario, who had gone between the sticks when Bryan Gunn went off with an injured knee with the score at 2-2. By the end of the match Millwall were out of the Simod Cup, having been beaten 2-3.

It was a long time before the next match; Birmingham, to be played in the second city, was cancelled along with many other matches due to the weather, and then scheduled was the next round of the FA Cup. So it was February before the Lions next kicked a ball in anger.

They probably wished this had been postponed too as Bradford won a scrappy affair 0-1 with a goal in the last minute. This goal denied the Lions a place at Wembley in April in the Festival of Football, which was being held to celebrate the Football League's centenary. Worse still it looked as if they would also be denied the consolation of at least a play-off spot as they dropped to fifth place and other clubs closed the gap behind them. They suffered another setback when they lost the rescheduled game at St Andrews 0-1 in a match played in a blizzard. With just thirteen matches remaining in the season, skipper Les Briley was not going to see the dream disappear without a fight. Calling the squad together he told them that if they wanted promotion then they had to show it from here on in. What happened next proved they had heeded his words.

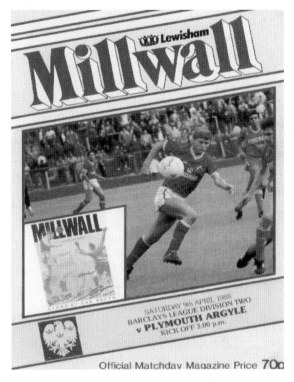

Official Matchday Magazine Price 70p

A programme cover from the 1987/88 season.

The return of Reading old boys Terry Hurlock and Steve Wood to the side doubtless inspired the 3-2 win at Elm Park. Sheringham scored twice and Hurlock smashed home a screamer against his old club, in a match where the Lions were behind twice. The rot had stopped and the promotion race was back on.

The Lions dominated their next match, at home to Oldham, but sloppy defending and a catalogue of missed chances saw the match end 1-1. The nervousness of both players and supporters were starting to show. A 1-0 away win at Swindon was followed by a 0-0 away draw against Shrewsbury and neighbours Crystal Palace stood next in line to try and halt the Lions' promotion push.

They were looking for promotion themselves and the match was without doubt one of those 'six-point' crunch matches. Before the match, Docherty strengthened his squad by signing Reading striker and Millwall old boy Dean Horrix. The latter had scored the goals that had taken Reading to Wembley for the Simod Cup final and, in signing for the Lions, had given up the opportunity of fulfilling every footballer's dream; of appearing in a Wembley final. 'I wouldn't have signed if I didn't think Millwall were capable of making it into the First Division,' Horrix said.

The match against Palace ended in a 1-1 draw. But did Jim Cannon punch in his last-minute equaliser or, as he said, did it hit him on the thigh? The draw really suited neither club but at least they were both still in contention.

Promotion hopes soared however with the 4-1 home demolition of Huddersfield. Playing like the jesters they resembled in their yellow and black harlequin shirts, Huddersfield were no match for the now-roaring Lions. Only the Huddersfield goalkeeper Seamus McDonagh, with some brilliant saves, prevented Millwall adding to goals from Cascarino and Sheringham (2) – one a stunning twenty-five-yard lob – and the first from Horrix since his return.

The end of March saw the Lions in fourth place and next into The Den was table-topping Aston Villa.

	P	W	D	L	F	A	Pts
Aston Villa	37	20	10	7	63	35	70
Blackburn Rovers	36	19	11	6	57	38	68
Middlesbrough	36	18	10	8	47	27	64
MILLWALL	37	19	7	11	59	43	64

A crowd of almost 14,000 saw the Lions move closer to the impossible dream with a 2-1 win.

Danis Salmon, who a day earlier had been the victim of an April Fool's gag when told he had been dropped from the team, opened the scoring with his only goal of the season. Millwall were laughing all the way to the dressing room when Teddy Sheringham put the icing on his own birthday cake, scoring his 21st goal of the season on his twenty-second birthday. Not a bad way to celebrate.

The next match, a 2-1 away win at Leeds, with goals from Cascarino and Hurlock, took the Lions to second place in the table, equal on points with Aston Villa. Unfortunately many Lions fans had to miss the match as British Rail refused to lay on a special train for the match and local coach companies would not supply transport either. So the decision was between a long car trip with a return in the early hours of the morning after the Monday night game or to stay at home and bite the fingernails.

Those who made the trip were rewarded with a magnificent team performance. The ice-cool display of McLeary and Wood in the centre of the defence was backed up perfectly by everyone else in a game not for the faint hearted. Anyone with a heart condition would have needed to stay away from the next game, at home to Plymouth Argyle, too. A goal down after two minutes, the Lions were back on terms when O'Callaghan netted from the penalty spot on seven minutes. Three minutes later a spectacular overhead kick from Cascarino put the Lions in front and a thumping header from the edge of the box by Sheringham two minutes after that should have signalled another win. Plymouth had other ideas and they had pulled one back through Summerfield on twenty-five minutes. Eight minutes after the break he had the hearts of most of the 11,000 crowd in their mouths as he rounded off a four-man move by putting the ball into the roof of the net. A linesman's flag was signalling for offside, however, and a nervous team, along with their nervous fans, breathed a collective sigh of relief. Another three points were safely in the bag and the Lions were now top of the table, one point clear of Middlesbrough and Blackburn, two clear of Aston Villa and three ahead of Bradford.

A wet and windy Tuesday night in Bournemouth is not the place you want to play football when your future depends on it but that was where the Lions found themselves. All 2,700 Millwall tickets had been sold and many more wanted to see the match so, in an effort to stop fans travelling without a ticket, the game was screened live to what on that night was an aptly named Cold Blow Lane. Goals from O'Callaghan and Hurlock within the first twenty-three minutes seemed enough to calm nerves that were starting to fray when Bournemouth scored five minutes later. Commentator Kenneth Wolstenholme must have been the only person, either at Dean Court or Cold Blow Lane, who seemed unaffected by events on the pitch. But even he must have felt something when referee Brian Hill pointed to the penalty spot with just a minute left on the clock. Thoughts of Birmingham sixteen years earlier raced through the minds of most Lions fans. Were they to be denied a place in the top flight yet again when they had been so near?

The answer was no. Brian Horne, diving to his right, saved the kick and the cheers could be heard all over south-east London as well as the South Coast.

The Lions were now four points clear but, with no game the following Saturday, had to wait another week to get back into action. In the down week the points gap had closed again.

Goals from Sheringham and O'Callaghan, his third penalty in three successive games, brought a home win against Stoke and the Lions were nearly there. Hull is not the place you would choose to spend a Bank Holiday Monday unless you lived there or were a Lions fan praying for the win that would give you the chance to win promotion the following Saturday

Captain Les Briley with the Second Division championship trophy.

against Blackburn. On ten minutes Sheringham's diving header was handled on the line and O'Callaghan scored from the spot for the fourth consecutive time. That was all that was needed! Results elsewhere gave the Lions an unassailable lead and their 103-year wait was over. The biggest knees-up along the Old Kent Road for years was being planned and the final match against Blackburn, which the Lions lost 1-4, did not matter.

A remarkable season in which the Lions recorded a club record of 34 away points, including 10 away wins and had no 0-0 home draws was brought to a close. A 17,000 crowd were at The Den to see their heroes take their long-awaited place with the big boys. The party carried over to a 2-2 draw with Arsenal four days later in a testimonial for Chief Scout Bob Pearson. The Lions were ready to roar in the First Division.

1987/88　　　　Football League Second Division

Date		Opposition	Score	Scorers
Aug	15	Middlesbrough	1-1	Sheringham
	22	BARNSLEY	3-1	Cascarino, Sheringham, Lawrence
	29	Leicester City	0-1	
Sept	1	BIRMINGHAM CITY	3-1	Lawrence, Walker, Stevens
	5	Bradford City	1-3	Hurlock
	12	IPSWICH TOWN	2-1	Walker, O'Callaghan (pen)
	16	Manchester City	0-4	
	19	Sheffield United	2-1	Byrne, O'Callaghan
	26	WEST BROMWICH ALBION	2-0	Cascarino, Sheringham
	29	Oldham Athletic	0-0	
Oct	3	SWINDON TOWN	2-2	Lawrence, Sheringham
	10	Crystal Palace	0-1	
	17	SHREWSBURY TOWN	4-1	O'Callaghan (pen), Sheringham, Cascarino, Opp OC
	20	Plymouth Argyle	2-1	Cascarino, Sheringham
	31	Huddersfield Town	1-2	Walker
Nov	3	BOURNEMOUTH	1-2	Cascarino
	7	Aston Villa	2-1	Cascarino, Briley
	14	LEEDS UNITED	3-1	Cascarino (3) (2 pens)
	21	Stoke City	2-1	Cascarino (2)
	28	HULL CITY	2-0	Sheringham, Byrne
Dec	1	READING	3-0	Cascarino (2), Lawrence
	5	Blackburn Rovers	1-2	Cascarino
	12	MANCHESTER CITY	0-1	
	19	Barnsley	1-4	Sheringham
	26	West Bromwich Albion	4-1	Sheringham (3), Briley
	28	SHEFFIELD UNITED	3-1	Sheringham, Cooke, Briley
Jan	1	LEICESTER CITY	1-0	Briley
	2	Ipswich Town	1-1	Cascarino
	16	MIDDLESBROUGH	2-1	Walker, Sheringham
Feb	6	BRADFORD CITY	0-1	
	9	Birmingham City	0-1	
	13	Reading	3-2	Sheringham (2), Hurlock
	20	OLDHAM ATHLETIC	1-1	Cascarino
	27	Swindon Town	1-0	Cascarino
Mar	5	Shrewsbury Town	0-0	
	12	CRYSTAL PALACE	1-1	Sheringham
	19	HUDDERSFIELD TOWN	4-1	Sheringham (2), Cascarino, Horrix
Apr	2	ASTON VILLA	2-1	Salman, Sheringham
	6	Leeds United	2-1	Cascarino, Hurlock
	9	PLYMOUTH ARGYLE	3-2	O'Callaghan (pen), Cascarino, Sheringham
	19	Bournemouth	2-1	O'Callaghan (pen), Hurlock
	30	STOKE CITY	2-0	Sheringham, O'Callaghan (pen)
May	2	Hull City	1-0	O'Callaghan (pen)
	7	BLACKBURN ROVERS	1-4	Sheringham

Full Members Cup

Round	Date	Opposition	Score	Scorers
1	Nov 10	West Ham United	2-1	Cascarino, Sheringham
2	Dec 8	LEEDS UNITED	2-0	Walker, Sheringham
3	Jan 19	NORWICH CITY	2-3	Cascarino (2)

League Cup

Round	Date	Opposition	Score	Scorers
1/1	Aug 18	Leyton Orient	1-1	Morgan
1/2	Aug 25	LEYTON ORIENT	1-0	Lawrence
2/1	Sept 23	Queens Park Rangers	1-2	Walker
2/2	Oct 6	QUEEN'S PARK RANGERS	0-0	

FA Cup

Round	Date	Opposition	Score	Scorers
3	Jan 9	ARSENAL	0-2	

1987/88   Football League Second Division

	P	W	D	L	F	A	Pts
MILLWALL	44	25	7	12	72	52	82
Aston Villa	44	22	12	10	68	41	78
Middlesbrough	44	22	12	10	63	36	78
Bradford City	44	22	11	11	74	54	77
Blackburn Rovers	44	21	14	9	68	52	77
Crystal Palace	44	22	9	13	86	59	75
Leeds United	44	19	12	13	61	51	69
Ipswich Town	44	19	9	16	61	52	66
Manchester City	44	19	8	17	80	60	65
Oldham Athletic	44	18	11	15	72	64	65
Stoke City	44	17	11	16	50	57	62
Swindon Town	44	16	11	17	73	60	59
Leicester City	44	16	11	17	62	61	59
Barnsley	44	15	12	17	61	62	57
Hull City	44	14	15	15	54	60	57
Plymouth Argyle	44	16	8	20	65	67	56
Bournemouth	44	13	10	21	56	68	49
Shrewsbury Town	44	11	16	17	42	54	49
Birmingham City	44	11	15	18	41	66	48
West Bromwich Albion	44	12	11	21	50	69	47
Sheffield United	44	13	7	24	45	74	46
Reading	44	10	12	22	44	70	42
Huddersfield Town	44	6	10	28	41	100	28

In the Promised Land
1988/89

Just how would the Lions adjust to life in the top division? That was the question on the lips of every fan as they looked at the fixture list and for the first time in their history planned to visit places that were previously only dreamed of.

Manager Docherty decided to go into the new campaign with the squad that won promotion. The only additions were the return of Neil Ruddock, who was once an apprentice with the club and was a £300,000 buy from Spurs and the last-minute signing of Ian Dawes from Queens Park Rangers for £150,000. The purchase of Dawes was necessary because it was discovered that regular full-back Nicky Coleman would be out for six months with a knee injury.

Would the players freeze when playing in exalted company in First Division grounds or would it inspire them? Would their opponents dread the thought of playing at The Den with the full vocal support of the Lions' fans against them? Time would tell.

Not only were there worries about whether the squad was good enough or big enough to cope with the demands of First Division football but also about the behaviour of the thousands of fans who would follow them all over the country. Their good behaviour was crucial to the club. To assist them in this matter, the club brought in ex-Manchester police chief John Stalker to advise them on all aspects of security.

Losing their final pre-season match at home, 0-1 to neighbours Crystal Palace, started the doom-mongering but by the end of the year only 6 games were lost from the 24 played.

The first game of the new season was away to Aston Villa. The Lions had won there the previous season but it still came as a bit of a surprise to find them two goals to the good in the first twenty-five minutes, Cascarino scoring both. However, a penalty given away by David Thompson, perhaps surprisingly selected ahead of Wood and Ruddock, and a goal scored when Dawes, making his Lions debut, failed to control the ball, saw the game levelled by half-time. The match finished with no more additions to the scoreline. A point away from home in your first ever First Division match was nothing to sneer at, but the Lions were clearly disappointed at not taking all three.

Just over 13,000 fans packed into The Den to see the Lions play their first First Division home match against Derby. The 1-0 win, with Sheringham scoring a simple tap-in on the stroke of half-time, says little for the way Millwall dominated the game and only an outstanding performance by Peter Shilton in the Derby goal kept the score down.

The storybook start continued when the Lions went to Selhurst Park for their match against Charlton, who were playing there at the time due to their ground problems. A headed Sheringham goal in the first minute started the ball rolling and additions from Cascarino and a thirty-five-yard screamer from Briley made the 3-0 win a comfortable stroll in the sun.

Now, instead of printing reports about hooligan fans, the press were busy writing about winning ways both on and off the pitch, telling of the club's initiatives of soccer schools and crèche facilities for the fans' children, the promotion of women's football and the work done against hooliganism and racism in sport. Surely their next match, at home to Everton, would give the Lions a much sterner test?

Teddy Sheringham celebrates after scoring the Lions' first goal in the First Division at The Den on 3 September 1988.

Before the game the club unveiled its new family enclosure and Junior Lions and their parents were allowed in free of charge for the match. The game itself was one that undermined the argument for a super league, for which Everton were to the fore and in which Millwall would be definite non-starters. Two goals from Cascarino in the first half gave the Lions a lead they never looked like losing and, although an own goal by McLeary closed the deficit, the value of the not-so-fashionable clubs in the league was well demonstrated.

On to Carrow Road and the clash with table-toppers Norwich. Going behind twice in the game the Lions equalised within a minute each time. Cascarino and O'Callaghan were the scorers and the club found themselves in the unbelievable position of third at the end of their first month in the top flight with Norwich manager Dave Stringer saying, 'Millwall will upset a lot of teams this season.'

Taking a break from league action the Lions took on Gillingham at The Den in the first leg of the Littlewoods Cup in a match that saw Neil Ruddock make his Millwall debut in place of the injured Les Briley. Although scoring twice in the 3-0 win – Sheringham scored the other – Ruddock never made the starting line up in a league match all season and only featured twice as a substitute. The Lions won the second leg, played a fortnight later, 3-1, with two goals from Sheringham and another from Danis Salmon. By doing so they earned themselves another match at Villa Park in the next round. Surprisingly, after his two-goal heroics, Ruddock did not even make the bench for the league match at home against Queens Park Rangers. Darren Morgan took his place. Morgan had an inspired afternoon, along with his fellow midfielder Terry Hurlock, who scored an unstoppable thirty-yard goal and set up two more for Cascarino in the 3-2 win that took the Lions to the top of the table. Even with Brian Horne superbly saving a Trevor Francis penalty, the scoreline flattered QPR and the Lions deserved their place as top cats, with a team that cost just a little over £500,000.

Tony Cascarino powerfully heads into the QPR goal in front of a packed crowd. This result put Millwall top of the First Division.

	P	W	D	L	F	A	Pts
MILLWALL	6	4	2	0	13	7	14
Norwich City	6	4	1	1	11	7	13
Liverpool	6	3	2	1	10	5	11
Southampton	6	3	2	1	10	6	11
Manchester United	6	3	2	1	7	3	11
Arsenal	6	3	1	2	17	11	10

With the match against Arsenal the following week called off due to other commitments for the Highbury club, it was two weeks before the Lions faced league action again. In a match that they never looked like losing but where the ball never ran kindly for them, the Lions were held 0-0 away at Coventry. This was perhaps to be expected in a match between what were now the second and third-placed teams. The Lions were now the only unbeaten team in the League.

It is a rare thing when Brian Clough is left speechless, especially when your Nottingham Forest side are two goals to the good, with Steve Hodge having scored either side of half-time. Yet the Lions are nothing if not resilient and were not going to give up their unbeaten status without a fight. There were only ten minutes of the match left when Sheringham scored to give the Lions a lifeline and only five when Ruddock, who was called from the bench to make his League debut after seventy minutes to replace the injured Lawrence, was thrown into the attack.

If fairy tales are made on the Old Kent Road then this was one of them as Ruddock hit home the equaliser and the Lions kept their games lost total at nil. The fans went home not quite believing what they had seen.

The run had to come to an end of course and it happened in the next game away to Middlesbrough but not without a fight and an initial scare for the Ayresome Park team. In a game that had everything you could ask for in a football match Middlesbrough were a goal to the good after just two minutes when Slaven scored with a twenty-yard effort. Goals from Sheringham and Cascarino put the Lions in front after twenty minutes and it stayed that way until half-time.

Immediately after the restart Boro equalised and then went in front after seventy-six minutes but the Lions were determined to hold onto their unbeaten record and gave as good as they got.

The game hinged on a penalty given against Alan McLeary and the game ended 2-4. Should the Lions have lost? Perhaps not, but they could have pride in their defeat and went to Villa Park for the next round of the Littlewoods Cup with their heads held high.

If losing once was unheard of, twice was almost a catastrophe but Aston Villa were in the mood to avenge their earlier league defeat.

Ruddock, starting in the side again, had put the Lions one up after ten minutes, once more demonstrating his long-distance shooting skills. But Villa were to run out 1-3 winners and Millwall went away to lick their wounds and show that losing was not becoming a habit. 'It will take more than a couple of defeats to burst our bubble,' said a confident Docherty before the Lions entertained Luton Town at The Den. His confidence was proven as his side were three goals up after twenty-five minutes; Sheringham, O'Callaghan with a penalty and Ian Dawes, with his first for the club, were the scorers.

They could easily have added to the total in the second half but the 3-1 final score was enough to keep Docherty bubbling with delight and the Lions continued unbeaten at home.

Well, only just. Barnsley were leading by a goal to nil with just two minutes remaining when Dean Horrix struck the equaliser in the first round of the Simod Cup. This was a match that Docherty used to rest some of his regular first-team players.

Extra time produced no further scoring so it was the turn of Brian Horne to show his goalkeeping skills as he saved three times in the penalty shoot-out. Although the Lions missed two of their efforts, Horrix, Briley and Ruddock were successful and Millwall were through to the next round.

Everyone wanted to go to Anfield to see the Lions take on champions Liverpool. The 3,900-ticket allocation was sold in just one hour. So once more the game was beamed back live to The Den to satisfy the thousands who wanted to see the match. It was an experiment monitored by the European football authorities as an initiative that could help English clubs back from their European ban.

Transfer rumours were now rife, not about who was coming to The Den but about who was leaving it. Sheringham, Cascarino, Hurlock, Carter and Horne were all subjected to newspaper speculation. David Byrne, finding it difficult to get a first-team place, had handed in a transfer request so it came as a bit of a shock when Docherty bought Paul Stephenson from Newcastle for £275,000 to strengthen the squad.

He did not take long to repay at least some of that fee when, to the delight of the travelling Millwall fans and those who struggled to watch the game on the six television screens back at The Den, he scored after ten minutes of his debut match against Liverpool, in what was a bruising encounter.

Although they conceded an equaliser five minutes later and were on the end of some strange refereeing decisions from a clearly intimidated Mr Kirkby, including a penalty appeal when Gary Ablett had climbed all over Sheringham, the Lions were eventually satisfied with the 1-1 draw.

In fact they came very close to winning the game as Cascarino had seen his header crash against the crossbar before Stephenson's goal and Sheringham had a shot bobble just inches wide. 'Our supporters were magnificent,' said a delighted Docherty, 'and the players responded.' Millwall had proved that they now deserved to be with the big boys and they wanted to stay there.

'Fans riot shame.' That was the newspaper heading after the next match, where twenty fans – hooligans was the newspaper description – were arrested after kicking in glass panels leading to the directors' box. Sports Minister Colin Moynihan said, 'It is tragic that a club like Millwall should have to put up with these ugly scenes after a great game.'

The match itself had seen the Lions tear a poor Newcastle side apart. The 4-0 scoreline, in which McLeary, Hurlock, Cascarino and O'Callaghan shared the goals, did not come close to showing how much of a mauling they had given the Magpies. Newcastle supporters had caused the off-field problems.

Tony Cascarino had been quoted as saying that the best was yet to come. With the way that Millwall were playing, especially Stephenson who teased his old teammates mercilessly, who would doubt them?

In fact they were denied a fifth goal when a clear penalty was denied them but nobody was complaining after such a well-deserved win.

The 2-2 away draw against Southampton that followed – O'Callaghan and Sheringham were the scorers – was a bit disappointing, especially as O'Callaghan had smacked a shot against the crossbar and Burridge, in the Southampton goal, had produced an outstanding save to deny Sheringham.

Once more the Lions had failed to turn their dominance into the goals that would have won the match but a point away from home can never be dismissed. Thoughts of actually winning the title, although a little premature, were nevertheless discussed by fans and football commentators alike.

Taking a break from League action, the month of November came to a close with a 2-0 win over Leeds at The Den in the second round of the Simod Cup. Briley and Cascarino scored the goals that set up an away fixture against Everton in the next round and the Lions were on a high.

They were brought back down to earth just four days later when West Ham came to The Den and won 0-1 with Paul Ince walking the ball into an empty net after an appalling back pass by Ian Dawes. It had been 167 games since the Lions had failed to score at The Den but this was going to be one of those days. Despite camping around the West Ham penalty area for most of the second half of the match that elusive goal never materialised.

They failed to score in the next game as well, a 0-2 defeat at White Hart Lane. It may have been hard to take but two glorious goals – a Waddle twenty-five-yard shot that crashed in off the underside of the crossbar and a Gascoigne free-kick special, gave Tottenham a deserved win. The Lions huffed and puffed but could not really complain about the result.

Normal service was resumed the following week, however, but it was hard going against a Sheffield Wednesday side that was content to play the ball outside of their own penalty area for most of the match. Maybe it was their intention to bore the Lions into submission. It certainly worked with the fans, but this tactic proved to be their undoing as a poor back pass allowed Sheringham, in his 150th appearance for the club, to score with just two minutes of the match remaining. 'They came with the ambition of winning a corner – and reaped their reward,' said Docherty after the match, in what completely summed up an afternoon that might have been better spent Christmas shopping.

Perhaps the players had mentally gone shopping the following Tuesday when a dismal display saw them out of the Simod Cup, beaten 0-2 by Everton. They fared no better at Plough Lane on Boxing Day where Wimbledon had an easy 0-1 win after another poor Millwall performance.

After four defeats from the previous five games it was good to see the Lions bring the year to a close with a win. Sheringham scored the only goal in a win over Derby at the Baseball Ground in a game where Brian Horne did not have a serious shot to save. The Lions did not find goal chances easy to come by either but a win is a win and the players and their fans could go and celebrate New Year's Eve in style. The year ended with the team still third in the table.

	P	W	D	L	F	A	Pts
Arsenal	18	11	4	3	40	20	37
Norwich City	19	10	7	2	28	19	37
MILLWALL	18	8	6	4	29	21	30

When your first game of a new year is against your near neighbours and they happen to be struggling near the bottom of the table you just have to fancy your chances. And so it was when the Lions travelled back to Selhurst Park, the adopted home of a Charlton Athletic side that never even attempted to play in their opponents' half of the pitch.

Millwall were not exactly ripping their opponents apart but the time-wasting and spoiling tactics that Charlton employed did not help to make the match much of a spectacle. The Lions had got used to waiting for a winning goal though, and this match proved that patience could be a virtue. With just ten minutes left, David Thompson replaced Paul Stephenson as a last throw of the dice. The lanky central defender duly obliged with his first Millwall goal, indeed his only goal of the season, five minutes later to secure a 1-0 victory.

The Lions' next match was a home FA Cup tie against Luton Town and again it was to produce a dramatic ending. Two up within the first quarter of a hour – Cascarino and Carter scoring within a minute of each other – and the Lions were coasting to victory. Even a controversial goal by Kingsley Black, which crashed down from the crossbar and the linesman signalled it had crossed the line, gave them no half-time worries.

Danny Wilson's penalty gave Luton some hope but normal service was resumed when Sheringham gave the Lions their lead back. However, with just seven minutes of the match remaining fate, and referee Mr Martin, took a hand. A floodlight failed and although there was a slight reduction of vision in one corner of the pitch no player of either side complained. Mr Martin though decided to take the players off and a frantic search for an electrician to fix the problem started.

Half an hour later an agitated crowd, who had feared the match might have been abandoned due to this controversial decision, were allowed to see the last seven minutes played to a conclusion and Millwall had won themselves a home draw against Liverpool in the next round. 'It's referees like this that cause trouble at football matches,' called a voice in the crowd. You had to agree he had a point.

So it was off to Old Trafford and a match against Manchester United that saw the return of Jimmy Carter from injury for his first start of the season. Although Millwall had their chances, sloppy defending gave away at least two goals and the Lions were well beaten 0-3.

The club now had ambitions to grow and consolidate itself as a major club in the division and announced before the first of consecutive televised matches that they were to build a new stadium at Senegal Fields. It was to take the club into a new era.

The first of the Sunday televised matches, a league game against second-placed Norwich, produced a great advertisement for football. A goal up after two minutes and two up five minutes later, Norwich looked as though they would run away with the game. Maybe it had been stage fright but the Lions got over their TV nerves and were back on level terms at half-time with goals from Cascarino and Carter.

The second half looked like producing only one winner and, except for the heroics of Norwich goalkeeper, Bryan Gunn, there would have been. However, with the referee about to blow for full time, Danis Salmon sliced a clearance high into the air and when it came down it fell at the feet of Robert Fleck who hit an unstoppable shot to win the game and leave Millwall fans feeling as sick as a… canary.

The Liverpool team that arrived at The Den the following Sunday for the televised FA Cup encounter must have watched the match because they changed the formation of their side. They frustrated the Lions before goals from Aldridge and Rush left them comfortable 0-2 winners. The two-match television exposure had shown the watching millions what the Lions were all about and brought a great deal of credit to the club and its fans.

The team needed to get back to winning ways so imagine the surprise of the fans when they took to the field at Loftus Road with the unexplained absence of striker Teddy Sheringham. Dean Horrix took his place in the starting line-up for the first time this season. Horrix led the line well against a Queens Park Rangers side that struggled in the mud and QPR old boy Jimmy Carter turned in a Man of the Match performance; he scored once and made another for Cascarino as Millwall won 2-1.

They were a goal up after fifteen minutes the following week when Arsenal came to The Den, Carter again the goal-scorer. Arsenal were not going to give up their chase for the championship without a fight and dominated the second half, scoring twice in the last twenty minutes to win the match.

With their next match postponed due to Nottingham Forest's FA Cup quarter-final appearance, the match against Middlesbrough, scheduled for early March, was brought forward. Sean Sparham made his first appearance of the season for the injured Ian Dawes.

An own goal, added to one from Briley, gave the Lions a much-needed three points and moved the Lions back into the top five. A 1-0 win over Coventry four days later – Cascarino was the goal scorer – took them into third place and looking forward to a trip to Highbury the following Tuesday with confidence high.

	P	W	D	L	F	A	Pts
Arsenal	26	16	6	4	52	25	54
Norwich City	26	14	8	4	39	28	50
MILLWALL	25	12	6	7	38	30	42

Arsenal 0 Millwall 6. Well that is how the newspapers the following morning should have read. Instead, the Lions and their fans went home wondering how it had finished 0-0. Briley and Hurlock, back from a two-match ban, dominated the midfield and only some unlucky finishing and poor refereeing decisions kept it that way. Sheringham had already been denied a penalty having been clearly pulled back by Adams when the referee disallowed a 'goal' from Briley. His shot, from fully thirty yards, rocketing into the back of the net, was disallowed for offside against Sheringham who was standing beside the corner flag.

Floodlight robbery! You had better believe it.

The Lions remained in third place after a 2-1 away win at Luton, where Carter scored both goals, in another match beamed back live to The Den due to Luton's away fan ban.

Hoping for European football in the following season, a friendly against Swiss side Servette showed how much the Lions had to learn. They lost the match 1-3 but the European dream continued when goals from O'Callaghan and Hurlock gave them a convincing win over Aston Villa. But the season was now to take a dramatic turn.

If the first ten games of the season saw the Lions roaring their way to success then the last ten saw them whimper away as the bubble finally burst. Just four points were taken from a possible 30 and only five goals were registered, three from Sheringham, one from Salman and an own goal.

It started when Everton managed a draw by equalising from a rather dubious penalty. This was followed by a 0-1 home defeat by Wimbledon, a match that saw Sheringham sent off, and 1-3 away loss against Sheffield Wednesday. A 0-0 home draw with Manchester United offered little respite as they lost at home to Liverpool (0-2), away to West Ham (0-3), home to Tottenham (0-5) and away to Nottingham Forest (1-4) in a match that gave Darren Treacy his Millwall debut and Steve Anthrobus his first game of the season.

All of this seemed insignificant though in the aftermath of the tragedy at Hillsborough that saw many Liverpool supporters lose their lives.

The final two games of the season were drawn. The first was a 1-1 scoreline away against Newcastle and the second a home match, which saw Wesley Reid get his first start, which produced the same score. It was against a Southampton side that fielded Neil Ruddock, who had moved there earlier in the season.

The Lions had finished their first ever season in the top division in tenth place and could hold their heads high as they flew off to Australia for a summer break. They had seen the club win the Community Club of the Year award, Cascarino win full international caps for the Republic of Ireland, McLeary and Hurlock win England 'B' caps and Brian Horne England Under-21 caps.

But the writing had been on the wall for those last ten games. Although some youngsters had been blooded, with Ruddock and Lawrence gone, the fans were looking to see who would be brought into the side for the following season to stop the same thing happening again to help the Lions push on to bigger and better things.

1988/89   Football League First Division

Date		Opposition	Score	Scorers
Aug	27	Aston Villa	2-2	Cascarino (2)
Sept	3	DERBY COUNTY	1-0	Sheringham
	10	Charlton Athletic	3-0	Sheringham, Cascarino, Briley
	17	EVERTON	2-1	Cascarino (2)
	24	Norwich City	2-2	Cascarino, O'Callaghan
Oct	1	QUEEN'S PARK RANGERS	3-2	Cascarino (2), Hurlock
	15	Coventry City	0-0	
	22	NOTTINGHAM FOREST	2-2	Sheringham, Ruddock
	29	Middlesbrough	2-4	Sheringham, Cascarino
Nov	5	LUTON TOWN	3-1	Sheringham, O'Callaghan (pen), Dawes
	12	Liverpool	1-1	Stephenson
	19	NEWCASTLE UNITED	4-0	McLeary, Hurlock, Cascarino, O'Callaghan
	26	Southampton	2-2	O'Callaghan, Sheringham
Dec	3	WEST HAM UNITED	0-1	
	10	Tottenham Hotspur	0-2	
	17	SHEFFIELD WEDNESDAY	1-0	Sheringham
	26	Wimbledon	0-1	
	31	Derby County	1-0	Sheringham
Jan	2	CHARLTON ATHLETIC	1-0	Thompson
	14	Manchester United	0-3	
	22	NORWICH CITY	2-3	Cascarino, Carter
Feb	4	Queen's Park Rangers	2-1	Carter, Cascarino
	11	ARSENAL	1-2	Carter
	21	MIDDLESBROUGH	2-0	Briley, Opp OG
	25	COVENTRY CITY	1-0	Cascarino
	28	Arsenal	0-0	
Mar	11	Luton Town	2-1	Carter (2)
	18	ASTON VILLA	2-0	O'Callaghan, Hurlock
	25	Everton	1-1	Sheringham
	27	WIMBLEDON	0-1	
Apr	1	Sheffield Wednesday	0-3	
	8	MANCHESTER UNITED	0-0	
	11	LIVERPOOL	1-2	Salman
	22	West Ham United	0-3	
	29	TOTTENHAM HOTSPUR	0-5	
May	3	Nottingham Forest	1-4	Opp OG
	6	Newcastle United	1-1	Sheringham
	13	SOUTHAMPTON	1-1	Sheringham

Full Members Cup

Round	Date		Opposition	Score	Scorers
1	Nov	9	BARNSLEY	1-1*	Horrix
2		29	LEEDS UNITED	2-0	Briley, Cascarino
3	Dec	20	Everton	0-2	

*a.e.t. Millwall won 4-3 on penalties

League Cup

Round	Date		Opposition	Score	Scorers
2/1	Sept	27	GILLINGHAM	3-0	Ruddock (2), Sheringham
2/2	Oct	11	Gillingham	3-1	Sheringham (2), Salman
3	Nov	2	Aston Villa	1-3	Ruddock

FA Cup

Round	Date		Opposition	Score	Scorers
3	Jan	7	LUTON TOWN	3-2	Cascarino, Sheringham, Carter
4		29	LIVERPOOL	0-2	

1988/89 — Football League First Division

	P	W	D	L	F	A	Pts
Arsenal	38	22	10	6	73	36	76
Liverpool	38	22	10	6	65	28	76
Nottingham Forest	38	17	13	8	64	43	64
Norwich City	38	17	11	10	48	45	62
Derby County	38	17	7	14	40	38	58
Tottenham Hotspur	38	15	12	11	60	46	57
Coventry City	38	14	13	11	47	42	55
Everton	38	14	12	12	50	45	54
Queen's Park Rangers	38	14	11	13	43	37	53
MILLWALL	38	14	11	13	47	52	53
Manchester United	38	13	12	13	45	35	51
Wimbledon	38	14	9	15	50	46	51
Southampton	38	10	15	13	52	66	45
Charlton Athletic	38	10	12	16	44	58	42
Sheffield Wednesday	38	10	12	16	34	51	42
Luton Town	38	10	11	17	42	52	41
Aston Villa	38	9	13	16	45	56	40
Middlesbrough	38	9	12	17	44	61	39
West Ham United	38	10	8	20	37	62	38
Newcastle United	38	7	10	21	32	63	31

From Top to Bottom
1989/90

The poor run of results at the end of the previous season meant that the fans were expecting changes and the first of these came in an unexpected way. Frank Sibley came in as reserve team manager to replace Roger Cross whose unexplained departure after the club tour of Australia had created a vacancy.

Talk of a super league had started and chairman Reg Burr, who had been elected to the Football League's management committee, spoke about the club being part of it and floated the club on the stock market with a £5 million share issue.

Rumours were rife about possible signings so it came as a surprise when the season kicked off with no new players in the side at all. The club had signed Eire international Gary Waddock from Belgium club Charleroi in a complicated transfer deal. This was due to Waddock's injury-related retirement from football two years previously but he did not get his first outing until later in the season. George Lawrence, out on loan at the end of the previous season, had left the club and joined Bournemouth as had David Byrne, who left before the previous season had ended.

Pre-season friendlies went well so spirits were high for the opening match of the season away at Southampton. The Lions won the match 2-1 with the goals from Briley and a last-minute winner from Cascarino, The Saints' goal was, inevitably, sandwiched in between from ex-Millwall man Ruddock. But it was youngster Steve Anthrobus, in for the injured O'Callaghan, who stole the show with a brilliant man of the match display.

For the first time in history all four south London sides were in the First Division together. Crystal Palace had won promotion and the second game of the season provided the Lions with their first derby match of the campaign – a home match against Charlton.

Two goals down with five minutes left, it looked like Millwall's first defeat would come early in the season but they had not forgotten their late goal-scoring ability from the previous match. Sheringham and Dawes showed they could still do it and the match finished in a thrilling 2-2 draw.

They left it late again in the following match, Carter scoring with just ten minutes left in the 1-0 home win over Nottingham Forest. But who cared? The Lions were second in the table, on the same points tally as leaders Chelsea and the future looked rosy.

So off to Plough Lane on a wet Tuesday night and the Lions left it late again. The 2-2 draw saw Wimbledon's Eric Young sent off and Steve Torpey make his Millwall debut. Two behind, the Lions had fought back with goals from Anthrobus – his first for the club, after forty-one minutes – and a Cascarino equaliser on eighty-five minutes.

Neighbours Charlton did the Lions a favour by beating Chelsea and Millwall found themselves at the top of the table at the end of August.

	P	W	D	L	F	A	Pts
MILLWALL	4	2	2	0	7	5	8
Chelsea	4	2	1	1	6	4	7
Charlton Athletic	4	1	3	0	6	3	6

By the time Millwall played again, Coventry had taken the top spot and it was they who came next into the Lions' Den. Once more the Lions scored a very late goal. Dawes notched it on ninety minutes with the only goal Millwall scored in a second half that saw striker David Speedie take over in the visitors' goal from the injured Steve Ogrizovic and be well protected by his defence.

Coventry took time out from their defensive duties to score as well but the Lions had proved they could put the ball in the net early in a game as well as late. Sheringham scored twice – the first after just forty-four seconds – and Anthrobus another before half-time and the Lions were back on top. 'The best is yet to come,' said manager Docherty. 'I'm sure this team can develop further.'

That development was halted the following week at Old Trafford where Manchester United ran out easy 1-5 winners, although Sheringham's goal had made the score 1-1 with what was the club's 1,500th league away goal.

They had not recovered from that mauling when they travelled to the Victoria Ground and were beaten 0-1 by Stoke in the first leg of the Littlewoods Cup first round tie. Steve Wood was sent off in the process and Gary Waddock got his first game in a Millwall shirt, coming on to replace Anthrobus.

He made his league debut in the home game against Sheffield Wednesday the following Saturday, coming on for the injured Briley after just twelve minutes, and played a starring role in the Lions' 2-0 win. He made the first goal for Carter while Cascarino scored the other.

However it all went wrong a week later against Norwich, who withstood a battering at The Den yet emerged 0-1 winners.

The Lions duly took their place in the next round of the Littlewoods Cup by beating Stoke 2-0 but again left it late. Cascarino, who looked yards offside, scored with just one minute of extra time left, Sheringham having levelled the tie just before half-time.

Things were looking up off the field as fans rushed to buy shares in the club's stock market flotation but on the field they seemed to have caught the habit of losing, at least in league matches.

True, they were a goal up against Everton, Sheringham again having scored, but the referee did them no favours in awarding a dubious penalty that produced the equaliser. He also ignored appeals for handball, which helped secure the second, in Everton's 1-2 win. A draw would perhaps have been a fair result but the signs were there that things were going wrong.

There were plenty of goals in the next game. Crystal Palace won 3-4 at Selhurst Park with a last-minute winner after leading for most of the match. Cascarino and Anthrobus were the Millwall goal scorers, although a Jeff Hopkins own goal, lobbing his 'keeper from twenty-five yards, had given the Lions the lead.

They lost again, 2-3, as they crashed out of the Littlewoods Cup to Third Division Tranmere. Hurlock scored both goals. Tranmere had been behind at Prenton Park. Docherty was not happy, especially when the team threw away another two league points in the 1-1 home draw against Luton after Dawes had given them a twelfth-minute lead, as the new electric scoreboard showed.

The Lions looked to be in free fall and Chelsea's 0-4 win at Stamford Bridge seemed to confirm it and although they played much better when beaten at home 1-2 by Arsenal the following week. Sheringham was the goal-scorer this time in a match where Arsenal midfield player David Rocastle almost choked to death after swallowing his tongue. The signs were ominous, especially with Liverpool due at The Den for a televised match the following week.

The panic button had not been pressed just yet but the side needed something to get their confidence back. Reserve goalkeeper Keith Branagan, bought by Docherty from Cambridge for £100,000 two years earlier, and Danis Salman had asked for transfers after getting frustrated with reserve-team football. Branagan went on loan to Brentford and although Salman remained he eventually moved to Plymouth just before the transfer deadline in March. It was hard to see what changes could be made, especially with injuries and suspensions taking their toll.

David Thompson's saving tackle against Liverpool.

So Docherty scoured the transfer market and brought in goalkeeper Peter Hucker, on a free transfer from QPR, who never managed to get a first-team game.

The Lions kept the same side and their barren run continued. Television viewers would have to admit though that they should have done better than just have Thompson's goal to show for their efforts as Liverpool won 1-2.

The scrappy 0-0 away draw at Queens Park Rangers saw Nicky Coleman make his first start after injury, but he was to make only two more all season. A 2-2 home draw with Southampton saw Paul Stephenson make his first start of the season and score one of the goals, Cascarino netting the other one.

The chances were still being missed though and poor defending was not helping. Southampton's equaliser came from the penalty spot after a mistake by Horne. At least another point had been secured and another came after the 1-1 away draw with Charlton, Anthrobus scoring his fourth of the season. However a missed Cascarino penalty would have secured all three.

The distraction of a cup match did not help as the Lions lost 1-2 to Second Division Swindon in the second round of the Zenith Data Systems Cup. Gary Waddock was the scorer and it would have been worse but for the heroics of goalkeeper Keith Branagan, back from his loan at Brentford.

Cascarino dismissed the idea that speculation of a move to Aston Villa was affecting his play. To prove it he scored against the Midlands side at The Den the following Saturday in a 2-0 win. Paul Stephenson scored the other goal in a match that saw Horne back in goal and the first start of the season for Steve Torpey, who had made a couple of appearances as a substitute earlier in the season.

Cascarino scored again in the next match, but it was only a consolation effort and Spurs were comfortable 1-3 winners in the Boxing Day match at White Hart Lane. Having lost 0-2 against relegation contenders Manchester City at Maine Road, the year ended with the Lions just five places from the bottom of the table.

	P	W	D	L	F	A	Pts
MILLWALL	19	5	6	8	27	33	21
Luton Town	19	4	8	7	21	25	20
Sheffield Wednesday	20	5	5	10	15	29	20
Manchester City	19	5	4	10	21	34	19
Charlton Athletic	19	3	7	9	15	24	16

Anxious supporters were no doubt lifted by the news that the club had shattered its transfer record with the £800,000 signing of striker Paul Goddard from Derby. Denials of the sale of either Cascarino or Sheringham came next and Docherty insisted that all three could play together. With Sheringham still out injured Goddard made his Lions debut on New Year's Day against his old club at The Den.

If it had been a fairy-tale Goddard would have scored against his former Derby teammates but true life is rarely like that. He must have left his scoring boots at the Baseball Ground and it was left to Dawes to produce the equaliser in the fifty-third minute as two more priceless points went begging. 'I know I can do a lot better,' said Goddard. The fans waited to see how much.

The club had been working tirelessly to rid itself of its hooligan image; the Community Club of the Year award that had been won the previous season showed how far they had come. But the BBC dragged the club's name back into the gutter with the televising of the TV drama, *Arrivederci Millwall*.

The drama was about five Millwall fans who travelled to Spain for the 1982 World Cup. After its showing the complaints flooded in, especially from Millwall fans themselves, who protested that the grotesque violence shown was unfair to the club and blackened their image. Club chairman Reg Burr said, 'It could have been called Arrivederci anything, so why Millwall? I would feel just as strongly, and just as saddened,' he added, 'if it were West Ham, Leeds or Glasgow Rangers.'

The fans had a chance to redress the balance when Channel 4 broadcast *No One Likes Us, We Don't Care* when they were able to voice their opinion on many things. This programme showed the club in the context of a changing community.

Meanwhile, back on the pitch, an epic FA Cup tie was about to unfold. Drawn away to Manchester City, the match ended 0-0 thanks to a splendid match by goalkeeper Keith Branagan, in the side due to a late stomach injury to Brian Horne that needed surgery. Three days later it was City's Andy Dibble who kept the tie alive with some brilliant saves in a game that finished 1-1 after extra time. Jimmy Carter scored the Lions' goal.

Millwall won the toss to decide the venue of a second replay six days later. But before then there was the matter of league points to be won against Nottingham Forest. Maybe it was their cup exertions that were to blame for the 1-3 defeat at the City Ground. The goal, by Sheringham, on as a substitute for Coleman when the Lions were three down, did little to halt their league slump. It did however help him warm up for the second FA Cup replay against Manchester City.

Docherty had the option of starting with his three strikers for the first time and decided to go with it. Cascarino was deployed wide on the left with Goddard and Sheringham as a central strike force and it paid immediate dividends.

After just two minutes Goddard had registered his first goal for the club. It was not a classic. He had a few bites at the cherry and he may well have punched it home. City certainly thought so and so did some of the crowd? But who cared, the goal was awarded and the Lions were on their way.

Seven minutes later Sheringham finished off a three-man move involving Dawes, Hurlock and Waddock when he spun around Redmond, sidestepped Hendry and thumped the ball into the bottom corner.

There were a few heart-stopping moments in the second half, especially when City pulled a goal back and Goddard had seen a shot hit the underside of the bar and come out. But the Lions wrapped the game up in a move involving all three strikers. Cascarino headed on Goddard's corner and Sheringham's shot on the turn sealed the 3-1 scoreline.

Delighted with the result, Docherty kept the same side for the home league fixture against Wimbledon the following Saturday. If it had worked once it would work again. Wouldn't it? Well actually no!

Jimmy Carter, who had turned down a move to Coventry and signed a new three-year deal with the Lions, watched most of this boring 0-0 draw from the bench. When called upon to replace Goddard with fifteen minutes left he must have wished he had stayed on it as he had a chance to win the match in the last minute but drove straight at Wimbledon goalkeeper Hans Segers. Another two points lost but maybe the FA Cup match against Cambridge would see the Lions roaring again.

The players must not have read the script though. The Fourth Division side were given a standing ovation by the Millwall supporters who saw their side lucky to escape with a 1-1 draw, Cascarino scoring just before half-time. Cambridge duly won the replay at the Abbey Stadium with a goal four minutes from the end of extra time, in a game spoilt by a vicious wind. Unfortunately it was Millwall defender David Thompson who scored it with an overhit and misdirected back pass that eluded Branagan, who had kept his side in the match with some wonderful saves.

Docherty had dropped Goddard for this game and cries of 'Docherty out' at the end of the match showed just what the fans were thinking of a Lions side that showed no confidence and a lack of purpose in their play.

Docherty reverted to his three-striker policy for the next match but it was Branagan who earned the Lions a point in the 1-1 away draw with Sheffield Wednesday, where Darren Treacy got his first league start of the season. Although it was Sheringham who scored in the ninth minute to level David Hirst's sixth-minute opener, Branagan's goalkeeping had saved his team from a battering.

Millwall were now in a relegation dogfight. Having shared the points with fellow strugglers Sheffield Wednesday they needed to take all three from a Manchester United side who came to The Den in a similar position.

They certainly tried hard enough and a Darren Morgan goal, in his only start of the season, went a long way to help but the injury-hit side, which started without Sheringham and lost Goddard during the game and had Morgan and Treacy as its midfield, eventually lost 1-2 and were now in serious trouble and the 'Docherty out' cries returned.

The fans got their wish just three days later as Docherty and his assistant Frank McLintock were sacked with what chairman Reg Burr called, 'the hardest decision I've had to make in twenty-seven years in football'. The man who had taken the Lions to the top of the First Division had gone to be replaced by… Bob Pearson. Pearson would not have been the first name on most supporters' lips to replace Docherty. In fact, it would have been more a question of Bob who?

The new manager had been at the club since 1974, mostly in a scouting capacity and admitted that, 'I have no coaching qualifications or management experience but I have worked with fourteen managers.' 'And,' he added, 'we are going to stay up.'

That prediction seemed a little premature at Highfield Road where, although they were a goal up after six minutes through Cascarino, Coventry were worthy 1-3 winners. Millwall's defence once more looked in tatters.

Pearson responded by bringing the players in for Sunday training with emphasis on removing the individual defensive errors that were causing problems. It failed to work though and the boos rang round the terraces of The Den again when they lost 1-2 to Queens Park Rangers having employed Pearson's new sweeper system to no avail. In fact, David Seaman in the QPR goal did not have a shot of note to save.

Cascarino was the goalscorer once more but it was the last he would score for the club, although he did hit the crossbar in the Lions' next match at Anfield. Liverpool won 0-1 with a late goal in what proved to be the Irishman's final appearance for the club.

Wesley Reid started his first League match of the season as Pearson tried to ring the changes. With the transfer deadline approaching, everyone looked on to see what would happen next.

First there was the matter of a match at Carrow Road where the Lions managed to gain another point in a 1-1 draw with Norwich. It might have been three points had Steve Wood not been sent off after a fight with Robert Fleck, who also got his marching orders. But it was not to be, although one ray of light came in the debut performance of defender Kenny Cunningham.

Transfer activity came with a rush. Dean Horrix, who had not had a first-team start all season, moved to Bristol City and tragically died in a car accident a few weeks later. The Lions played an all-London side at the end of the season as a tribute to him.

Steve Anthrobus moved to Wimbledon, Danis Salmon went to Plymouth and Darren Morgan joined his ex-boss John Docherty at Brentford on loan. Tony Cascarino's move to Aston Villa finally found fruition after a £1.2 million bid was accepted.

Balancing up the moves, Pearson brought in Welsh international striker Malcolm Allen from Norwich – he had played in the match the previous Saturday – for £400,000 and Eire's World Cup captain, central defender Mick McCarthy, for £500,000 from French club Lyon. McCarthy originally signed on loan and the move was made permanent in the close season. Both players were on the bench in the home match against Everton although Allen did make an appearance as a substitute for Briley.

Millwall had taken the lead when Goddard scored his only league goal for the club just before half-time with a brilliant curling shot. But Everton equalised almost immediately and went on to win 1-2 and relegation came a little closer. With just eight games left until the end of the season there was still time to avoid the drop and three points against fellow strugglers Luton would go a long way to help.

Pearson dropped Sheringham for Allen and McCarthy played as well in what was a dour game at Kenilworth Road. McCarthy scored just before half-time, but unfortunately his header was in the wrong end – not an auspicious start for your new club. When Luton went two up midway through the second half the death knell for the club could be heard.

Briley pulled a goal back immediately but it was too little too late and a win in their next match, at home against Crystal Palace, was vital as the Lions now found themselves bottom of the table.

	P	W	D	L	F	A	Pts
Manchester City	30	7	10	13	31	45	31
Charlton Athletic	31	6	9	16	26	43	27
MILLWALL	31	5	10	16	36	53	25

Things were now looking very desperate and with their next match at home to local rivals Crystal Palace, Millwall needed a win to have any hope of saving their First Division status.

Everyone made the right noises before the game but it is goals that count. Although Allen scored his first in Millwall blue and both he and Stevens hit a post, Palace were already two up and the game was won. Players and supporters alike wondered if the Lions would ever win again. The simple answer was no!

A 1-1 draw in the next game at home to Manchester City, with Thompson scoring, was their last point. In fact they did not score another goal until Allen found the net in the last game of the season, which was lost 1-3 to Chelsea. Before that they had lost away to Derby (0-2) in the game that finally sealed relegation, Aston Villa (0-1) and Arsenal (0-2) and a home match against Spurs (0-1).

By now Pearson had lost his managerial position. The question was; was it ever really his? Bruce Rioch had been appointed before the Spurs match although he insisted that he would just be a face in the crowd until the season was over.

There was nothing he could do now but assess the situation and he looked at all of the playing staff over the last few games. Coach Frank Sibley left as Rioch installed Ian McNeill as his assistant and the Lions' flirtation with the top flight was over, at least for the time being.

Where did it all go wrong? According to Reg Burr, 'Our problems occurred pre-season.' A season that had started with a growl ended with a whimper. The side had gone twenty consecutive games without a win – in fact they won only five all season – and Rioch had some pre-season work to do to make sure it did not happen again.

1989/90   Football League First Division

Date		Opposition	Score	Scorers
Aug	19	Southampton	2-1	Briley, Cascarino
	22	CHARLTON ATHLETIC	2-2	Sheringham, Dawes
	26	NOTTINGHAM FOREST	1-0	Carter
	29	Wimbledon	2-2	Anthrobus, Cascarino
Sept	9	COVENTRY CITY	4-1	Sheringham (2), Anthrobus, Dawes
	16	Manchester United	1-5	Sheringham
	23	SHEFFIELD WEDNESDAY	2-0	Carter, Cascarino
	30	NORWICH CITY	0-1	
Oct	14	Everton	1-2	Sheringham
	21	Crystal Palace	3-4	Cascarino, Anthrobus, Opp OG
	28	LUTON TOWN	1-1	Dawes
Nov	4	Chelsea	0-4	
	11	ARSENAL	1-2	Sheringham
	19	LIVERPOOL	1-2	Thompson
	25	Queen's Park Rangers	0-0	
Dec	2	SOUTHAMPTON	2-2	Cascarino, Stephenson
	9	Charlton Athletic	1-1	Anthrobus
	16	ASTON VILLA	2-0	Cascarino, Stephenson
	26	Tottenham Hotspur	1-3	Cascarino
	30	Manchester City	0-2	
Jan	1	DERBY COUNTY	1-1	Dawes
	13	Nottingham Forest	1-3	Sheringham
	20	WIMBLEDON	0-0	
Feb	3	Sheffield Wednesday	1-1	Sheringham
	10	MANCHESTER UNITED	1-2	Morgan
	17	Coventry City	1-3	Cascarino
	24	QUEEN'S PARK RANGERS	1-2	Cascarino
Mar	3	Liverpool	0-1	
	17	Norwich City	1-1	Sheringham
	21	EVERTON	1-2	Goddard
	24	Luton Town	1-2	Briley
	31	CRYSTAL PALACE	1-2	Allen
Apr	7	MANCHESTER CITY	1-1	Thompson
	14	Derby County	0-2	
	16	TOTTENHAM HOTSPUR	0-1	
	21	Aston Villa	0-1	
	28	Arsenal	0-2	
May	5	CHELSEA	1-3	Allen

Full Members Cup

Round	Date		Opposition	Score	Scorers
2	Dec	13	Swindon Town	1-2	Waddock

League Cup

Round	Date		Opposition	Score	Scorers
2/1	Sept	19	Stoke City	0-1	
2/2	Oct	3	STOKE CITY	2-0	Sheringham, Cascarino
3		23	Tranmere Rovers	2-3	Hurlock (2)

FA Cup

Round	Date		Opposition	Score	Scorers
3	Jan	6	Manchester City	0-0	
3R		9	MANCHESTER CITY	1-1	Carter
3/2R		15	MANCHESTER CITY	3-1	Sheringham (2), Goddard
4		27	CAMBRIDGE UNITED	1-1	Cascarino
4R		30	Cambridge United	0-1	

1989/90   Football League First Division

	P	W	D	L	F	A	Pts
Liverpool	38	23	10	5	78	37	79
Aston Villa	38	21	7	10	57	38	70
Tottenham Hotspur	38	19	6	13	59	47	63
Arsenal	38	18	8	12	54	38	62
Chelsea	38	16	12	10	58	50	60
Everton	38	17	8	13	57	46	59
Southampton	38	15	10	13	71	63	55
Wimbledon	38	13	16	9	47	40	55
Nottingham Forest	38	15	9	14	55	47	54
Norwich City	38	13	14	11	44	42	53
Queen's Park Rangers	38	13	11	14	45	44	50
Coventry City	38	14	7	17	39	59	49
Manchester United	38	13	9	16	46	47	48
Manchester City	38	12	12	14	43	52	48
Crystal Palace	38	13	9	16	42	66	48
Derby County	38	13	7	18	43	40	46
Luton Town	38	10	13	15	43	57	43
Sheffield Wednesday	38	11	10	17	35	51	43
Charlton Athletic	38	7	9	22	31	57	30
MILLWALL	38	5	11	22	39	65	26

Oh! Teddy Teddy!
1990/91

Having assessed the situation, Rioch made an immediate move and, along with McNeill, changed his backroom staff. In came Steve Harrison as first-team coach, Ian Evans took over as reserve-team coach and Tom Walley was put in charge of the youth team, as Rioch looked to change the structure of the club.

A strict disciplinarian, Rioch made other changes too. Out went jeans and designer stubble and in came suits, shirts and ties and shaven faces. Also out went the long-ball style of play that Docherty had employed during his tenure as manager and in came a pass-and-move game that epitomised Rioch's style.

He also changed midweek matches from Tuesdays to Wednesday evenings, saying that it gave the players more time to recover from the weekend game.

There were also changes within the club itself. The fences, which were still a feature at most football grounds, were lowered and the spikes on top of them removed.

As part of their community scheme a job club was opened to help the unemployed find work and the 'Lions Lifeline' scheme, a way of bringing extra money into the club and based on a similar scheme at Crystal Palace, was introduced.

Of course there were the usual changes in playing personnel. Phil Babb, a youngster who never made the first team but went on to play for Coventry and Liverpool as well as gaining international honours for Eire, left to join John Docherty, who was now at Bradford City. Goddard, McLeary and Wood were transfer listed and new signings Alex Rae – a bargain buy at £100,000 from Falkirk – and John McGlashan, who cost £25,000 from Montrose, joined the club. They were the first Scottish players to be signed by the club for twelve years and Rioch described them as, 'very exciting young prospects'. Discussing his transformation of playing style Rioch added, 'the players that can't adapt, for whatever reason, will have to go and I will find people who can play the way I want to.'

Six wins and a draw in their pre-season matches showed that the players had adapted well to the new style of play and the start of the new season augured well. But before they kicked a ball in anger, the squad, and perhaps especially the fans, had to get used to being without midfield dynamo Terry Hurlock, who had made a surprise move to Glasgow Rangers just forty-eight hours before the big kick-off.

Neither should have worried. The team that had forgotten how to win a league match started the new campaign with an emphatic 2-1 win over Watford. Alex Rae made his Millwall league debut and Malcolm Allen scored both goals against his old club in a new striking partnership with Teddy Sheringham.

Just over 10,000 fans were at The Den to see the first home game of the season against Barnsley and they were not to be disappointed; Allen scored from thirty yards out, Rae opened his account and further goals from Carter and Sheringham made it an easy 4-1 win for the Lions.

Brian Horne had made his first appearance in goal, replacing the injured Keith Branagan and not surprisingly Rioch kept an unchanged side for the next match away at Newcastle. Could the

Lions make it three wins in a row against a Newcastle side that had been virtually invincible at St James' Park the previous season?

A goal each for Allen and Sheringham in the 2-1 win showed they could. When Rae scored after just eighty-one seconds of the home match against Ipswich it looked like they were on their way to a fourth. But Ipswich had other ideas and were good value for their part in a match that ended 1-1. Bromley striker Jon Goodman had joined the club in a £30,000 move before the game and he was to play his part later in the season.

The following Wednesday it looked as though the Lions would suffer their first defeat of the season when Hull City came to The Den and took a 1-3 lead by half-time. Millwall had actually gone ahead through Sheringham, heading home a cross from Paul Stephenson who was making his first start of the season in place of the injured Briley. In a match that see-sawed from brilliant to bizarre, he could have had five before Hull had scored.

A shocked Millwall battled away and Carter gave the fans some hope with a wickedly deflected shot with twelve minutes left. They were delighted when Waddock, making his first start of the season in place of the ill Alex Rae, scrambled a dramatic equaliser ten minutes later for the match to end 3-3.

The Lions could not shake off the drawing habit when they finished the game against Charlton 0-0. It was only the brilliance of home goalkeeper Mike Salmon that kept the score that way, in a match where Millwall had Keith Stevens sent off five minutes from time and Kenny Cunningham got his first start of the season. John McGlashan also played in his first Millwall league match, coming on for the injured Darren Morgan.

It was Brian Horne's turn to make sure the Lions finished 0-0 in their next match, the first leg of a second round Rumbelows Cup match away at Bournemouth. He saved a Luther Blissett penalty in the last minute, although he had made a string of fine saves throughout the match to save lacklustre Millwall from defeat.

Horne was at it again the following Sunday in another 0-0 draw, this time away to Swindon. The Lions had now drawn five games in a row, ending the first month of the season in sixth place.

	P	W	D	L	F	A	Pts
Sheffield Wednesday	7	5	2	0	17	6	17
Notts County	7	5	0	2	15	10	15
West Ham United	8	3	5	0	10	6	14
Swindon Town	8	4	2	2	10	8	14
MILLWALL	7	3	4	0	12	7	13

The club had also put in its application with Lewisham Council for planning permission to build the new ground on the Senegal Fields site and were waiting now to see what the reaction would be. Back on the playing field at Cold Blow Lane, normal service was at last resumed as Kevin O'Callaghan, back from the injury that had kept him out of the entire previous season, started his first game and inspired the Lions to a 2-0 win over Portsmouth. Rae and Sheringham scored in the last twenty minutes.

Three days later it was the turn of West Bromwich Albion, who found themselves on the end of a 4-1 mauling by the Lions. Showing why Queens Park Rangers had offered £1 million for his services and Bruce Rioch insisted that he was going nowhere, Sheringham scored a hat-trick – he actually scored four as he also scored an own goal for WBA. Alex Rae added the fourth and then another two when the Lions booked a place in the third round of the Rumbelows Cup by beating Bournemouth 2-1.

So it was with high hopes that Rioch took his team to Middlesbrough to face his old club. Although Rae scored for the Lions he also scored for 'Boro, and a John Hendrie cracker saw Millwall lose, 1-2, for the first time in the campaign.

Alex Rae coolly slots in the fourth goal in a remarkable comeback against Sheffield Wednesday. After being two goals down at half-time the Lions won 4-2.

The away game at Notts County that followed showed a change in formation as Mick McCarthy, playing for the first time this season, joined Wood in the centre of the defence and McLeary was used in a sweeper role. It paid dividends as O'Callaghan scored the only goal of the game and the win kept the Lions' promotion challenge roaring on.

Sticking to the adage of not changing a winning team, Rioch did just that when the Lions met Bristol City at The Den on the following Wednesday night. It looked to have paid dividends when Waddock put them in front after just eight minutes. However, Brian Horne showed that he could be as bad as he could be good when first he knocked the ball into his own net after a back pass from McCarthy and then his attempted clearance failed to clear the penalty area. City ended up 1-2 winners.

It would be easy to blame Horne but in reality the whole team were poor. They could not manage to put more than two passes together all night and things did not look good for the Lions with unbeaten Sheffield Wednesday visiting The Den the following Saturday.

Rioch rang the changes for this match. Out went the sweeper system along with Horne, Cunningham and McCarthy, who were replaced by Branagan, Dawes and Allen as the side reverted to playing 4-4-2. It did not seem to make much difference, however, as Wednesday were two goals to the good by half-time. Whatever Rioch said to his players in the dressing room certainly made a difference though. Goals from Carter and Sheringham brought the game level and when Allen scored their third with just two minutes left the improbable became possible. When Rae added a fourth it became an unbelievable 4-2 win.

So on a high they travelled to Aston Villa for the next round of the Rumbelows Cup. Although they played well, a penalty and the inevitable Cascarino goal put them out of the competition.

The frustration continued at Blackburn, who won 0-1 with their only shot on target. The Lions had plenty of possession but fail to convert it into goals.

Things went from bad to worse as a one-goal lead given to them by Allen became a 1-2 home defeat against Oxford United and surely things had to change for the visit of West Ham to The Den the following week. Perhaps it was inevitable that before the match Millwall's carefully built new image was shattered as fans fought a running battle outside the ground and the match had to be delayed by fifteen minutes.

The only changes to the team were the return of Horne and Stephenson to the starting line up and it was Stephenson's goal early in the second half that gave the Lions the lead. That they did not increase it or indeed were not in front earlier was due to the goalkeeping ability of Ludek Miklosko in the visitors' goal. The Lions fans went home disappointed with a 1-1 draw. 'We have not quite got the balance of the side right,' said Rioch. 'But it will come.'

He would have to do it without buying players though as it was made quite clear that there was no money to spend. The club's acquisition of the Tavern Leisure chain of pubs had taken money out of the club without bringing any back in.

Rioch tinkered with the team again for the trip to Plymouth Argyle, bringing in Goddard, who had been on the bench for the previous two matches, for Allen. Although the decisive goal in their 2-3 defeat was a penalty – Sheringham and Rae were the Millwall goalscorers – the Lions never really got going. 'Some of our individual performances were nothing short of being shocking, especially in the first half,' said Rioch. 'It will not be tolerated at this club. You are looking for players to give you consistent performances.'

To prove he meant what he said, Rioch put Allen, Dawes, Morgan, Thompson and Hucker onto a transfer list that already included McLeary, Wood and Goddard, and sold Torpey and Treacy to Bradford City for a combined fee of £100,000.

He then brought Briley, who had recovered from an operation on an injured ankle, McCarthy and Cunningham back into the side for the away match against Brighton. Although they again could not turn their supremacy into goals, the 0-0 draw redeemed them a little from the previous week.

The same team faced Bristol Rovers at The Den the following week and only a last-minute Sheringham goal saved some red faces in another 1-1 draw. It was with some appreciation that the match at Oxford the following week was cancelled due to the weather and hopefully the break would help the team get things right for the visit of Watford.

It didn't!

Rioch changed the team again. This time he brought in youngster Alan Dowson for the only first-team game he played for the club, John McGlashan got his first start in a match, having been used just once before as a substitute, and Wood and O'Callaghan were restored to a side that stumbled to an humiliating 0-2 home defeat to the side at the bottom of the table.

There followed the distraction of the Zenith Data Cup match at Norwich, where Rioch again changed the side, bringing in Dawes, Waddock, Stephenson and Allen. Their performance deserved more than the 1-1 draw. Sheringham scored in extra time and the team subsequently lost 5-6 in a penalty shoot-out.

It was no surprise that the same side took the field at Molineux but old habits are hard to break and although Sheringham scored, they gifted the match to Wolves 1-4 with a series of shocking misses and defensive blunders.

Without a win in eight games it came as a relief when two Sheringham goals gave them a 2-1 Boxing Day win over Leicester in a match that saw Jon Goodman get a taste of first-team action at The Den coming on as a substitute for Allen. The same side fought out a 0-0 draw with top-of-the-table Oldham, to end the year in ninth place.

	P	W	D	L	F	A	Pts
West Ham United	24	14	9	1	35	13	51
Oldham Athletic	23	14	6	3	47	24	48
Sheffield Wednesday	23	11	10	2	46	27	43
Middlesbrough	23	12	4	7	37	20	40
Notts County	23	11	6	6	35	27	39
Wolverhampton Wanderers	23	8	10	5	37	28	34
Bristol City	22	10	4	8	37	33	34
Barnsley	23	8	9	6	32	24	33
MILLWALL	23	8	8	7	33	29	32

Whatever New Year resolutions the players made had an immediate effect when the same side, except with Goodman making his first start in place of Allen, won 2-0 at Port Vale. Goodman certainly enjoyed his first full game, scoring on the stroke of half-time after his earlier run and cross had set up Sheringham to put the Lions in front.

With Jimmy Carter complaining of an upset stomach after a dodgy curry, the team had to change for the home FA Cup tie against Leicester. Stephenson took his place. Sheringham was presented with a silver salver before the match for breaking Derek Possee's all-time goalscoring record.

Leicester took a third-minute lead that they held until the last two minutes when Sheringham and Stephenson scored to give the Lions a place in the next round. The result surely hinged on the refereeing decisions of Kelvin Morton who, having booked five players, four of them from Millwall, sent off two Leicester players either side of the Millwall goals.

A programme from the 1990/91 season.

Just how 'dodgy' Carter's stomach had been was brought into question when a few days later he was wearing Liverpool red after the Anfield club's £800,000 bid was accepted.

Millwall's promotion race looked back on course when they won 2-1 away at Barnsley. Goodman's pace ran the Barnsley defence ragged and a Sheringham penalty and a goal from Rae wrapped up the points. But the push took a knock when Newcastle came to The Den and went away with a 0-1 win after an outstanding display by John Burridge in the Newcastle goal helped them get away with daylight robbery.

Rioch went into the transfer market again, buying goalkeeper John Donegan for £30,000 from Irish club Kilkenny and strikers John Humphrey from Leatherhead and John McGinlay on loan from Bury. Paul Goddard moved to Ipswich – the man who had cost the Lions £400,000 per goal scored left for free.

Remembering the four goals that the team had put past Sheffield Wednesday in the league match at The Den earlier in the season the fans were looking forward to seeing more of the same when they met in the fourth round of the FA Cup. What they saw nobody could really believe.

The only change to the side saw O'Callaghan come in for the injured Briley and he instigated most of the Lions attacks, especially in the first half. But it was his fellow winger Paul Stephenson who got the Lions off to a dream start by scoring after just fifty-seven seconds.

However, poor defending was to blight the Lions' efforts throughout the match and they soon found themselves 1-2 behind. Alex Rae levelled the scoring just before half-time and everyone settled in for an interesting second forty-five minutes.

Sheffield soon re-established their advantage but inevitably Sheringham evened things up again. When Wednesday scored again with just five minutes left it looked all over. Nobody reckoned with the never-say-die efforts of Alex Rae, however, and his last-gasp effort, in the dying seconds, squared the match 4-4. The lights may have gone out in the stands at half-time but the efforts of all the players certainly lit up the pitch.

You could not expect the same thing to happen in the replay four days later and Sheffield duly won the match 0-2. But if a Sheringham effort had gone in instead of hitting the bar who knows what might have been?

Back in league action the Lions were purring again when goals from Sheringham, Goodman and Rae gave them a comfortable 3-0 away victory against Ipswich. David Thompson got his first match of the season and Paul Goddard was the butt of endless mocking from the Millwall fans.

Plymouth were the next team to receive a mauling at The Den. Sheringham, who scored all of Millwall's goals in their 4-1 win, gave them a lesson in goalscoring. He thus became the first

Millwall player to score four in a game since John Sheppard in the 1950s. He also broke Derek Possee's league goals record of 79 when he curled home his fourth and by the end of the season had broken John Calvey's all-time Millwall league and cup goals record of 98, which Calvey established over two spells with the club in 1895-99 and 1904-05.

The game was also significant for another reason: it was the first league game in the country to be sponsored by a local fanzine; in this case *No-one Likes Us*.

Unfortunately Sheringham did not score in the next game, away to West Ham. The goal was left to Goodman but it was the Lions' only one in a game they lost 1-3. A 0-0 draw away at Oxford United and another loss, this time 1-0 away to Bristol Rovers, dented their automatic promotion hopes.

They were soon back on track when goals from Goodman, Briley – his first of the season – and inevitably Sheringham completed a 3-0 win over Brighton. But it was not all good news for the Lions as McCarthy, back after injury, tore his knee ligaments after just twelve minutes and faced a lengthy layoff.

A 0-0 draw away at Portsmouth and a 1-0 home win against Swindon, where O'Callaghan was the scorer, kept them in contention. But a mistake by goalkeeper Branagan saw a two-goal lead established by Thompson and Goodman at home against Middlesbrough thrown away. The 2-2 draw saw two points go begging and Briley limped out of the action with a hamstring injury.

Rioch immediately brought in Mike Fillery on loan from Oldham and he went straight into the team against West Bromwich Albion at The Hawthorns in what would be his only game for the club. It ended in a 1-0 win with Sheringham scoring his 100th goal for the club.

He scored two more in the 2-1 away win at Leicester where Paul Kerr, a £130,000 buy from Middlesbrough on transfer deadline day, made his Millwall debut. Rioch also made John McGinlay's loan move permanent when he paid Bury £50,000 for the striker's services.

Sheringham continued his remarkable goal-scoring feats when he added another to his tally in the 2-1 home win over Wolves. Stevens, with his only goal of the season, scored the other.

Malcolm Allen, restored to the side instead of Goodman, scored the goal in the 1-1 draw on Oldham's plastic pitch but they changed places for the next match, at home to Charlton. Here Sheringham scored his third hat-trick of the season in the Lions' 3-1 win.

Promotion nerves now set in. Port Vale won 1-2 at The Den (Thompson was the scorer) and a 1-1 draw at Hull, where McGinlay made his League debut, saw the Lions clinging to a play-off place. Kerr scored his first goal for the club at Hull but McCarthy had to go in goal after Branagan was injured after seventeen minutes.

Kerr scored again in the next match, which the Lions lost 1-2 at home to play-off rivals Notts County, so they travelled to Bristol City to play a game they had to win. After being a goal down at half-time, a devastating twenty-minute spell in the third quarter, during which Sheringham scored his fourth hat-trick of the season and Thompson also netted, saw a 4-1 win as the end result.

Sheringham scored again against Sheffield Wednesday but it was only a ninetieth-minute consolation as the home side won 1-2. He scored his 38th of the season from the penalty spot and Rae added another as the 2-1 win over Blackburn Rovers sealed fifth place. A collective sigh of relief was heard over The Den, as the fans got ready for the two-legged match against Brighton in the Play-off semi-final.

	P	W	D	L	F	A	Pts
Oldham Athletic	46	25	13	8	83	53	88
West Ham United	46	24	15	7	60	34	87
Sheffield Wednesday	46	22	16	8	80	51	82
Notts County	46	23	11	12	76	55	80
MILLWALL	46	20	13	13	70	51	73

Bruce Rioch presenting the Player of the Season Award to record goalscorer Teddy Sheringham.

Why Rioch chose to have both Briley and McCarthy on the bench for the first leg at the Goldstone Ground was the talking point among the fans but it did not seem to matter when Stephenson gave the Lions an eighteenth-minute lead. Although Goodman had another goal disallowed the fans were waiting for the onslaught.

It came in a manner that they had not bargained for as Brighton scored again and again to leave a shell-shocked Lions 1-4 down. Nine months of hard work had evaporated away.

McGinlay scored his only goal of the season in the second leg to put the Lions one up but they had a mountain to climb. Brighton eventually won the match 1-2.

Sheringham won the golden boot with 38 goals, which equalled the club record. In fact he finished the season with a number of records: 111 goals in all competitions, 93 Football League goals and 8 Football League (Rumbelows) Cup goals.

The Lions, though, had to face another season in the Second Division. But with the youth team winning the FA Youth Cup and reaching the final of the Southern Junior Floodlight Cup the future looked good. Just how Rioch would meet the challenge of the coming season we were about to find out.

1990/91   **Football League Second Division**

Date		Opposition	Score	Scorers
Aug	25	Watford	2-1	Allen (2)
Sept	1	BARNSLEY	4-1	Allen, Rae, Sheringham, Carter
	8	Newcastle United	2-1	Allen, Sheringham
	15	IPSWICH TOWN	1-1	Rae
	19	HULL CITY	3-3	Sheringham, Carter, Waddock
	22	Charlton Athletic	0-0	
	30	Swindon Town	0-0	
Oct	3	PORTSMOUTH	2-0	Rae, Sheringham
	6	WEST BROMWICH ALBION	4-1	Sheringham (3), Rae
	13	Middlesbrough	1-2	Rae
	20	Notts County	1-0	O'Callaghan
	24	BRISTOL CITY	1-2	Waddock
	27	SHEFFIELD WEDNESDAY	4-2	Carter, Sheringham, Allen, Rae
Nov	3	Blackburn Rovers	0-1	
	7	OXFORD UNITED	1-2	Allen
	10	WEST HAM UNITED	1-1	Stephenson
	17	Plymouth Argyle	2-3	Sheringham, Rae
	24	Brighton & Hove Albion	0-0	
Dec	1	BRISTOL ROVERS	1-1	Sheringham
	15	WATFORD	0-2	
	22	Wolverhampton Wanderers	1-4	Sheringham
	26	LEICESTER CITY	2-1	Sheringham (2) (1 pen)
	29	OLDHAM ATHLETIC	0-0	
Jan	1	Port Vale	2-0	Sheringham, Goodman
	12	Barnsley	2-1	Sheringham (pen), Rae
	19	NEWCASTLE UNITED	0-1	
Feb	2	Ipswich Town	3-0	Sheringham, Goodman, Rae
	16	PLYMOUTH ARGYLE	4-1	Sheringham (4)
	24	West Ham United	1-3	Goodman
	27	Oxford United	0-0	
Mar	2	Bristol Rovers	0-1	
	9	BRIGHTON & HOVE ALBION	3-0	Goodman, Briley, Sheringham
	12	Portsmouth	0-0	
	16	SWINDON TOWN	1-0	O'Callaghan
	20	MIDDLESBROUGH	2-2	Thompson, Goodman
	23	West Bromwich Albion	1-0	Sheringham
	30	Leicester City	2-1	Sheringham (2)
Apr	3	WOLVERHAMPTON WANDERERS	2-1	Stevens, Sheringham
	6	Oldham Athletic	1-1	Allen
	10	CHARLTON ATHLETIC	3-1	Sheringham (3)
	13	PORT VALE	1-2	Thompson
	16	Hull City	1-1	Kerr
	20	NOTTS COUNTY	1-2	Kerr
	27	Bristol City	4-1	Sheringham (3), Thompson
May	4	Sheffield Wednesday	1-2	Sheringham
	11	BLACKBURN ROVERS	2-1	Sheringham (pen), Rae
	19	Brighton & Hove Albion	1-4	Stephenson
	22	BRIGHTON & HOVE ALBION	1-2	McGinlay

Full Members Cup

Round	Date		Opposition	Score	Scorers
2	Dec	19	Norwich City	1-1*	Sheringham
				*a.e.t Millwall lost on penalties	

League Cup

Round	Date		Opposition	Score	Scorers
2/1	Sept	25	Bournemouth	0-0	
2/2	Oct	10	BOURNEMOUTH	2-1	Sheringham (2)
3		31	Aston Villa	0-2	

FA Cup

Round	Date		Opposition	Score	Scorers
3	Jan	5	LEICESTER CITY	2-1	Sheringham, Stephenson
4		26	SHEFFIELD WEDNESDAY	4-4	Rae (2), Stephenson, Sheringham
4R		30	Sheffield Wednesday	0-2	

1990/91   Football League Second Division

	P	W	D	L	F	A	Pts
Oldham Athletic	46	25	13	8	83	53	88
West Ham United	46	24	15	7	60	34	87
Sheffield Wednesday	46	22	16	8	80	51	82
Notts County	46	23	11	12	76	55	80
MILLWALL	46	20	13	13	70	51	73
Brighton & Hove Albion	46	21	7	18	63	69	70
Middlesbrough	46	20	9	17	66	47	69
Barnsley	46	19	12	15	63	48	69
Bristol City	46	20	7	19	68	71	67
Oxford United	46	14	19	13	69	66	61
Newcastle United	46	14	17	15	49	56	59
Wolverhampton Wanderers	46	13	19	14	63	63	58
Bristol Rovers	46	15	13	18	56	59	58
Ipswich Town	46	13	18	15	60	68	57
Port Vale	46	15	12	19	56	64	57
Charlton Athletic	46	13	17	16	57	61	56
Portsmouth	46	14	11	21	58	70	53
Plymouth Argyle	46	12	17	17	54	68	53
Blackburn Rovers	46	14	10	22	51	66	52
Watford	46	12	15	19	45	59	51
Swindon Town	46	12	14	20	65	73	50
Leicester City	46	14	8	24	60	83	50
West Bromwich Albion	46	10	18	18	52	61	48
Hull City	46	10	15	21	57	85	45

The Wind of Change
1991/92

It was perhaps inevitable that, after his goalscoring exploits of the previous season, Teddy Sheringham would be starting the new one somewhere else. A £2 million bid from Nottingham Forest saw him add his talents to Brian Clough's side, leaving behind a scoring record of 111 goals from 244 games. Not a bad scoring average by any means!

Having come so close to promotion most fans thought that even with his departure a little tinkering of the squad by Rioch would make sure of it this campaign. However, instead of tinkering with the squad, the manager decimated it.

In on free transfers came goalkeeper Aidan Davison from Bury and midfielder John Hall from Watford. More midfield players followed and Ian Bogie from Preston for £145,000, John Colquhoun for £400,000 from Hearts and Phil Barber, a £100,000 buy from Crystal Palace, all joined the club.

Defender Colin Cooper made a £300,000 move from Middlesbrough to The Den, as did strikers Chris Armstrong, a £75,000 buy from Wrexham and the experienced Mark Falco, who cost £175,000 when signing from Queens Park Rangers.

Of course, with so many new faces there had to be departures. Both Nicky Coleman and Sean Sparham had to stop playing due to serious injuries, Gary Waddock failed to agree terms and neither could Darren Morgan and both were released and so, sadly, was Les Briley, who was given a free transfer along with Kevin O'Callaghan, whose injury problems never really healed.

Before the season started Rioch explained what was needed to get out of the Second Division. 'Consistency has to be the most important factor of all and that's what we'll be striving for,' he said, adding, 'we can play push and run to great effect. If I can ally that with consistency we'll cause a few teams considerable problems.'

They were certainly consistent in pre-season, losing five of their six matches and drawing the other one, and it was a much-changed side that kicked off the season, losing 0-1 at Middlesbrough. Davison, Cooper – made captain against his old club – Colquhoun, Falco and Barber all made their League debuts. With both Bogie and Armstrong also coming on as substitutes the fans saw seven new faces and a team desperately short of match practice and knowledge of each other. Only playing together would address the problems.

And so it was on a sunny August afternoon that the fix started. At least it looked that way, as the same side, with the exception of McLeary for Wood, took the field against Sunderland. Two goals from Barber, sandwiching one each from Falco and Kerr, gave the fans something to look forward to in an exciting 4-1 win. In fact it might have been a clean sheet if the referee had not ordered Sunderland's penalty to be retaken for encroachment after Davidson had brilliantly saved the original kick. 'This is just the start,' said Rioch. 'We'll get better, fitter and stronger.'

It seemed that those words had not reach Plymouth however, as they took a two-goal lead, due in part to some poor Millwall defending. The Lions fought back, though, and Rae tapped home after a Colquhoun shot had hit the bar to give them some hope at half-time. An own goal looked to have given Millwall a share of the points until Wood, a replacement in the second half for McLeary, put the ball into his own net with no time left in the match.

Phil Barber rifles home his first goal for Millwall against Sunderland, August 1991.

The 2-3 defeat showed there was still a lot of work to be done and when Brighton took all three points from The Den the following Wednesday night it was confirmation of the fact.

The match started bizarrely. Full-back Gary Chivers started in goal after 'keeper Perry Digweed had injured himself in the warm up and reserve Mark Beeney was still rushing from the stands to the changing room when the game kicked off. John McGlashan breaking his ankle did not help matters but Falco's goal could not disguise a disjointed and anxious performance from the Lions in the 1-2 defeat.

Those defensive frailties were still to be seen three days later when, in spite of taking a fourth-minute lead through a Kerr penalty, the Lions lost 1-2 at home to Cambridge United. This match saw Chris Armstrong and Ian Bogie start their first league game of the season.

This result produced a few rumbles of 'Rioch out' from a disenchanted section of the crowd that wondered what would happen when they faced the other university city side, Oxford, at the Manor Ground a week later.

Rioch brought back Mick McCarthy, who had been out because of injury, to shore up a fragile defence against a side without a point. Goals from Colquhoun, his first for the club, and Rae looked like keeping it that way. Unfortunately those old defensive errors crept back in and the match ended 2-2. Two more precious points had been thrown away.

The lessons still had not been learned three days later. Having taken a two-goal lead away at Bristol City with goals from McCarthy and Colquhoun, they once more drew 2-2. It might have been a late penalty and a disallowed Rae goal that lost them the additional two points but things were clearly not right with the side. However, Colquhoun was quoted as saying, 'We are starting to play well and I'm sure it's only a matter of time before the victories start coming.' The fans had started wondering how long that time would take.

It looked like no time at all when a 2-1 win over Newcastle at The Den cheered them no end. They might have come back from a goal down and the second of Kerr's two goals may have come in the final minute but, without some outstanding saves from Aiden Davison and the aid of the Millwall crossbar, things could have been very different. 'There's a thin line between success and failure,' said Rioch. How right he was to be proved.

Maybe the home tie of the Rumbelows Cup against Swindon would prove to be a little light relief from the problems the Lions were having in their matches, but they found themselves two down after half an hour and things were looking bleak. The situation changed when Swindon defender Nick Summerbee was sent off for two bookable offences. Stevenson scored just before the break and Armstrong's first goal for the club, soon after the restart, gave them some hope of progressing through the return match at the County Ground thirteen days later.

It did not. Although Colquhoun gave the Lions an eleventh-minute lead they lost the match 1-3 and the tie 3-5.

Before then was the matter of two league games. The first, at Oakwell, saw the Lions come away with a well-deserved 2-0 win against a Barnsley side that defended poorly. Two goals from Rae – he would have had a hat-trick if his late thirty-yard shot had gone in instead of hitting a post – were enough to give the Lions all three points. It was the Lions' first clean sheet of the season and saw them end the month of September six from the bottom of the table. It was also Steve Wood's last game for the club before his £400,000 move to Southampton.

	P	W	D	L	F	A	Pts
MILLWALL	10	3	2	5	17	17	11
Barnsley	12	3	2	7	11	20	11
Bristol Rovers	10	2	2	6	13	19	8
Plymouth Argyle	10	2	2	6	12	21	8
Oxford United	10	2	1	7	13	19	7
Newcastle United	11	1	4	6	13	23	7

Off the pitch, the club were having their problems too. Their venture into the pub game with Tavern Leisure was not as successful as had been hoped and the club's own shares had dropped from the opening bid of 20p to just 2.5p, so there was little money around to spend. Chairman Reg Burr did, however, say that if Rioch could find the right player at the right price a 'calculated gamble' could not be ruled out.

They needed to find one quickly as Colin Cooper's first goal for the club was no more than a consolation in their 1-3 home defeat against Blackburn Rovers in the first league match of October.

The next match was won 3-2, away against Southend, with Colquhoun's late strike, after he had a goal disallowed, proving to be the winner. The other goals came from Rae and Stephenson but the defence was still shaky and the 0-0 away draw with Ipswich would have been different but for some exceptional saves from Davison.

They may have been looking forward to the trip to Plymouth for the Zenith Data Cup match but the shock news that coach Steve Harrison had been sacked for 'personal conduct unacceptable to the club' might have had something to do with the 0-4 scoreline that followed.

Another demoralising home defeat followed, 1-2 against Derby, where Kerr was the scorer, although there were a lot of contributory factors to this result. With the scores level and Armstrong having hit the Derby crossbar twice, goalkeeper Davison was injured; he broke a rib that punctured his lung and Colin Cooper took over with just ten minutes of the match left. Referee Ian Hemley had already made a string of extraordinary decisions. Some of the tackles on Armstrong and Colquhoun would not have been out of place in a wrestling ring.

Both the culprits should have been sent off, as should Kerr, who later decided on his own form of retribution, but only yellow cards were shown. To add insult to injury Derby scored the winner in the dying seconds. Complaints about the Derby players' behaviour from Millwall fans led to three of them being fined by the FA but it was the three undeserved points they took that hurt the most.

Maybe the players took out their frustration of that result against Watford the following Tuesday at Vicarage Road. With Keith Branagan recalled from his loan at Gillingham to replace the injured Davison, the 2-0 win, with goals from Rae and Kerr, relit the fire of hope in the hearts of the Millwall faithful. But the match itself was not pretty to watch.

The panicky defence had not disappeared, however, and, despite being in front, thanks to Armstrong's first league goal, they only drew the next match, at home to Portsmouth, 1-1. 'I don't know how we survived,' admitted Rioch after the game.

At Prenton Park the following Tuesday they lost again, although the 1-2 scoreline did not tell the whole story. Paul Kerr's penalty was all they had to show for a performance that deserved at least a share of the points.

Encouraged by their efforts, a 2-0 win at Port Vale was well deserved and the two goals scored by Mark Falco were just reward for a brilliant second-half display. The match also saw a knee injury to Colin Cooper that looked like putting him out of action for some time.

This allowed for the recall of Ian Dawes to the side. Dawes had lost his place to Keith 'Rhino' Stevens in mid-October, but was selected for the home match against Wolves. Goals from Barber and McGinlay, playing his first game of the term because of a pre-season injury, secured a 2-1 win in a hard-fought game.

McGinlay scored again in the 1-1 away draw with Grimsby and the Lions' impressive away form continued, as did their poor home performances as they lost 0-1 to Bristol Rovers. The 'Rioch out' calls started again. 'It was almost inevitable that Rovers would take the lead,' said Paul Kerr. It certainly was!

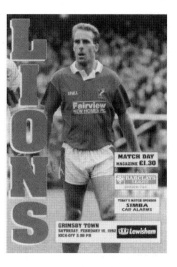

A programme from the 1991/92 season.

Kerr was the scorer in the 1-1 away draw with Leicester and the cancellation of the game against Charlton the following week due to fog offered the chance of some regrouping. It also allowed for the introduction of Dutch midfield player Etienne Verveer from Swiss club FC Chur for 'a small fee'.

Verveer, or 'ET' as he would become known, made his debut in the away match at Brighton and scored the fourth of Millwall's goals. Two came from McGinlay and the other from a Kerr penalty that saw the sending off of Brighton's Gary O'Reilly in a thrilling 4-3 win.

The Lions' impressive away form continued, as did the equally poor home form, and this was highlighted when Watford came to The Den on Boxing Day. Watford cruised to a 0-4 win that was as easy as it was embarrassing for Millwall fans to watch.

It looked like it was going to continue when the Lions found themselves a goal behind when they entertained Plymouth at The Den two days later but two 'Big Macs', McCarthy and McGinlay, had other ideas. Their goals helped the Lions to a 2-1 win and the side ended the year in mid-table.

The New Year did nothing to shake off the team's inconsistencies. This was proved when the New Year's Day match at Swindon was lost 1-3 with McGinlay scoring, and the team then went on to a 4-0 win at Huddersfield in the FA Cup just days later. The match, with goals from Thompson, Verveer and two by Rae, saw the return from injury of Aiden Davison in goal and Colin Cooper as one of the substitutes.

Expectations were high for the trip to Sunderland and when Rae scored to send the teams in level at half-time the fans were looking forward to something special in the second half as McGinlay had also hit the crossbar. What they got was another humiliating defeat and, although Kerr scored for the Lions, they went home with their tails between their legs having lost 2-6. 'We've got to improve our defensive awareness, without sacrificing our attacking flair,' wrote Rioch in his programme notes for the match against Middlesbrough. Having restored 'Boro old boy Cooper to the defence they did just that with a convincing, if somewhat nerve-wracking, 2-0 win with McGinlay and Rae again the scorers.

They were looking to taking this newfound confidence to Norwich but the late cancellation of the FA Cup match meant that by the time the next match arrived, at home to Ipswich, the old problems had returned. A late surge that produced goals for Rae and Kerr, a penalty, could not

An elegant penalty wins the game against local rivals Charlton Athletic.

prevent the Lions from losing 2-3. Facing the rescheduled Norwich match with a defeat rather than a win on their minds was not ideal.

Although they lost the match 1-2 the Lions had more than enough chances to win. A missed Kerr penalty – he also scored the goal – helped them throw away a game they should have easily won. 'We let this game slip away because we missed too many chances,' said a dejected Alex Rae, who himself should have scored a hat-trick.

So it was off to the Baseball Ground. If revenge for the game in October was on the team's mind they certainly gained it in the best way possible, notching a 2-0 win with goals from McGinlay and Rae. Jon Goodman, playing his first game of the season, was a constant handful, Verveer was outstanding in midfield and the team as a whole were good value for money in a well deserved win. Alex Rae, whose twenty-five-yarder left Peter Shilton clutching thin air said, 'I've always wanted to score against Shilton and it was nice to do it with one like that.'

Expectations were high as goal-shy Grimsby were next up at The Den, but the visitors were a goal up after just thirty seconds and the Lions could do no more than equalise through Rae. The 1-1 draw no doubt added new impetus to the 'Rioch out' brigade and their number grew at Twerton Park the following Saturday when goals from Goodman and Armstrong could not stop Bristol Rovers from winning 2-3.

While the winning strike may well have been an own goal by Phil Barber and Rovers' Devon White had given a new meaning to the phrase 'more power to your elbow' by sending Colin Cooper to hospital with severe cuts to his tongue and mouth after one of his elbow-led challenges, the Lions were again guilty of squandering enough chances to have won the match. Therefore the subsequent 1-0 win over Charlton, courtesy of a Kerr penalty, was a welcome relief.

By now Rioch had added to the squad by signing American international goalkeeper Kasey Keller, who immediately left to join the American Olympic squad. Now having six goalkeepers in the squad, Branagan and Carl Emberson were allowed to go on loan to Fulham and Dulwich respectively.

Promotion hopefuls Leicester were next at The Den but they were made to look ordinary as the Lions ran out 2-0 winners. It may have been the early goal, a Cooper twenty-five-yard free-kick after five minutes, that settled the nerves of the Lions but they could have added more than Goodman's tap-in to the final score.

The return match with Charlton followed, ten days after the first, at Upton Park. Those old bad habits returned, though, with the Lions losing 0-1. Missed chances and some poor defending cost them dearly and when Tranmere arrived at The Den the following Saturday and won 0-3 after a lacklustre performance, poor finishing and some comic defending from the Lions brought back the calls for Rioch's head. With the next game lost, away at Portsmouth 1-6, the writing was on the wall.

So poor were the Lions in fact that it took them over an hour to have their first direct shot at goal and there were only five minutes left when Verveer put the ball in the net. By this time the team had been completely humiliated.

It may have saddened Reg Burr when he accepted Rioch's resignation the following Monday after he had been constantly barracked at a reserve match that afternoon, but most fans were pleased to see him go. Whether it was his constant tinkering with the side, sometimes forced on him by injuries, bad luck or, as some suggested, player power, that eventually was Rioch's undoing perhaps no one will ever know. He did, however, leave the club a legacy of some very talented young players who would eventually come good.

When Mick McCarthy was summoned to the chairman's office the following day he thought it was to pay him off. Instead he was offered the vacant manager's role. 'I'm going to give it a hell of a go,' was the blunt Yorkshireman's answer. 'Victory over bottom placed Port Vale at The Den would be nice for starters.' To show he meant business he made eleven changes to the thirteen players that played at Portsmouth. Some of them were positional, but the gamble paid off.

It may have only been a 1-0 win – Allen scored the goal in his first start of the season after a long lay-off due to a knee injury (he was on the bench at Portsmouth), and on his birthday too – it may have been more of a growl than a roar, but on a treacherously windy day it got McCarthy's managerial career off to a good start. More importantly it gave the team some belief in themselves.

Perhaps the most significant change of all was moving Colin Cooper from left-back to centre-back. McCarthy called it, 'the best decision I made in a match situation' and Cooper's future displays did not prove him wrong.

Alex Rae took McCarthy's exhortation to become 'more aggressive' too literally and was sent off in the next match, away against Wolves, but the 0-0 draw was well deserved. It was especially merited with the team down to ten men for the last fifteen minutes. 'I've never been sent off before in my career,' said Rae. 'I'm not that kind of player.' If only he had a crystal ball.

Not wishing to be caught out as April Fools, a 2-1 win over Oxford United at The Den – Stephenson and Goodman were the scorers – kept the ball rolling although they had to fight hard for their win after going behind after just nine minutes. 'I don't know whether it's me taking over or Bruce leaving,' said McCarthy, 'but the players have responded magnificently and I'm delighted we have taken seven points out of nine.'

Naturally the bubble would now burst and a match spoilt in part by the high wind, and also by the constant ball in the air, saw the Lions lose 0-1 away to Cambridge in their next game. This match also saw the first appearance of Andy Roberts in a first-team shirt when he replaced Stephenson ten minutes from the end of the game, and John McGlashan also made his first start (after recovering from a broken ankle) in a match the Lions did not deserve to lose.

The transfer deadline had passed without much activity at The Den. The only movement saw goalkeeper Brian Horne go to Watford on loan. McCarthy continued his Millwall revolution without adding anyone to his squad, although Kerr, Bogie and Thompson were all put on the transfer list.

Roberts made his first start in a home match against Swindon that ended 1-1 – Allen was the scorer – but their old failings returned three days later when a dismal performance saw them lose 2-3 at home to Bristol City. Barber put the Lions in front and a late own goal made up the Millwall scoreline.

It might have taken seventy-seven minutes to score against the side with the leakiest defence but Allen's goal that produced the 1-0 away win at Newcastle pleased both him and his manager. It seemed that he was making up for lost time when he did it again in the draw at home to Barnsley. It may have been a penalty but when you have not played for eleven months any goal is worth having, although the Lions missed a hatful of chances to win the game. 'I feel we've got enough quality at the club to do well next season,' said McCarthy after the match.

The old defensive problems showed themselves at Ewood Park when, having taken a lead through Goodman, the team contrived to throw the game away; Blackburn eventually won 1-2.

A 2-0 win at The Den against Southend, with late goals from Armstrong and Allen, brought the season to a close in a match where Kasey Keller made his Millwall debut. It had been a frustrating if eventful season and the team never really lived up to its potential, finishing fifteenth in the division.

	P	W	D	L	F	A	Pts
MILLWALL	46	17	10	19	64	71	61

The inability to convert chances into goals had haunted the team all season and it was something McCarthy knew he would have to work on. He had managed to put the teeth back into the Lions but now he needed to spend the summer finding a way to make them bite. 'We've got to stamp out the defensive mistakes, sharpen up our finishing and be a lot stronger mentally and physically,' he said, and the fans were eager to find out how he was going to do it.

The launch of 'The Lions Card' was to help raise money for the new stadium and give discounts to fans that took it up. Everything was now gearing itself up for the start of a new era at the club.

1991/92   **Football League Second Division**

Date		Opposition	Score	Scorers
Aug	17	Middlesbrough	0-1	
	24	SUNDERLAND	4-1	Barber (2), Kerr, Falco
	31	Plymouth Argyle	2-3	Rae, Opp OG
Sept	4	BRIGHTON & HOVE ALBION	1-2	Falco
	7	CAMBRIDGE UNITED	1-2	Kerr (pen)
	14	Oxford United	2-2	Rae, Colquhoun
	17	Bristol City	2-2	McCarthy, Colquhoun
	21	NEWCASTLE UNITED	2-1	Kerr (2)
	28	Barnsley	2-0	Rae (2)
Oct	5	BLACKBURN ROVERS	1-3	Cooper
	12	Southend United	3-2	Colquhoun, Rae, Stephenson
	19	Ipswich Town	0-0	
	26	DERBY COUNTY	1-2	Kerr
	29	Watford	2-0	Kerr, Rae
Nov	2	PORTSMOUTH	1-1	Armstrong
	5	Tranmere Rovers	1-2	Kerr (pen)
	9	Port Vale	2-0	Falco (2)
	16	WOLVERHAMPTON WANDERERS	2-1	McGinlay, Barber
	23	Grimsby Town	1-1	McGinlay
	30	BRISTOL ROVERS	0-1	
Dec	7	Leicester City	1-1	Kerr
	21	Brighton & Hove Albion	4-3	McGinlay (2), Kerr (pen), Verveer
	26	WATFORD	0-4	
	28	PLYMOUTH ARGYLE	2-1	McCarthy, McGinlay
Jan	1	Swindon Town	1-3	McGinlay
	11	Sunderland	2-6	Rae, Kerr
	18	MIDDLESBROUGH	2-0	Rae, McGinlay
Feb	1	IPSWICH TOWN	2-3	Rae, Kerr (pen)
	8	Derby County	2-0	Rae, McGinlay
	15	GRIMSBY TOWN	1-1	Rae
	22	Bristol Rovers	2-3	Goodman, Armstrong
	26	CHARLTON ATHLETIC	1-0	Kerr (pen)
	29	LEICESTER CITY	2-0	Cooper, Goodman
Mar	7	Charlton Athletic	0-1	
	11	TRANMERE ROVERS	0-3	
	14	Portsmouth	1-6	Verveer
	21	PORT VALE	1-0	Allen
	28	Wolverhampton Wanderers	0-0	
Apr	1	OXFORD UNITED	2-1	Stephenson, Goodman
	4	Cambridge United	0-1	
	8	SWINDON TOWN	1-1	Allen
	11	BRISTOL CITY	2-3	Barber, Opp OG
	18	Newcastle United	1-0	Allen
	22	BARNSLEY	1-1	Allen (pen)
	25	Blackburn Rovers	1-2	Armstrong
May	2	SOUTHEND UNITED	2-0	Armstrong, Allen

Full Members Cup

Round	Date		Opposition	Score	Scorers
2	Oct	22	Plymouth Argyle	0-4	

League Cup

Round	Date		Opposition	Score	Scorers
2/1	Sept	25	SWINDON TOWN	2-2	Armstrong, Stephenson
2/2	Oct	8	Swindon Town	1-3	Colquhoun

FA Cup

Round	Date		Opposition	Score	Scorers
3	Jan	4	Huddersfield Town	4-0	Rae (2), Thompson, Verveer
4	Feb	5	Norwich City	1-2	Kerr

1991/92   Football League Second Division

	P	W	D	L	F	A	Pts
Ipswich Town	46	24	12	10	70	50	84
Middlesbrough	46	23	11	12	58	41	80
Derby County	46	23	9	14	69	51	78
Leicester City	46	23	8	15	62	55	77
Cambridge United	46	19	17	10	65	47	74
Blackburn Rovers	46	21	11	14	70	53	74
Charlton Athletic	46	20	11	15	54	48	71
Swindon Town	46	18	15	13	69	55	69
Portsmouth	46	19	12	15	65	51	69
Watford	46	18	11	17	51	48	65
Wolverhampton Wanderers	46	18	10	18	61	54	64
Southend United	46	17	11	18	63	63	62
Bristol Rovers	46	16	14	16	60	63	62
Tranmere Rovers	46	14	19	13	56	56	61
MILLWALL	46	17	10	19	64	71	61
Barnsley	46	16	11	19	46	57	59
Bristol City	46	13	15	18	55	71	54
Sunderland	46	14	11	21	61	65	53
Grimsby Town	46	14	11	21	47	62	53
Newcastle United	46	13	13	20	66	84	52
Oxford United	46	13	11	22	66	73	50
Plymouth Argyle	46	13	9	24	42	64	48
Brighton & Hove Albion	46	12	11	23	56	77	47
Port Vale	46	10	15	21	42	59	45

What Beautiful Diamonds 1992/93

The beginning of June saw the bulldozers move onto the Senegal Fields site and work got under way for the building of the new stadium. Early resistance to the scheme had changed to apathy or at least resigned acceptance, while the dream of playing in a brand new stadium became a step nearer. Around 1,000 fans had bought the new Lions Card, raising nearly £250,000 towards the building costs. It was hoped that many more would do so as the season started.

This was also the first season of the new Premier League, so the club found itself back in Division One, if only by default.

McCarthy's plans were set on building a side that would be worthy of playing in such a stadium and preferably in the top division. He signed central defender Tony McCarthy from Irish club Shelbourne for £100,000 and midfielder Andy May from Bristol City in a straight swap for David Thompson. Paul Kerr moved to Port Vale for £140,000 and John Colquhoun to Sunderland for £250,000. Keith Branagan joined Bolton on a free transfer and Alan McLeary went on loan to Sheffield United, while midfield player Paul Holsgrove arrived from Dutch club Hercules FC. An injured back that had troubled Mark Falco all of the previous season finally forced him to give up the game and youngsters Sean Devine and John Hall were released.

The club had new sponsors in the shape of Fairview Homes, who were to purchase and redevelop the old ground as a housing project. They also had a new strip, a darker blue shirt with widening white bands around the bottom half of it.

McCarthy took the team on a pre-season tour of Ireland but it was when they returned home and played Slade Green that the fans got their first glimpse of the shape of things to come – the diamond midfield system. 'We've prepared well and I'm optimistic that we'll be up there challenging for one of the promotion spots,' said McCarthy. 'We didn't do ourselves justice last season and all the players are determined to put that right.' A reasonable pre-season showed he could be right.

The season started with an away trip to Watford where Andy May made his League debut and Keith Stevens was given the captain's armband. The Lions were a goal up, scored by John McGinlay on twelve minutes, after Watford goalkeeper Perry Suckling had made a mess of the new back pass rule that banned goalkeepers from handling the ball when deliberately passed back to them. However some strange decisions by referee Gurnam Singh, including the thirteenth minute sending off of Allen and a penalty awarded against Stevens for shielding the ball, contributed to them losing 1-3.

The same side took on Leyton Orient at Brisbane Road in the first leg of the Coca-Cola Cup first round in what was the Lions' 100th game in the competition under its many guises. Roberts, with his first for the club, and Stevens were the scorers in a 2-2 draw.

The first home game of the season, against Oxford United, gave the fans a chance to see the 'diamond' in action at The Den. The 6,746 in attendance were not disappointed with the 3-1 win, which saw Kasey Keller take over from Davison in goal. Oxford were ripped apart time and again by Armstrong's pace and he helped himself to one of the goals. He also helped Rae, a substitute for the injured May, and Allen to score theirs.

A programme cover from
the 1992/93 season.

Brian Horne went on loan to Middlesbrough and Carl Emberson was loaned to Cambridge; however, McLeary's loan at Sheffield United was called off and he was back, but not chosen to play, for the second leg of the Coca-Cola Cup match with Leyton Orient. The only change from the previous Saturday was Rae for the injured Andy May.

Although Millwall won the match 3-0 with two goals from Allen and another from Armstrong, the scoreline did not really show the massacre that was before the fans' eyes. It set up a game in the next round against Arsenal. 'We were never in it,' admitted a shell-shocked Orient manager Peter Eustace after the game, in which Paul Holsgrove made his debut coming on from the substitutes bench.

Jon Goodman replaced the suspended Allen for the 0-0 away draw against Barnsley although it needed an outstanding display from Keller and a penalty miss to keep it that way. This was to be Chris Armstrong's last game for the club as he was sold to Crystal Palace for £1 million plus striker Jamie Moralee.

There were a host of changes for the side that played at home to Charlton in the revised Anglo-Italian Cup. This round-robin event saw Holsgrove get his first start, Bogie and Stephenson get their first game of the season, the return of McLeary in defence and the debut of youngster Tony Dolby, who replaced Rae in the second half.

Having taken the lead through Cunningham – his first for the club – nobody could work out how the Lions managed to lose 1-2. Charlton scored both their goals in the last five minutes.

A 2-1 win at home to Swindon, after being a goal down, delighted McCarthy. It was not just the goals from McGinlay and Goodman but the way in which they fought back to take control of the game against a talented Swindon side. Two 0-0 draws followed, at home to Birmingham and away to Peterborough, although the only thing missing from both games were the goals that Millwall's impressive displays deserved.

So when Notts County arrived at The Den, it came as no surprise that the goals flowed. Six of them to be precise, scored by Goodman, Allen (2), Barber (2) and Dolby with his first for the club on his first start. The Lions even managed to keep a clean sheet. 'We've been threatening to do that to somebody for a while,' said an understandably delighted McCarthy. So it was in high spirits that they went to Highbury for the first leg of the Coca-Cola Cup second round where Arsenal were lucky to escape with a 1-1 draw.

A late Campbell equaliser to Roberts' goal brought some relief to an Arsenal side grateful that they only conceded once. 'Millwall were superb,' said Arsenal and ex-Millwall manager George Graham.

Perhaps their efforts in the match were reflected in the next game away to Brentford. A 1-1 draw, with Allen scoring the goal, was all they could manage, although they created enough chances in the second half to have won the match.

On to Portsmouth for the second Anglo-Italian Cup match and again McCarthy changed the side. This time he brought in Davison, Holsgrove, Stephenson and Rae and played himself for the first time this season. He also gave debuts to youngster Paul Manning, Dutch trialist Romano Sion and Jamie Moralee, who had injured himself when he butted a wall just before his transfer to the club. Rae's goal in the 1-1 draw was not enough to keep them in the competition and international football at The Den was over, at least for this season.

Brian Horne returned to the club when Middlesbrough decided to take his loan deal no further and John McGinlay left to join Bolton Wanderers. The side returned to a more usual look when they travelled to Sunderland but perhaps their minds were on the coming return match with Arsenal: the 0-2 scoreline reflected this.

The match against Arsenal was as exciting as it was enthralling and showed how far the side had come in such a short space of time. Normal time ended with the score at 1-1, Barber's scoring shot going in off Lee Dixon. Through extra time there were no additional goals, so it was down to the dreaded penalty shoot-out. When Keller pulled off a world-class save from the first penalty from Dixon it looked like it could be the Lions' night but Seaman made a spectacular save from Allen.

Campbell, Dawes and Smith all scored to leave the tie at 3-3 when Seaman made another incredible save from Cooper. Millwall's glory hopes were over – for now. 'Of course I'm disappointed,' said McCarthy. 'But the fact that we caused one of the top clubs in the country so many problems is very encouraging.'

Unfortunately some mindless idiots, who threw coins onto the pitch (one hitting Nigel Winterburn), marred the night. Millwall's on-pitch activities were overshadowed by off-pitch ones once again.

Brian Horne was on his loan travels again, this time to Stoke City and the team got ready for the visit of Cambridge for their next league match. The mental and physical effort of the previous Wednesday had obviously taken its toll; the Lions were two down after half an hour with the first coming after just ninety seconds. However, a rousing second-half display saw them gain a credible 2-2 draw with goals from Allen and Goodman.

In fact, when John Francis was sent off with twenty-five minutes remaining, it looked like they had an opportunity of winning the game but it was not to be. Next came the away match against neighbours Charlton, who had lost just one league game all season, in a game shown live on television.

Having never won a live televised match, the fans must have wondered what the outcome would be of this one and they got a pleasant surprise. If the watching television audience wanted to know what Millwall were about they knew after seeing them dominate the match with their slick passing and movement off of the ball.

Jamie Moralee made his first start for the club and scored his first goal after Alex Rae, in his 100th appearance for the club, had opened the scoring with a thirty-yard cracker. Why the game finished 2-0 when it was such a one-sided contest is anyone's guess. Having won their first game on television, though, the Lions were looking forward to the next one, a week later at home to Wolves. 'If I get the chances I'll score goals,' said a confident Moralee. 'I'll score more than Chris Armstrong.' The fans waited to see the outcome of this boast!

Meanwhile Carl Emberson had gone on loan to Rotherham and Alan McLeary was loaned to Wimbledon.

The match against Wolves would probably not have gone ahead had it not been on television as a torrential downpour left the pitch looking more like a paddy field. The fact that once more Millwall played some scintillating football on it was to their credit. Cooper's first goal of the season and another from Moralee was no more than they deserved, as was the ovation they got at the end of their 2-0 win over a side that had been unbeaten before the game.

Watching from the main stand was Irish international John Byrne, and he signed for £250,000 from Sunderland the following Monday. He made his debut coming on as a substitute in the 0-1 defeat at Bristol Rovers. It looked like the Lions would take a point from the game until Andy Roberts was sent off. 'We were crap,' was McCarthy's view of the game. But the Lions had made enough chances to have won the match before Roberts' dismissal.

They took their revenge on the team from the other side of Bristol four days later; City found themselves losing 4-1 at The Den in a game that saw Byrne start a match for the first time. All five goals came in the first half and those scored by Cooper, Allen, May – his first and last for the club and against his old side as well – and Moralee were the icing on an impressive all-round display in a match that Bristol City contributed to with their never-say-die attitude.

A trip to the Baseball Ground to face a Derby side that had won six of their last seven matches came next and Millwall found themselves behind at half-time. This Millwall side had added resilience to their repertoire though and goals from Moralee and Rae gave them a 2-1 win. This won them the Barclays Performance of the Week award and moved them to fifth in the league table, only one place behind West Ham who were their next opponents.

Travelling goalkeeper Brian Horne had now gone on loan to Sunderland and McLeary was back from his loan at Wimbledon.

Keith Stevens led the side out in his 400th Millwall appearance against the Hammers in yet another live televised match, and they made it a happy one with a 2-1 win with goals from Allen, a penalty after a trip on Cunningham, and Barber. The 12,445 in attendance and the watching television audience certainly had their money's worth in a game that had everything associated with local derbies: near misses, bookings and plenty of excitement in a hard-fought contest. The televised winning streak continued.

Millwall continued their policy of loaning out fringe players when Paul Stephenson went to Gillingham.

The trip to Luton saw John Byrne score his first and only goal for the club in a 1-1 draw that would have been different but for the heroics of Kasey Keller in the Kenilworth Road mud. He more than earned his wages again in the 0-1 defeat at Portsmouth a week later although the Portsmouth goal had more than a touch of offside about it.

Struggling to get back their early season form the Lions were hoping that the visit of Southend to The Den would be the turning point. But the 1-1 draw – Barber scored the goal – was all an out-of-sorts Millwall could muster. It would have been worse if Cooper had not miraculously cleared with an acrobatic overhead kick from Tilson's chip three minutes from time. So it was back to the drawing board for the home match against Grimsby.

McCarthy dropped Allen and replaced him with Bogie and it looked to have worked when Moralee put the Lions in front after just nine minutes. But when Grimsby equalised it was like watching the bad old days of the previous season.

Maybe it was nerves but the old defensive frailties were back and, just when it looked like they would hang on for a point, Moralee scored his second, just two minutes from the end. It was not a bad way to celebrate your twenty-first birthday. The 2-1 score line probably flattered the home side but the relief was heard all around the ground.

A 1-1 draw against runaway leaders Newcastle would seem a credible result yet cries of 'we were robbed' could be heard all over south London. Leading after a goal from Moralee, Millwall looked capable of holding on for a win when linesman John Jones raised his flag in the seventy-fifth minute. The millions of television viewers would have seen the ball handled by Newcastle's

Robert Lee but the linesman decided that it was a Millwall player who had touched the ball. When questioned after the game he added that he had given it for handball and pushing, although the push look more to have been on Cunningham than anyone else.

Mr Jones was certainly the only person, in or out of the ground, who saw things that way but the resulting penalty brought a disappointing end to the match for McCarthy and his team. 'That decision cost us two points,' he said afterwards, 'and who knows, by the end of the season it might cost us promotion and a lot of money.'

A 1-1 away draw on Boxing Day against Tranmere – Goodman was the scorer – and a 2-0 home win over Leicester, with goals from Moralee and Goodman, two days later meant the Lions ended the year in fourth place.

Meanwhile Brian Horne stopped his loan travels and made a permanent move to Portsmouth on a free transfer, while John McGlashan went on loan to Fulham and Carl Emberson continued gaining experience with a loan move to Colchester.

	P	W	D	L	F	A	Pts
Newcastle United	23	17	2	4	45	21	53
Tranmere Rovers	22	12	5	5	42	26	41
West Ham United	23	11	6	6	43	25	39
MILLWALL	23	10	9	4	35	20	39

They did not play again until 9 January because their FA Cup match against Southend was called off because of the weather on the Essex coast. This meant that they had been able to have an extended rest before travelling to Notts County. It seemed to have done some good with Moralee and Goodman again being the scorers with the Lions coming from behind to win 2-1. From here it was off to Southend for the rearranged FA Cup match.

Losing the match 0-1 was bad enough and the fact that ex-Lions goalkeeper Paul Sansome made some exceptional saves did not help. In fact, apart from the goal, Southend did not have one shot on target so dominant were the Lions, but they were unable to break down a resolute Southend defence aided by a gale-force wind, a badly cut-up pitch and some strange refereeing decisions from referee Ian Borrett.

Sadly it was the trouble at the match that took the headlines once again as Millwall fans were accused of causing trouble at the match, although inflammatory policing and Southend's ticketing policy – they sold seats to their own fans that had already been bought by Millwall fans – had to take some of the blame.

Unfortunately many of the off-field activities of the club were not so well publicised. For example, the Salter Road home of Fisher Athletic, at that time playing in the Beazer Homes South League, was under threat of closure; the club put together, and won, a tender for the ground and promised that they could continue playing there as well as providing a home for the Millwall Lionesses.

Back to league action, and the Lions hoped to continue their unbeaten televised match run when Brentford came to The Den. It did not take them long to show that it would continue. In fact it took just fifty-two seconds to be precise, when Rae opened the scoring and goals from Cooper, Goodman (2) and Moralee (2), completed a 6-1 rout of the Bees. It could have been more; Moralee hit the post and numerous shots were kicked off of the goal line in another fine display for the television audience.

The American international John Kerr was taken on trial and he was later to earn a place in Millwall history. For now though it was the bargain-basement buys, Moralee and Goodman, who were taking all the striking plaudits. And the goals just kept on coming. Ten days later Peterborough stepped off their coach for the next match at The Den and probably wished they had stayed at home. They were soundly beaten 4-0.

Alan McLeary made a rare appearance and Tony McCarthy, on his debut, was one of the scorers. Barber, Rae and Goodman were the others. John McGlashan, who just days earlier had gone to Cambridge on loan, had surprisingly joined The Posh for £70,000 but under the terms of his transfer did not play in the game.

It came as a bit of a surprise then when they were beaten 0-3 in their next game, away at Oxford United. The sending off of Rae did not help their cause though.

Normal goalscoring service was resumed the following Saturday when Watford found themselves on the wrong end of a 5-2 walloping. Four up at half-time, with Moralee, Rae, Cooper and Goodman all finding the net, it was inevitable that the second period would be a bit of an anti-climax. But Moralee notched a second just to keep things ticking over and Mick McCarthy's thirty-fourth birthday was ready to be savoured. 'We were a bit cavalier at times,' the Millwall manager said, 'but it was great.'

It was not so great at St Andrews the following Tuesday when Birmingham stopped the Lions from scoring in a 0-0 draw and then they lost away to Swindon 0-3. Meanwhile John Kerr had done enough in his trial to show that he was worth taking on for McCarthy to add him to his strike force.

If the wheels had started to wobble they fell off the following week at The Den, when Barnsley went away 0-4 victors. What had looked like a goal-scoring machine had suddenly been stopped in its tracks.

In an attempt to change things around Allen and Byrne were restored to the starting line-up. It looked to have worked when Allen put the Lions in front against Cambridge at the Abbey Stadium but the match ended 1-1. Although still in third place in the table things were not looking too good as they entered the final furlong of this season's campaign. The table at the end of February looked like this:

	P	W	D	L	F	A	Pts
Newcastle United	32	20	7	5	55	26	67
West Ham United	32	17	9	6	56	29	60
MILLWALL	32	14	11	7	53	35	53

Trying to help the players relax and gain some rest before the run in the management took them off to Portugal for a week. Meanwhile Paul Stephenson was off in a different direction, Brentford to be exact, for £30,000.

Perhaps they were still in a holiday mood for their first game back as they only managed a 0-0 draw against Sunderland at The Den but things looked brighter when a goal from Barber gave them a 1-0 win away at Bristol City. It was a match in which Kasey Keller was outstanding.

It took a ninetieth-minute penalty from Allen to secure the 1-0 win over a resolute Derby at The Den and the Millwall faithful now looked forward to the televised match against Southend at Roots Hall. They were hoping to avenge their FA Cup defeat, stay on the good side of the police and keep their unbeaten live televised match record.

At least they managed two of these and looked to have got back their appetite for scoring goals. A goal down, they scored three in eleven minutes from Barber, Stevens and Goodman, but with Cooper sent off for a tackle on Collymore just before half-time and the return of those old defensive jitters, the match ended 3-3.

The 1-0 home win against Luton the day before the transfer deadline was welcome if not convincing. Jamie Moralee, who hauled himself off the treatment table to score for the injury- and suspension-hit Lions, said, 'I was determined to play and getting the goal was a bonus because I had been stuck on thirteen for ages.'

With the next game being the televised match away against West Ham, there was a flurry of transfer activity. John Byrne went on loan to Brighton. Arriving at The Den was Danny Wallace, on loan from Manchester United, Tommy Gaynor on a free from Nottingham Forest and Gavin Maguire from Portsmouth for a tribunal-fixed £115,000.

Maguire and Gaynor both made their debuts at Upton Park; Gaynor came on as a substitute for Maguire with fifteen minutes left. The Lions got off to the perfect start with Moralee scoring

A panoramic view of the final game at The Den, Cold Blow Lane.

after just forty-five seconds. But the Hammers scored two goals in thirty seconds to ease ahead until Stevens scored. The match ended 2-2. Once again the armchair audience had been treated to a thriller and Millwall had hung onto their unbeaten television record.

Wallace made his debut in the next match, at home to Portsmouth, but it was Kerr who took the applause. He came off the bench to replace Allen and scored his first goal for the club. It was the equaliser in a 1-1 draw. He kept his place in the starting line-up in the away match against Grimsby but the goals were eluding Millwall again and they lost 0-1 to a last-minute penalty.

With the new ground nearing completion and needing extra finance the club launched a two for one special rights issue on the Stock Exchange. But it was what was happening on the pitch that the fans were more interested in.

A 0-0 home draw with Tranmere was a travesty of justice after Kerr's winner was ruled out. Then a 0-3 away loss against ten-man Leicester saw them slip out of the play-off places. The promotion dream was finally shattered when Newcastle came to The Den and went away 1-2 winners. The Lions had been worthy of at least a draw but had only Phil Barber's fluky goal to show for their efforts.

With the odds stacked against them starting life in their new stadium playing Premier League football, the Lions went into their last three games still believing they could do it. But the likelihood was that they would have to win all of them to get into a play-off position. A local derby, even at home, is not the ideal match to play for the first one but Jon Goodman's goal against Charlton was enough to give them a 1-0 win and hope was still there. Mark Kennedy had his Millwall debut in the game and almost scored when he came on as a substitute but at least the dream was still alive – just.

The dream died at Molineux however. Allen's goal was just a consolation as Wolves won 1-3, and all that was left was the final match ever to be played at Cold Blow Lane. Paul Manning finally got his taste of league football and Etienne Verveer got his first action of the season after recovering from a serious knee injury.

With a farewell programme printed and all sorts of things happening on the pitch before the match and a carnival atmosphere (even a fan dressed in a full Lion outfit), it was little wonder that Bristol Rovers won the match 0-3. It seemed that they only had to turn up to win as nothing the Millwall players did turned out right. Allen even missed a penalty.

Had the emotion got to the players that day? Perhaps. But a pitch invasion, started as a friendly farewell, ended in mass destruction of the ground, cut the match short and spoiled the day for many. An emotional farewell was marred by a small element that once again ruined things with wanton vandalism.

The club had come to the end of an era and a new one was about to start. Had it been the injuries, the suspensions, the lack of goals or a combination of all three, all of which seemed to come together at the wrong time, that ended the promotion dream? We shall, of course, never know but the future was looking good with the reserve and youth teams having another good season. The reserve team won the Football Combination and the youth team the Southern Junior Floodlit Cup.

McCarthy was upbeat about the coming season and the end of the present one said, 'I thought we had a great season. If I'd said at the start of the season that we'd finish seventh with 70-odd points some people would have said I was out of my tree.' Then he added, 'We'll be sticking to the diamond system. We've got a good team and now is the time to look forward to next season.' Just what that season would bring, and in their new ground, the fans were waiting for.

	P	W	D	L	F	A	Pts
Newcastle United	46	29	9	8	92	38	96
West Ham United	46	26	10	10	81	41	88
Portsmouth	46	26	10	10	80	46	88
Tranmere Rovers	46	23	10	13	72	56	79
Swindon Town	46	21	13	12	74	59	76
Leicester City	46	22	10	14	71	64	76
MILLWALL	46	18	16	12	65	53	70

Eighty-three years at Cold Blow Lane had come to an end with a family extravaganza after local clubs and the Lewisham festival had played on what was left of the pitch. The sale of every piece of the ground took place and now there was nothing left except memories.

1992/93   **Football League Division One**

Date		Opposition	Score	Scorers
Aug	15	Watford	1-3	McGinlay
	22	OXFORD UNITED	3-1	Allen, Armstrong, Rae
	29	Barnsley	0-0	
Sept	5	SWINDON TOWN	2-1	McGinlay, Goodman
	12	BIRMINGHAM CITY	0-0	
	15	Peterborough United	0-0	
	19	NOTTS COUNTY	6-0	Allen (2), Barber (2), Dolby, Goodman
	26	Brentford	1-1	Allen
Oct	3	Sunderland	0-2	
	10	CAMBRIDGE UNITED	2-2	Allen, Goodman
	18	Charlton Athletic	2-0	Rae, Moralee
	25	WOLVERHAMPTON WANDERERS	2-0	Cooper, Moralee
	31	Bristol Rovers	0-1	
Nov	4	BRISTOL CITY	4-1	May, Cooper, Moralee, Allen
	7	Derby County	2-1	Rae, Moralee
	15	WEST HAM UNITED	2-1	Allen (pen), Barber
	21	Luton Town	1-1	Byrne
	28	Portsmouth	0-1	
Dec	5	SOUTHEND UNITED	1-1	Barber
	12	GRIMSBY TOWN	2-1	Moralee (2)
	20	Newcastle United	1-1	Moralee
	26	Tranmere Rovers	1-1	Goodman
	28	LEICESTER CITY	2-0	Goodman, Moralee
Jan	9	Notts County	2-1	Goodman, Moralee
	17	BRENTFORD	6-1	Goodman (2), Moralee (2), Rae, Cooper
	27	PETERBOROUGH UNITED	4-0	Goodman, Rae, A.P. McCarthy, Barber
	30	Oxford United	0-3	
Feb	6	WATFORD	5-2	Moralee (2), Rae, Cooper, Goodman
	9	Birmingham City	0-0	
	13	Swindon Town	0-3	
	20	BARNSLEY	0-4	
	27	Cambridge United	1-1	Allen
Mar	6	SUNDERLAND	0-0	
	9	Bristol City	1-0	Barber
	13	DERBY COUNTY	1-0	Allen (pen)
	21	Southend United	3-3	Stevens, Goodman, Barber
	24	LUTON TOWN	1-0	Moralee
	28	West Ham United	2-2	Moralee, Stevens
Apr	3	PORTSMOUTH	1-1	Kerr
	6	Grimsby Town	0-1	
	10	TRANMERE ROVERS	0-0	
	14	Leicester City	0-3	
	17	NEWCASTLE UNITED	1-2	Barber
	24	CHARLTON ATHLETIC	1-0	Goodman
May	1	Wolverhampton Wanderers	1-3	Allen
	8	BRISTOL ROVERS	0-3	

Anglo-Italian Cup

Round	Date		Opposition	Score	Scorers
GM	Sept	2	CHARLTON ATHLETIC	1-2	Cunningham
GM		29	Portsmouth	1-1	Rae

League Cup

Round	Date		Opposition	Score	Scorer
1/1	Aug	18	Leyton Orient	2-1	Stevens, Roberts
1/2		26	LEYTON ORIENT	3-0	Allen (2), Armstrong
2/1	Sept	22	Arsenal	1-1	Roberts
2/2	Oct	7	ARSENAL	1-1*	Opp OG

*a.e.t. Arsenal won on penalties

FA Cup

Round	Date		Opposition	Score	Scorer
3	Jan	13	Southend United	0-1	

1992/93   Football League Division One

	P	W	D	L	F	A	Pts
Newcastle United	46	29	9	8	92	38	96
West Ham United	46	26	10	10	81	41	88
Portsmouth	46	26	10	10	80	46	88
Tranmere Rovers	46	23	10	13	72	56	79
Swindon Town	46	21	13	12	74	59	76
Leicester City	46	22	10	14	71	64	76
MILLWALL	46	18	16	12	65	53	70
Derby County	46	19	9	18	68	57	66
Grimsby Town	46	19	7	20	58	57	64
Peterborough United	46	16	14	16	55	63	62
Wolverhampton Wanderers	46	16	13	17	57	56	61
Charlton Athletic	46	16	13	17	49	46	61
Barnsley	46	17	9	20	56	60	60
Oxford United	46	14	14	18	53	56	56
Bristol City	46	14	14	18	49	67	56
Watford	46	14	13	19	57	71	55
Notts County	46	12	16	18	55	70	52
Southend United	46	13	13	20	54	64	52
Birmingham City	46	13	12	21	50	72	51
Luton Town	46	10	21	15	48	62	51
Sunderland	46	13	11	22	50	64	50
Brentford	46	13	10	23	52	71	49
Cambridge United	46	11	16	19	48	69	49
Bristol Rovers	46	10	11	25	55	87	41

Building a New Home

In the days when a football club was newly established and trying to make a place for itself in the football world, it was common for it to move homes perhaps several times before a permanent ground was found. Millwall were no exception to this, as you have already read in chapter one. The two grounds Millwall have played in during the period covered by this book were built from scratch and here we give the reason and history for the building of them.

Having made the decision to move from their North Greenwich home, Millwall's directors had been quietly looking at various sites in east and south London before settling on an area in New Cross. This was a part of the Cold Blow Farm that was already being eaten up by railway sidings and railway lines taking goods in and out of the local docks that surrounded the proposed ground and was in fact used to grow rhubarb and cabbages.

The estimated cost to build the ground was around £10,000 and renowned football ground architect Archibald Leitch, who had previously worked on projects at Tottenham, Chelsea, Fulham and Huddersfield in England and at Celtic and Rangers in Scotland, designed it. The builders were Humphries of Knightsbridge. To bank up the terraces labourers brought in cartloads of rubble. Lord Kinnaird, the then-president of the Football Association opened The Den, as the ground was to be called, on 22 October 1910.

The first game was a Southern League fixture against Brighton & Hove Albion, who were the reigning champions, and the Lions went down 0-1. Attendances for the Lions doubled overnight and fans that once travelled by ferries and foot tunnel to the island to watch Millwall now had the club on their doorsteps, with the islanders doing the reverse journey.

The grandstand, which for the first time at any of their previous grounds ran the whole length of one side, had 3,500 bench seats and initial estimates were of 32,000 spectators in the ground. This gradually increased as improvements were carried out. The terraces were concreted over just after the First World War ended but roofing was not added until the late 1930s so those in attendance really suffered in inclement weather.

Groundsman Elija Moor's experiences with the grounds on the island stood him in good stead, so the pitch at Cold Blow Lane was laid on tons of sand for better drainage. In fact the first game postponed or abandoned through rain came on Boxing Day 1959 when the match with Stockport County was called off after fifty-nine minutes with County leading by a goal to nil (when the game was rearranged the Lions won 3-2).

The record attendance gradually improved, although it was mostly when the club played FA Cup ties that the club consistently attracted over 30,000 gates. The first game to go over 40,000 was played on 20 February 1926 against Swansea Town and exactly eleven years later the record of 48,672 was achieved against Derby County. As far as league games were concerned, for some reason the newspapers either estimated or rounded up the figures released.

At the MFC museum we have actual attendance figures from the Football Museum in Preston, who have preserved these records since the Football League started collating them in 1925. The highest Football League gate was on 23 October 1948 when 44,627 were at The Den for the visit of Notts County, an amazing figure when you realise this was for a Third Division match.

In 1924 and again in 1930 Millwall received royal visits by the Duke of York (later King George VI), who came to watch the Clevedon Charity Cup Finals.

When Charlie Hewitt took over as manager in 1936, the families that had run Millwall since its reformation were dragged into the twentieth century. Reg Smith was put in charge of installing electricity, while Hewitt sought out the quaintly named Synchromatic Time Recording Co. who had offices in London and Liverpool. They built a giant clock that was erected on the highest part of the North Terrace, which was affectionately known by the fans as the halfway line no matter where along the terrace you stood.

The clock was built on a steel lattice framework, its total height over 30ft with a 16ft dial and hands of 10ft and 7ft long and it was driven by 'the new fangled' electricity. Greenwich Observatory controlled the time and the local newspapers gave the price for building it at £600. It was the largest clock at any football ground in the United Kingdom.

When roofing was added on the three open sides in 1938 the clock was moved to the north-west corner and Millwall now estimated that 20,000 could see games under cover.

The Den suffered terribly during the war years, particularly during April 1943. First a bomb blew a huge crater in the north terrace, showering the pitch with debris and so badly damaging the huge clock that it had to be dismantled and we assume scrapped.

A hasty clear-up enabled the London Senior Cup final between Dulwich Hamlet and Tooting & Mitcham United to go ahead but a short time after the game had finished smoke was seen rising around the grandstand, which developed into an inferno that completely destroyed the wooden structure. The likely cause was thought to be a discarded cigarette. Although the club received compensation from the war damages commission, the regulations meant Millwall had to gain a licence to get the rebuilding work done and fill in the crater. The club suffered huge losses of revenue as this was classed as non-essential work.

In 1947 the board developed plans to build a two-deck grandstand extending out and over the adjacent Southern Railway line. But this never came about and a one-tier structure containing 3,480 seats was built, although it was not finally completed until 1962.

With the lease on The Den due to expire in 1956, Millwall purchased the freehold from British Railways in 1951 for £30,000. Floodlights were erected and were officially turned on for a friendly with Manchester United on 5 October 1953. Interestingly The Den is one of only five Football League grounds – Blackpool, Burnley, Notts County and Torquay United are the others – where the players enter the arena from a goal end rather than from the side.

The Den was given a facelift in anticipation of First Division football back in 1966 when the then chairman, Mickey Purser, said, 'We shall be spending £120,000 during the next five years on a facelift at The Den. If we get full support from the supporters' club it will take two years only.'

This facelift included installing new floodlights, rebuilding the terraces and building a 'members room', to hold 1,000 people, equipped with bars and a dance floor. A cover over the whole ground was planned, although never executed, but there were no plans for a large amount of seating due to lack of demand.

During the early 1970s the club gained better access to the ground with the closure and dismantling of the two railway bridges over Cold Blow Lane and the railway lines around The Den.

This need for better access led to a proposed major redevelopment, when the ground could have become a super stadium, in 1979. The then chairman, Len Eppel, announced a £12 million scheme in association with supermarket chain Asda, for a 25,000 all-seater covered stadium that was to include car parking facilities, a sports hall, ice rink and two cinemas, but the planning permission was never given.

After tragedies at other grounds, safety restrictions were gradually imposed everywhere and the crowd limit at The Den had been reduced to less than 20,000 when chairman Reg Burr sold the ground to property developer Fairview Homes for around £6 million. Houses have now been built over the area where the ground stood. The New Den is just a proverbial goal kick away across the old Surrey Canal, which is now filled in and has become the Surrey Canal Road.

The building of new stadia today is now commonplace but back in 1993 it was so rare it was big news, in fact even making improvements to an existing stadium was a rarity.

The last London club to move to a new ground of their own was Leyton Orient back in 1937, so what brought about this unusual occurrence? What went into the making of a new ground, its planning and building? Perhaps most importantly of all, what was the reaction of the fans?

The Taylor Report, commissioned to look into the state of English stadia in the wake of the Hillsborough tragedy, had, among other things, recommended that stadia were all-seater. The Football Association then made it mandatory that all clubs, and especially those in the then First and Second Divisions, should have all-seater stadia, giving time limits for this to happen.

For Millwall to have complied with this at Cold Blow Lane would have meant a maximum crowd capacity of 11-15,000 at a then estimated cost of £9 million, with a maximum grant of only £1 million available from the Football Trust.

Obviously redevelopment of The Den would be uneconomical, the capacity too low and the ability of the club to fund such an operation impossible, not to mention the disruption to the ground and inconvenience to the fans while it was going on. A move to a new ground was the only viable answer, so a new site was looked for, budgets prepared and designs looked at that would fit all the necessary requirements.

The site was close to the Cold Blow Lane ground, therefore supporters would not have any greater distance to travel and the site had been used back in the 1960s as a training ground for the players.

One problem that needed looking at was the fact that the area had originally been marshland. George Fisher, who had played for Millwall in their first Wembley appearance, mentioned the problem when saying that the area was prone to flooding. He had lived in one of the houses that were built on the cobbled streets around the area himself.

The design of the stadium was important and designer Nick Parkinson, who also refashioned Ibrox Park, made the original plans for it to have 25,000 seats that were later changed to 20,000 to fit in with the £15 million budget. In an effort to keep something like the old atmosphere found at Cold Blow Lane, the supporters were to be seated as close to the pitch as possible.

The four two-tiered cantilever stands would provide an uninterrupted view of the pitch as the floodlights would be built into the roof of the East and West stands and incorporated in the East Stand would be thirty executive boxes. Facilities were also built into the West Stand for seventy-four disabled fans, with lifts built to assist them to reach the area set aside for them. In all, the ground was able to accommodate 200 disabled fans and live commentary for blind fans was to be made available.

Under the stands, a covered concourse would house refreshment facilities, including bars and toilets, 345 of them to be precise, including eighteen for the disabled. The concourse originally allowed for free movement between the stands but this was changed after the first season for segregation purposes.

There were twelve pay telephones around the ground and televisions were set up in the concourse area so that replays of the previous week's game could be shown before the match and re-runs of first-half highlights could be shown. The match would also be shown live on these screens so there was no need to miss any of the action, if you were going to buy some refreshments for example.

This was in addition to the scoreboard, replaced near the end of the 2001/02 season by a Jumbotron, which also showed the match live, and the introduction of *Lions World*, a magazine-style programme with features on the club and player interviews, which commenced at the same time.

Apart from housing the club offices and players' dressing rooms, the West Stand had entertainment facilities that could be used on non-match days for any number of things and were used on match days to house the executive suite, a sponsors' lounge and a supporters' restaurant, now called Kitchener's after Barry Kitchener, Millwall's longest-serving player. This stand would seat 5,400 fans – 1,000 in the lower tier and 4,400 in the upper tier. It was also to house a club museum but this still needs to find a permanent home.

A club shop was built on the corner of the North and West stands with an additional outlet in the South Stand, now enlarged and moved to the East Stand and replaced by additional box office facilities. A supporters' bar, now called 'Arry's Bar after Harry Cripps, was also built and later enlarged.

To help with the easy access of fans to the ground, eleven box office selling points were built for ticket sales and additional points in the South Stand supplemented these in 2002. Thirty-six turnstiles and fifty-two exits ensured that the fans could get in and out of the ground quickly and safely and on-site car parking for 236 cars was provided with an overflow at a neighbouring industrial site, which sadly is no longer available.

A walkway from South Bermondsey station would also allow fans to arrive at the ground without the need to come through the nearby streets but unfortunately, due to various political and financial problems, this had only just been started to be built at the end of the 2002/03 season.

The playing surface has a full drainage system, pop-up sprinklers for watering and undersoil heating. The groundsman at the time, John Plummer, seemed to spend all his waking hours and probably some of those when he should have been asleep ensuring that it was right for the opening game. All his hard work paid off when he won the Southern Regional Groundsman of the Year award for pitches at the end of the first season at The New Den.

Located next to the ground was a sports hall, now used by the Millwall Community Scheme, which apart from a full fitness gym has badminton, five-a-side football, netball, hockey and tennis courts both inside and outside plus a bar and cafeteria.

Of course all this needed to be paid for and about £5 million came from the sale of Cold Blow Lane, £2.5 million from The Football Trust and another £2.5 million from Lewisham Council. Various grants, advanced ticket and executive box sales, share issues and the fans through the Lions Card scheme would help make up the shortfall.

Using the ground to hold other entertainments was also mooted. The London Broncos and the London Monarchs teams were invited to use the ground, although this never happened. Thinking about the playing surface it was probably a good thing. There was though a charity American Football match played in aid of Childline between the London Mets and the Tampa Bay Guardians that did not help the pitch too much, proof if it were needed, that the right decision about American football had been made.

Ogden Entertainment Services, a New York-based company, were taken on to run and market the stadium with their promise to bring in star attractions for pop concerts and the like, which would bring in extra revenue. James Brown was due to appear on 30 August but the concert was mysteriously cancelled due to lack of work permits.

Although the corporate facilities of the club are used frequently for all sorts of things and the ground used for filming – for example *Dream Team* is filmed at the ground – these other events failed to materialise apart from a boxing match, the WBO Heavyweight Championship between Michael Bentt and Herbie Hide, an England v. Poland Under-21 match and a firework display.

The view of the fans on the move was naturally divided. Many did not want to move and others saw it as a necessity but the club promised to keep them informed as to what progress was being made and to talk to them about their ideas for the ground. There were misgivings uttered by the fanzines and the Independent Millwall Supporters Association, but in the main everyone knew that the move was inevitable. The plans for the ground were approved in April 1992 and the wheels for the move were set in motion.

Knowing some fans had doubts about the move chairman Reg Burr said, 'No one in their right mind would have gone through all this if it wasn't absolutely necessary.' And he added, 'we could have sat on our hands and done nothing but it really is the only way forward for this club.'

Barry O'Keefe, chairman of IMSA claimed, 'It's nothing short of an outrage. The first thing we knew about it was when we went along to Lewisham Town Hall to see the detailed plans and even then we thought it must have been a mistake.'

After seeing the plans, talking to Burr and having the reasons for the move explained in more detail with alternatives outlined, including a move to The Valley and a ground-share with Charlton Athletic, O'Keefe changed his mind, especially about the Lions Card scheme. 'The alternatives are unthinkable,' he said. 'We are pleased the club have agreed to consult with us and they have taken quite a few of our ideas on board.'

Two of these ideas had to be immediately rejected. Standing accommodation, because it would not be authorised, and the joining of three of the stands to create a bowl like effect, due to cost restrictions, but others were incorporated into the final design of the stadium.

A name for the new ground was now an issue. The New London Stadium and the obvious Senegal Fields were mentioned but these names created a mini revolt among the fans. The solution was found in calling it The New Den, although the word 'new' is hardly used these days.

On Monday 22 June 1992 the bulldozers of Birmingham-based firm Tilbury Douglas moved in and work on the new ground started, to the resigned acceptance of businesses and residents in the area as well as a number of supporters. But with around 1,000 fans already having bought a Lions Card, raising £25,000, resistance from the fans was dwindling. 'It's a tight schedule,' said project manager Keith Stuart. 'But we are confident that we can meet it.'

Talking about the fans' worries about the ground being characterless and prefabricated Burr said, 'I think they are going to be pleasantly surprised. The facilities at The New Den will be second to none.' A model of the stadium was made available for the fans to see and this also helped to allay some of their fears.

By mid-August 1992 the pitch had been marked out and the drainage pipes laid, and it was anticipated that the structure of the stands would be nearing completion by the end of the year. Tim Orchard of Ogden International was quick to say what his company would do, claiming that, apart from star acts performing at the stadium, it would also sell big-name burgers, pizzas and drinks. Unfortunately none of these claims saw fruition.

There was a scare that building work would be halted or at least slowed down in September when people from English Heritage looked over the site. Thankfully they found nothing of interest and the work continued.

By October the undersoil heating pipes that would allow hot water to flow around the pitch, keeping it playable in cold weather, had been laid and things were starting to take shape. In fact, this had been a suggestion that came from one of the fans' meetings. The structures of the stands were up and, although it still looked like a building site, there was certainly a stadium in the making.

A major boost to the finances for the project now came from an unexpected source. Ogden Entertainment Services agreed to contribute £1 million towards the construction costs. It certainly showed that they had confidence in the venture and although there were several million pounds still to find Burr was sure it would not be a problem.

Time constraints on any building work are always a problem. Getting a football stadium ready for the start of a season really highlights that fact. So the stand terracing was made of pre-cast concrete and lowered into position by crane.

Media interest was gaining hold and several newspapers as well as *News at Ten* ran features on the project.

The fans had been invited to visit the site and many took the opportunity to look at the construction. This in itself won over many of the doubters. It may even have helped to boost the shares up to 5p by the end of the year. Unfortunately all this activity brought another worry to the fans. Would they be priced out of the new stadium?

'I don't think that we are going to price our hard-core fans out of it,' said Burr. 'That's certainly not my intention at all. At the moment people are paying £8 to stand in a fairly decrepit ground with not particularly good facilities.' He then said that prices for the new ground would be £10 in the North and South Stands, £15 in the lower East and West Stands and £20 in the upper sections. 'Next season, as long as they are Lions Card holders or season ticket holders it will

The magnificent New Den at its completion.

cost exactly the same to sit in a brand new multi-purpose stadium,' he added, pointing out that discounts that were available in this way.

By February 1993, although there was still some exterior work to complete, the main activity was centred on the internal needs of the ground. Electrical fixtures and plumbing was being put in and the offices were being fitted out so that the club staff could move into the ground in May. The sports centre was also progressing well, the roof had been put on it and the internal blockwork was almost complete.

At this time Burr decided that the fans needed not just a written update of what was happening but the chance to ask questions which he could answer face to face. So along with Mick McCarthy he held, on consecutive nights at Lewisham Theatre, an open meeting, both hosted by Capital Radio DJ Mick Brown. It was either very brave or foolhardy but it allowed the fans to air their views and they did not shirk answering them.

The seating would virtually be the last of the exterior work to be done and although this would have to be done after the roofing this was started at the end of March. The seats would be blue, with the words 'THE DEN' depicted in the South Stand by yellow seats – the club's home and change strip colours. The pitch by now was totally enclosed by buildings as the corner infill buildings had been put in place.

And then, there it was. The seats were in, the food kiosks and bars were ready, the members of staff were in their offices, the car park tarmac had been laid and the grass was a lovely shade of green. Here was a stadium fit for the Premier League. Now all that was needed was a Premier League team to play in it.

Facing the Consequences 1993/94

All through our lives we have to face the consequences of our actions and the effect those actions will have on others as well as ourselves. The decisions of a football manager are no different, except for the fact that there are a few thousand other people who are affected in different ways and, of course, they all feel the consequences of your actions.

Imagine then, the decisions and subsequent consequences Mick McCarthy had to take when starting the season not only in a new stadium, one built with the aspirations of Premier League football high on the agenda of not just the fans but the players and board of directors, but also that it was the one hundredth season of competitive football for the club, having turned professional in 1893. His first decision was on personnel. Both Wallace and Gaynor had failed to impress in their brief loan spell at the club and were not taken on for the new season, Alan McLeary left the club, going to Charlton on a free transfer and Aiden Davison had gone to Bolton Wanderers. But perhaps most important of all was the transfer of Colin Cooper to Nottingham Forest for £1.75 million.

Joining were James Saddington, a £10,000 buy from non-League Cambridge City at the end of the previous season, Bruce Murray, an American international striker, midfielder Lee Luscombe from Brentford and Richard Huxford, a defender from Barnet, all for free.

Another player no longer available to take the field at The New Den was Mick McCarthy himself, who decided to hang up his boots and concentrate on the management side of his contract.

There was also a new strip: blue shirt with white pinstripes and a new shirt sponsor, Captain Morgan.

A successful pre-season tour of Ireland took the side to their final pre-season matches and the opening of The New Den on Wednesday 4 August against Sporting Lisbon, who were managed by Bobby Robson. After the preliminaries, which included another £1 million cash injection from the Football Trust and the ceremonial opening of the ground by Labour leader John Smith, a near full house saw the side lose 1-2. Although everyone there has his or her own memories of the night, John Kerr will take away the memory that he was the first player to score in the stadium. 'It was a great feeling,' he said after the game. 'When it hit the back of the net my first reaction was to check if it was offside and by the time I realised the goal stood I was in the middle of a huge crowd of players.' Kasey Keller was also the first to save a penalty, although Lisbon scored from the resulting rebound.

Next to come were Hungarian champions Honved and they left with the same 1-2 win, Kerr scoring again. It would have been a draw but for a spectacular headed own goal from Ian Dawes, but they were good workouts and it gave McCarthy a chance to look at some of the young players at the club as well as his new arrivals and fringe players.

The new stadium had received the thumbs up from the media and a large majority of the fans. Now it needed the team to do the business where it mattered, in the league.

This season had seen the adoption of squad numbers for Premier League teams with the players' names on the back of their shirts and some of the Division One clubs did the same. It

A panoramic view inside the new ground.

was to be some time before the Lions put this system into practice. There was also a new rule change that allowed a goalkeeper to be added to the substitutes' bench along with two outfield players.

The opening match of the season was away at Stoke on 14 August, against the wishes of the club, which had asked that their opening league match be at home for the obvious reasons of playing it in their new ground.

McCarthy had other problems though. Rae, Barber, Bogie, May, Moralee and Goodman were all injured and, with the exception of Bogie, missed the match. Allen was transferred to Newcastle for £300,000 just before the team left for the Potteries. The manager need not have worried though as the Lions had a dream start to the season, winning the game 2-1.

Ian Bogie, who played despite a broken hand, opened the scoring and Bruce Murray scored the winner, his first for the club on his league debut, after a Tony McCarthy own goal had levelled things.

London Weekend Television chose to show the home match against Southend live the following Sunday and the football public had the chance to see The New Den in all its magnificence. Richard Huxford had his League debut in this match, coming off of the bench to replace Dolby, but the team was the same as that which beat Stoke.

A first league win in their new home was what everyone was looking forward to but Southend obviously had not read the script and went away easy 1-4 victors. Kerr was the Millwall scorer when he put the side in front after twenty-two minutes. 'It was the worst performance I've seen since I took the job,' said McCarthy and he was not exaggerating. Maybe the occasion got to the players but it would be the only league match that the Lions would lose at home all season.

McCarthy changed the side for the trip to Wolves. Huxford and Barber got their first starts of the season and Luscombe made his debut when he replaced Bogie in the second half. Although they lost the match 0-2, the sending-off of Maguire after just six minutes did not help the Lions. The season went downhill even further when they lost 0-4 to Leicester three days later.

Building work at Filbert Street meant there were no Millwall supporters there to see the match and they were probably glad not to be there, although they missed the debut of promising youngster Ben Thatcher. It left the Lions second from bottom of the table at the end of the first month.

	P	W	D	L	F	A	Pts
Bristol City	3	1	0	2	3	4	3
Luton Town	3	1	0	2	3	4	3
MILLWALL	4	1	0	3	3	11	3
Bolton Wanderers	3	0	2	1	1	4	2

A new addition to the squad came in the shape of striker Warren Patmore, who had spent the last two years as a golf professional, although he had previously played for Cambridge United. He was immediately sent to Irish club Cobh Ramblers to gain experience along with youngster James Connor. Another addition to the club but not on the playing side was McDonald's Restaurants, who sponsored the Junior Lions and the Family Enclosure.

The Anglo-Italian Cup was still going and this season's round robin event saw the Lions in a group with Crystal Palace and Charlton, who provided their first opponents. An entertaining 2-2 draw saw the return of Rae, Moralee and Verveer from injury and it was the latter's goal that put the Lions two up after Roberts' twelfth-minute opener. But they were unable to hold onto their lead after a spirited Charlton comeback.

That performance helped to get things back on track in the league and Barnsley were well-beaten 2-0 at The New Den with goals from Kerr and Rae. But it was Verveer who impressed with a majestic midfield display; he was obviously making up for lost time.

McCarthy was still looking for a replacement for the departed Cooper and it was not to be young central defender Mark Foran, who left to join Sheffield United for £25,000. But the boss found his man in the experienced Pat Van Den Hauwe, who he signed on a free from Spurs.

And then the goals dried up and red cards took their place.

The first came in the 0-0 derby match against Charlton at The Valley, where Van Den Hauwe made his debut. Perhaps there should have been two cards because the Lions' new defender was lucky to get away with his abrupt stopping of Shaun Newton after just fifteen seconds and with the yellow card he received when stamping on Gary Nelson twenty minutes later. The red came when Alex Rae and Peter Garland had no more than a push and a shove at each other and both took an early bath. In truth the match itself had little to speak of, with excitement at an all-time low, and can quickly be assigned to the undistinguished bin.

Next came the Anglo-Italian Cup match against Crystal Palace at Selhurst Park. Two local derbies, two red cards and no goals for the Lions in the space of four days does not make good reading. This time the sending off was for Carl Emberson, who was also making his Millwall debut, for tripping Chris Armstrong.

The resulting penalty, which makeshift 'keeper Lee Luscombe had no chance with, gave Palace a two-goal lead and turned the match into no more than a training exercise. Although Tony Dolby hit a post, Palace were comfortable 0-3 winners and the 2,713 fans who bothered to turn up probably wished they had stayed at home.

It was back to league action at The New Den and the arrival of big-spending Derby County. Although the game ended 0-0, memories of the previous season's encounter came to the fore as Derby players got away with vicious tackles while Millwall players picked up cards. In the case of Stevens it was a red one for a second bookable offence.

Van Den Hauwe was also lucky to stay on the pitch after a clash with Marco Gabbiadini, but at least the spirit seemed to be back in the side. There was no doubt that the ten-man team, costing just £400,000, had outplayed their £10 million opponents.

Unfortunately though the goals were missing and they stayed missing for the away games against Watford in the first round first leg match of the Coca-Cola Cup and the league game against Peterborough, both of which ended 0-0.

The goal drought was about to end with two matches against Watford in quick succession at The New Den.

The first came in the league, which also saw the debut of young defender Mark Beard and coincided with the return of Jon Goodman after a hernia operation. Goodman, who only

Opening Celebration

Welcome to
THE NEW LONDON STADIUM

MILLWALL v
SPORTING CLUBE DE PORTUGAL
WEDNESDAY 4 AUGUST 1993
KICK-OFF 8PM

at The Den

Captain Morgan

PRICE £3

Another splendid production for the first game at the new ground.

played because of a late injury to John Kerr, scored a hat-trick and Roberts added another in the Lions' 4-1 win. 'I stayed up late to watch the Bruno fight because Mick told me I wasn't playing,' said Goodman. 'I had a big breakfast as well and turned up at the ground about 1.15 p.m. Mick told me John Kerr was injured and I was in. I didn't have time to be nervous. I was probably the most relaxed I've ever been before a game and it paid off.'

This match also saw the return of Andy May from injury and he played a ten-minute cameo role as substitute. Unfortunately he picked up an injury in training and faced a further lengthy lay-off.

The fans turned up the following Wednesday for the second leg of the Coca-Cola Cup match hoping for more of the same. What they got nobody could have predicted. It would have been too much to ask Goodman to perform again in such a short space of time after his operation. In fact he was not even on the bench, but the return of Keith Stevens from suspension meant that Cunningham could move to left-back from the centre of defence, allowing Tony Dolby to take the number nine shirt after filling in for the injured Ian Dawes.

Watford, perhaps smarting from their defeat a few days earlier, were two up after nineteen minutes and coasting when Paul Furlong kicked out at Cunningham after a perfectly fair tackle and was rightly sent off, as was a fan who came onto the pitch to show his displeasure to the Watford striker. Two minutes later Huxford scored his first and only goal in a Millwall shirt and five minutes thereafter Murray, who had replaced the injured Van Den Hauwe after a quarter of an hour, equalised.

The fans were still taking their seats at the start the second half when Murray burst into the box past two heavy challenges and collided with Watford goalkeeper Simon Sheppard. He was immediately surrounded by Watford players, was kicked in the melee that followed, reacted angrily and was sent off along with Watford's David Holdsworth. Mark Beard then hit the bar but it was Watford who took the lead again, when a poor Stevens back pass allowed Hessenthaler to score.

With ten minutes left Moralee scored to take the tie into extra time, the first fifteen minutes of which Millwall dominated without penetrating a stubborn Watford defence. The second period of extra time went the same way and it looked like Watford would hold out to win the tie on the away goals rule but, with just forty-two seconds remaining, Moralee flicked on a free-kick and Verveer pounced to put the ball in the net and win the tie. A game that had more twists and turns to it than a Brazilian free-kick was finally over.

It was little wonder that the side would see changes after such a game on the following Saturday when West Bromwich Albion were the visitors. The game was won 2-1, with a goal from Goodman and a penalty from Rae – back after suspension – after he had been brought down.

Ian Bogie went on loan to Leyton Orient but it was the arrival of striker Dave Mitchell from Turkish side Altay Spor Kuluba for £100,000 that caused a stir, and the Australian international made his Millwall debut when he came on for Goodman in the match at Bolton. The away day blues continued and, although the Lions did not play badly, they just could not score and the game was instantly forgotten, except perhaps by old boys John McGinlay, who scored two of his side's four goals and Aiden Davison, who kept his old teammates from scoring after he took over in goal from Keith Branagan, who injured himself in the pre-match warm up. No doubt there was a faint smile on Bolton manager Bruce Rioch's face as well.

Mitchell made his first start four days later at home to Notts County and almost opened his goalscoring account when he hit the bar with a header. Warren Patmore made his debut when coming on for Goodman in what would be his only Millwall appearance and hit the bar with a header as well. A Rae penalty and a Verveer diving header gave Millwall a 2-0 win but they did not look very convincing. 'We haven't got a snowball in hell's chance if we go on playing like that,' said McCarthy.

The televised home match against Middlesbrough came next and Mark Kennedy made his first start for the club and hit a post. Millwall's goal was credited as an own goal, Rae's shot deflecting off Derek Whyte, who was later sent off for a foul on Kennedy. The end result was 1-1. The Lions were on television again the following week when they played Birmingham at St Andrews, where they lost 0-1, but in neither of these games were they very impressive.

Sandwiched between these two televised games was the third round tie of the Coca-Cola Cup at Queens Park Rangers. Once again they failed to score, losing 0-3 and with their next match away at Nottingham Forest in just three days everyone expected the away goal blues to continue. But they were mistaken.

Goals from Goodman, Murray and Stevens saw the Lions to a well-deserved 3-1 win. 'One win doesn't mean we've cracked it,' said Keller and everyone waited to see how their next away games went.

Before that there was the matter of a home match against Oxford United, who included John Byrne in their line up. Byrne had been transferred there during the week and also on the move was Paul Manning, who went on loan to Slough Town.

With Byrne gone and a lack of goals still staring him in the face you would have thought that McCarthy's priority would be to find a player to put that right. Instead he signed two defenders, Neil Emblen and Michael Harle, from Sittingbourne for a combined fee of £200,000.

The game against Oxford ended 2-2 although the Lions should have won. They gave the lead away twice and again missed chances but McCarthy must have known something was to happen with this goalscoring problem. Mark Kennedy scored both goals, his first for the club, and McCarthy was also looking forward to the return of Dave Mitchell from international duty.

Kennedy only played a bit part in the next match, away to Bristol City, but played his part in a second-half comeback that helped the Lions to a 2-2 draw. On a waterlogged pitch and in driving rain they had an awful first half but goals from Rae and Beard, his first for the club, after a verbal roasting at half-time from McCarthy, saw them complete a memorable comeback.

Neil Emblen made his debut in the home match against Tranmere Rovers, replacing the injured Van Den Hauwe, and looked a class act from the start. The rest of the team certainly helped him to remember the day with an emphatic 3-1 win with goals from Mitchell – his first for the club – Goodman and Kennedy and a display of football that Tranmere could not cope with.

They did not look as good against Grimsby a week later but Mitchell's second goal in two games gave them a 1-0 win which some excellent saves from Keller did a lot to preserve. It meant that the Millwall faithful went home happy.

Meanwhile Ian Bogie's loan to Leyton Orient ended as he made it permanent in a £100,000 deal. Warren Patmore moved to Northampton for free and James Saddington and Lee Luscombe went on loan to Sittingbourne. With two away fixtures to follow everyone wanted to know if the Lions' rediscovered scoring touch would continue. They need not have worried. A 2-0 win at Oxford United was secured when Verveer, back from injury, came off the bench to add to Jackson's own goal. And a stunning Rae hat-trick, which secured a 3-1 win over Notts County, who had taken the lead just after half-time, moved the Lions into fourth place in the table, a jump of seven places since their home match with Oxford.

They moved up another place when beating Stoke 2-0 at The New Den the following Sunday but they left it late with Rae and Kennedy scoring in the last five minutes.

The Boxing Day game at home to Portsmouth ended in a 0-0 draw. In fact, the Lions could easily have lost what was a cracker of a game and they did lose their final game of the year 1-2 at Sunderland. Roberts was the scorer.

Fortunately neither of these results changed their League position and they saw out 1993 in third place.

	P	W	D	L	F	A	Pts
Crystal Palace	22	13	4	5	42	24	43
Tranmere Rovers	23	12	5	6	35	24	41
MILLWALL	24	11	7	6	33	28	40

The New Year's Day table-topping clash at home to Crystal Palace was memorable for more than the fact that it was Keller's seventieth consecutive football League match. After a scrappy first half, a ten-minute spell of Verveer magic devastated Millwall's promotion rivals.

First he provided the cross for Goodman to score and then added the second himself with an overhead bicycle kick. It was all over when three minutes later Rae scored from the penalty spot after Mitchell was pulled to the ground.

The majority of the 16,779 crowd went home happy but all of them must have marvelled at Verveer's awesome display. 'His display was out of this world,' said Palace manager Alan Smith and nobody could disagree with him.

The Lions' game at Luton was called off the following weekend so it was the night of Monday 10 January and the televised FA Cup game when Arsenal came to The New Den before he could try and work his magic again.

They certainly came close to an upset but Tony Adams bundled the ball into the net with just a minute of the match remaining. Keller had dropped the ball having been fouled by Merson. It was clearly seen by all but not given by the referee and there was no way back. They certainly deserved a replay but this time it was not to be.

Looking for experienced cover for Keller, McCarthy had signed Tim Carter from Hartlepool on a one-month loan just before the Arsenal match and he made his debut in the next game, at home to Bolton, due to a thigh injury Keller had picked up.

He had an excellent match and his saves contributed to a 1-0 win. Rae scored the goal in a game that saw Andy May make his long-awaited comeback when he come on as a second-half substitute. He made his first start of the season in the next game, a 0-0 away draw with West Bromwich Albion but he probably wished that he had not as he was sent off after reacting to a shove in the back in what was to be his last appearance of the season.

With no game the following weekend due to the FA Cup defeat by Arsenal Millwall played a friendly against Swedish side IFK Gothenburg. The 1-1 draw allowed McCarthy to field fringe players Carl Emberson, Michael Harle and Danny Chapman. Apart from Alex Rae's equaliser and a Moralee shot that hit the post, the Lions rarely threatened but it was a useful workout for both teams.

Lee Luscombe, having failed to impress since his arrival from Brentford, left to join Wimbledon and John Humphrey and Brett Smith, two youngsters who never quite made it, also left.

Tim Carter went back to Hartlepool because his loan period was up and swiftly returned on loan again. But the arrival that caused great excitement among Lions fans was that of folk hero Terry Hurlock, who was given a three-week trial by McCarthy after receiving a free transfer from Southampton.

The biggest crowd of the season, just over 600, turned up at Dulwich Hamlet's Dog Kennel Hill ground, where the reserve team were now playing to save wear and tear on The New Den pitch, to see him in a reserve game against Crystal Palace. His performance earned him a contract until the end of the season.

Six goals in the televised game at Middlesbrough followed but, unfortunately, Millwall only scored two of them: a Rae penalty and Moralee's first of the season. How they threw away their first-half lead no one can really say but a lacklustre performance, the muddy conditions and some poor refereeing decisions did not help.

A programme from the 1993/94 season.

It was back to winning ways with a 2-1 win at home to Birmingham. Verveer scored both goals but it only hid the fact that the goals were coming from the midfield and not the strikers. In truth, there had not been a settled strike force due to a bad run of injuries. One player who would not be adding to the goal tally was Tony Dolby, who was loaned out to Barnet.

The Birmingham game saw the welcome return from long-term injury of Ian Dawes when he replaced Ben Thatcher, who was injured in the match. Dawes also started in the next one, away to Southend.

There was a long gap between the two games due to four games being postponed; The Birmingham game was on 12 February and Southend on 2 March. Perhaps that contributed to the Lions looking a little rusty in the 1-1 draw. Mitchell scored the goal but there was off-field activity to keep the fans interested during this enforced break.

Richard Huxford went to Birmingham on a loan swop with Paul Tait but Tait had a toe injury and never featured in a first-team game.

The Southend game was notable for another reason, the return of cult midfielder Terry Hurlock to the Millwall starting eleven. The fans could not wait for his heralded return to The New Den in the televised match against Leicester. How the game ended 0-0 is anyone's guess in a game that went from unreal, to farce, to ridiculous.

The game was just eight minutes old when Hurlock was sent off for kicking Iwan Roberts in the face and then getting his retaliation in first as the striker lay on the floor. Leicester captain Steve Agnew should have followed him when he stamped on Andy Roberts but it was Van Den Hauwe who was next to take an early bath for elbowing David Oldfield. Oldfield also went five minutes before the break for smashing into Alex Rae's back after the midfield player had caught him in the face.

At the same time Leicester full-back Neil Lewis was penalised for a foul on Phil Barber and thought the red card had been shown to him as well and left the pitch, only to return some two minutes later after being told it had not.

The game took on the characteristics of a football rather than boxing match in the second half and the nine-man Lions held on although they were lucky when Leicester's Julian Joachim hit a post with four minutes left. The fans in the ground and those watching on television were left with a lot to talk about.

The 0-0 away match against fellow promotion contenders Derby County was a dull affair, especially after the previous week. Although the Lions played some attractive football they were still finding it hard to turn possession of the ball into goals. Bruce Murray was not going to be the answer to the problem and was loaned to Stockport County.

Although the Lions scored twice in their next match, a 2-1 win over Charlton, the goals again eluded the strikers as both came from Alex Rae. The second was a last-gasp winner. An own goal gave them a 1-0 home win over Peterborough, where Huxford, back from his loan at Birmingham, came back into the side because of injuries to most of the defenders in the squad. Paul Tait made the return journey to St Andrews.

What a way to get your 800th Football League home win!

The Peterborough game had caused a stir with some of the Millwall faithful as it had been moved from its original Saturday slot to the following Tuesday to accommodate the Bentt v. Hide fight. IMSA's Barry O'Keefe said, 'We were told that football would not be affected by any other activities at the stadium.'

This prompted an angry response from Reg Burr who said that the Saturday was the only available slot on American television and they were paying for the whole thing. He added, 'Genuine supporters will understand that in order to generate the revenue to buy players and not sell them, we need this sort of revenue. That is the crux of the matter.'

Whether McCarthy used this revenue or not he spent money for the promotion push and on transfer deadline day bought Greg Berry for £200,000 from Wimbledon and paid West Ham £75,000 for goal machine Clive Allen. Something must have been wrong with the machine though as he failed to score during his stay at The New Den.

Other deadline day moves included Tim Carter signing on a permanent basis and Gavin Maguire going to Scarborough on loan, with defender Stephen Swales coming in exchange.

Allen and Berry made their debuts in the 0-2 defeat at Watford, where they came on as substitutes and made their first starts in the 2-2 home game with Luton. Berry scored on his home debut, and Moralee got the other, but the side were still missing several chances.

A last-minute equaliser from Mitchell in the 2-2 draw at Portsmouth kept the promotion dream alive. Cunningham, with his first of the season, was the other scorer, but the result does not tell the tale.

Once again Millwall dominated the match but a dubious penalty and a bizarre goal from Darryl Powell, when a clearance from Van Den Hauwe hit him and looped into the net, summed up Millwall's day.

Two goals from Mitchell gave the Lions a 2-1 home win over Sunderland but losing 0-1 away to league leaders Crystal Palace (old boy Chris Armstrong scoring the decisive goal), started the promotion nerves jangling as the points for a play-off spot got tighter.

The televised clash against second-placed Nottingham Forest the following Sunday was another thriller and another 2-2 draw. Moralee and Mitchell had twice given the Lions the lead but they could not hold on against ten-man Forest who had Des Lyttle sent off. The team were now just outside the play-off positions.

A win against Wolves the following Wednesday night was vital and relief found its way round the ground when Dave Mitchell secured a 1-0 victory. But fellow promotion contenders, Tranmere, put a dent in Millwall's campaign when they won 2-3 at Prenton Park. Although they nearly pulled back a three-goal deficit they could not add to goals from Moralee and Kerr.

A 1-1 draw away at Luton – Kerr again the scorer – and a 0-0 home draw with Bristol City left nerves in tatters but Mitchell's late goal in the 1-0 win at Barnsley and results elsewhere moved the Lions back to third place. A 0-0 home draw with Grimsby in the last game of the season kept them there.

	P	W	D	L	F	A	Pts
Crystal Palace	46	27	9	10	73	46	90
Nottingham Forest	46	23	14	9	74	49	83
MILLWALL	46	19	17	10	58	49	74

It was now a two-legged play-off against Derby that had to be negotiated but before that there was a match played as part of Keith 'Rhino' Stevens' testimonial year. A Millwall team that included guests Barry Kitchener and Teddy Sheringham drew 6-6 with a Select Managers side. Clive Allen scored his only goal in a Millwall shirt.

Steven scored the final goal from the penalty spot and two of the opposition goals were scored by Reading manager Mark McGhee. These two would both be involved in another Stevens testimonial match a few seasons later only this time for different reasons.

The first leg of the play-off took place at the Baseball Ground and McCarthy, in what he later called 'the worst matchday decision I've made' chose to play with three central defenders.

Having used the system and lost against the reserves in practice matches the writing was on the wall and the 0-2 defeat the Lions suffered could have been far worse.

The second leg was always going to be an uphill struggle but had Rae's eleventh-minute shot gone in instead of hitting the crossbar things might have been different. Five minutes later Gabbiadini scored and it was all but over when Johnson added a second and a pitch invasion took the players off for nineteen minutes.

When play resumed Van Den Hauwe could only watch in disbelief when he touched a harmless through ball past Keller and the ball trickled into the net. Berry pulled a goal back and when referee Brian Hill pointed to the penalty spot for a foul on Rae a comeback, at least for the night, looked possible.

What Hill did not see was a second crowd invasion starting in which Derby players were attacked by invading spectators (one can hardly call them supporters). Play was stopped for another thirteen minutes and when the players came back out again Hill restarted the game with a drop ball in the centre circle while Dave Mitchell was standing on the penalty spot waiting to take the penalty kick.

The pitch invasion restarted at the end of the game – Hill stopped it two minutes early – and the violence spilled into the car park and surrounding streets. A Radio Derby car was smashed and thousands of pounds worth of damage caused. There were the inevitable calls for a ground closure, the reintroduction of fences and an FA inquiry.

Burr contemplated resigning as chairman. 'My heart says stay for the 15,000 or so loyal fans who have supported us and behaved well all season,' he said afterward, 'but my head says do I really need this?'

The media calls for punishment to the club certainly did not help the situation and neither did their exaggeration of the numbers that had invaded the pitch. But with the club's future called into question, sponsorship deals undermined and the name of Millwall again dragged through the mud, it was a sad end to the first season in the new stadium, Stevens' testimonial year and a season that had promised so much. The youth team once again had reached the FA Youth Cup final where they were beaten by Arsenal.

1993/94   Football League Division One

Date		Opposition	Score	Scorers
Aug	14	Stoke City	2-1	Bogie, Murray
	22	SOUTHEND UNITED	1-4	Kerr
	25	Wolverhampton Wanderers	0-2	
	28	Leicester City	0-4	
Sept	4	BARNSLEY	2-0	Rae, Kerr
	11	Charlton Athletic	0-0	
	18	DERBY COUNTY	0-0	
	25	Peterborough United	0-0	
Oct	2	WATFORD	4-1	Goodman (3), Roberts
	9	WEST BROMWICH ALBION	2-1	Goodman, Rae (pen)
	16	Bolton Wanderers	0-4	
	20	NOTTS COUNTY	2-0	Rae (pen), Verveer
	24	MIDDLESBROUGH	1-1	Opp OG
	31	Birmingham City	0-1	
Nov	3	Nottingham Forest	3-1	Stevens, Murray, Goodman
	6	OXFORD UNITED	2-2	Kennedy (2)
	13	Bristol City	2-2	Rae, Beard
	20	TRANMERE ROVERS	3-1	Kennedy, Mitchell, Goodman
	27	GRIMSBY TOWN	1-0	Mitchell
Dec	4	Oxford United	2-0	Verveer, Opp OG
	11	Notts County	3-1	Rae (3)
	19	STOKE CITY	2-0	Rae, Kennedy
	27	PORTSMOUTH	0-0	
	28	Sunderland	1-2	Roberts
Jan	1	CRYSTAL PALACE	3-0	Rae (pen), Verveer, Goodman
	15	BOLTON WANDERERS	1-0	Rae
	22	West Bromwich Albion	0-0	
Feb	6	Middlesbrough	2-4	Rae (pen), Moralee
	12	BIRMINGHAM CITY	2-1	Verveer (2)
Mar	2	Southend United	1-1	Mitchell
	6	LEICESTER CITY	0-0	
	12	Derby County	0-0	
	15	CHARLTON ATHLETIC	2-1	Rae (2)
	22	PETERBOROUGH UNITED	1-0	Opp OG
	26	Watford	0-2	
	30	LUTON TOWN	2-2	Moralee, Berry
Apr	2	Portsmouth	2-2	Cunningham, Mitchell
	6	SUNDERLAND	2-1	Mitchell (2)
	9	Crystal Palace	0-1	
	17	NOTTINGHAM FOREST	2-2	Moralee, Mitchell
	20	WOLVERHAMPTON WANDERERS	1-0	Mitchell
	23	Tranmere Rovers	2-3	Moralee, Kerr
	26	Luton Town	1-1	Kerr
	30	BRISTOL CITY	0-0	
May	3	Barnsley	1-0	Mitchell
	8	Grimsby Town	0-0	
	15	Derby County	0-2	
	18	DERBY COUNTY	1-3	Berry

Anglo-Italian Cup

Round	Date		Opposition	Score	Scorers
GM	Sept	1	CHARLTON ATHLETIC	2-2	Roberts, Verveer
GM		14	Crystal Palace	0-3	

League Cup

Round	Date		Opposition	Score	Scorers
2/1	Sept	21	Watford	0-0	
2/2	Oct	6	WATFORD	4-3	Huxford, Verveer, Moralee, Murray
3		27	Queen's Park Rangers	0-3	

FA Cup

Round	Date		Opposition	Score	Scorers
3	Jan	10	ARSENAL	0-1	

1993/94   Football League Division One

	P	W	D	L	F	A	Pts
Crystal Palace	46	27	9	10	73	46	90
Nottingham Forest	46	23	14	9	74	49	83
MILLWALL	46	19	17	10	58	49	74
Leicester City	46	19	16	11	72	59	73
Tranmere Rovers	46	21	9	16	69	53	72
Derby County	46	20	11	15	73	68	71
Notts County	46	20	8	18	65	69	68
Wolverhampton Wanderers	46	17	17	12	60	47	68
Middlesbrough	46	18	13	15	66	54	67
Stoke City	46	18	13	15	57	59	67
Charlton Athletic	46	19	8	19	61	58	65
Sunderland	46	19	8	19	54	57	65
Bristol City	46	16	16	14	47	50	64
Bolton Wanderers	46	15	14	17	63	64	59
Southend United	46	17	8	21	63	67	59
Grimsby Town	46	13	20	13	52	47	59
Portsmouth	46	15	13	18	52	58	58
Barnsley	46	16	7	23	55	67	55
Watford	46	15	9	22	66	80	54
Luton Town	46	14	11	21	56	60	53
West Bromwich Albion	46	13	12	21	60	69	51
Birmingham City	46	13	12	21	52	69	51
Oxford United	46	13	10	23	54	75	49
Peterborough United	46	8	13	25	48	76	37

Goodbye Reg
1994/95

The inquiry that followed the events at the end of the previous season eventually imposed a sentence of the club playing two matches behind closed doors, a fine of £100,000 suspended for two years, a deduction of three League points, suspended until the end of the season and various ground changes to be implemented.

No longer could fans move around the ground. They were restricted to the stand in which they had bought tickets, and the North Stand would now be for visiting supporters only. Millwall fans had been able to use part of it the previous season.

The South Stand became a members-only stand. A new Millwall Supporters Club was started, and supporters had to have a membership card to buy tickets in this stand, although there was no cost to be a member. There was talk of fencing being reintroduced although thankfully this never materialised.

Those finally identified as having taken part in the violence were banned from the ground and chairman Reg Burr said, 'We have to tell the people responsible for the trouble to bugger off and leave us alone, or sit down and watch the match and behave themselves.' Whatever the reasons, Burr decided that he would step down as chairman at the end of the season, although he originally denied it and announced his decision in the spring of 1995.

He had joined the club as a director in 1974 and although he left the board in 1982 he led a consortium that took over the club in 1986 and oversaw the promotion to the old First Division and the move to the new stadium.

He became life president at the end of the season.

There were the usual changes on the playing staff as well. Terry Hurlock left by mutual consent and went to Fulham while Paul Holsgrove's contract was not renewed and he went to Reading. Carl Emberson went to Colchester for £25,000, but the surprises were the departure of Jamie Moralee and Geoff Pitcher, who both went to Watford for a joint fee of £450,000, and a £1 million bid took Neil Emblen to Wolves. After just 12 league appearances this looked like shrewd business but the fans were upset by it.

Burr explained that the money was only going to offset losses incurred because of the violence that had happened at the end of the previous season, although many disagreed with that explanation.

Arriving were midfielder Dave Savage, who had signed at the end of the previous season for £15,000 from Irish club Longford Town and defender/midfielder Steve Forbes, who came from Sittingbourne for a nominal fee.

There was also a new strip, blue with white sleeves. The change shirt was red with a black pinstripe in contrast to the previous season's yellow shirt and, after some procrastination, Captain Morgan agreed to continue their shirt sponsorship.

The club also decided to withdraw from the Anglo-Italian Cup even though it had been revamped for the new season.

This season also saw a change in the promotion and relegation issues. The Premier League was reducing in size to twenty clubs so there were to be four clubs relegated and only two promoted, the divisional winner and the winner of the play-offs from the next four teams. This prompted a statement from Burr, who recommended five down and three up and suggested that five up and five down should be implemented from the following season.

A successful pre-season tour of Ireland was completed with home games against FC Porto from Portugal, which they lost 0-1, and Real Sociedad from Spain, which ended in a 1-1 draw. They both proved useful workouts and gave the fans a chance to see the new additions to the squad that included Jason Van Blerk, an Australian international defender who came on trial from Dutch side Go Ahead Eagles and was subsequently signed for £300,000.

McCarthy also took the decision to abandon his diamond midfield for a more conventional 4-4-2 system for no other reason than as he said, 'I just fancied a change.'

The season kicked off on 13 August with a home match against Southend. The game saw the welcome return of Andy May from his injury nightmare and Dave Savage made his Millwall debut. Memories of the previous season's home opener were quickly dispelled when goals from Mitchell, Goodman and a Tilson own goal gave the Lions a comfortable 3-1 win.

The long trip to Sunderland the following Saturday produced a 1-1 draw. Rae scored the goal and, although the Lions played well, they owed their point to an outstanding performance from Kasey Keller. Keller, who was barracked throughout the match because of his part in Sunderland player Don Goodman's dismissal the previous season, made some impressive and important saves.

Reg Burr was in the news again as he answered the club's critics about racism there and he introduced Millwall's kick out racism campaign. 'This is not just a public relations exercise,' he said. 'We are going to take strict action against anyone identified using racist abuse.'

The visit to The New Den of Derby County the following Saturday was naturally a worry, coming so close to the trouble at the end of the previous season. The media examination of the match was bound to be intense and Burr insisted that the club would treat the game like any other match. 'We are not making a drama out of it,' he announced. 'All we ask is that people conduct themselves like they would at any other game.' There was no crowd trouble and the team saw off their opponents with an emphatic 4-1 win.

It could have been very different, however, as the Lions lost May and Mitchell to bad injuries in the first fifteen minutes but goals from Rae and three from Kerr – the first hat-trick to be scored by a substitute – ensured victory, with Jon Goodman, who made all four goals, destroying the Rams' defence with his pace and trickery.

The 1-0 defeat at Bolton was agony after what had looked like being a goal-less draw until the eighty-eighth minute. Danny Chapman, who made his first-team debut in place of the injured May, will remember it. A 0-0 draw away at Reading brought about by poor finishing from Millwall and excellent goalkeeping by Reading's Shaka Hislop followed.

The team's inexperience showed in the 2-2 home draw with West Bromwich Albion but they came back to equalise twice. Both goals came from Goodman, and Millwall were unfortunate not to have won in the end.

A lacklustre display from the Lions and sloppy defending brought about the first home defeat of the season when Burnley won 2-3. It was also the Lions' 1,000th Football League defeat. Dave Savage scored his first senior goal and Rae scored the second from the penalty spot but the Lions never looked like they would win the match. Pantomime season seemed to have come early when referee Mike Bailey sent off Burnley's Ted McMinn for two bookable offences and then changed his mind when he realised that he had only booked him once.

Jason Van Blerk, whose arrival at The New Den had been held up in bureaucratic red tape, finally made his Lions debut when he came as a substitute for Savage at Tranmere. The Lions dominated the match so it was hard to see how they lost 1-3. Roberts was the scorer. There is no doubt that the referee's refusing to give a penalty when Tranmere's Mungall punched a Cunningham cross past the post when the score was 1-1 was a big factor.

Much more disappointing, however, was the fact that the Lions could not turn their dominance into goals and an old failing raised its ugly head once again in a match that saw the return of Van Den Hauwe from injury.

The second round of the Coca-Cola Cup had the Lions matched against Sunderland with the first leg played at The New Den. The game ended in a 2-1 win for the Lions, with goals from Goodman and Kennedy, but it will be a night remembered for two goalkeepers.

Keller was sent off for handball when stopping a Sunderland attack that could have levelled the game but he should have been joining his opposite number, Tony Norman, who had somehow managed to stay on the pitch when he flattened Dave Mitchell some twenty minutes earlier. He had already saved a Rae penalty kick.

A thoroughly boring 0-0 home draw with Luton followed and losing 0-3 to Middlesbrough a week later did nothing to build confidence. The 1-1 draw in the second leg of the Coca-Cola Cup game with Sunderland lifted the gloom a little. Goodman scored the goal that mattered and Van Blerk got his first start of the season in a side still missing key players due to injuries.

Still suffering from a lack of events at the new stadium the club parted company with Ogden and looked to organise events themselves. Although they were holding indoor cabaret nights they were still finding it impossible to hold events outside in the stadium.

It is a long way from Sunderland to Bristol and the game against City, which the Lions lost 0-1, was made harder with the loss of Goodman before the game and an injury to Mitchell at half-time. The sending off of Alex Rae after half an hour did not help and Tim Carter, making his first start of the season replacing the suspended Keller, made some excellent saves. But once again poor defending and bad finishing led to their downfall.

McCarthy needed to do something to brighten up his side and with Murray going back to the USA to play for Atlanta after having his contract terminated and Richard Huxford going to Bradford City on loan, he made his move and brought in on loan defender Tony Witter from Queens Park Rangers and striker Richard Cadette from Falkirk. They both made their debuts in the 1-1 home draw with Stoke. Also arriving at The New Den was midfielder Steven Roche from Irish club Belvedere.

Even though they took the lead through Goodman, the Lions were nervy and showed their lack of confidence. The crossbar and post saved them from losing the game on three separate occasions. James Connor, also making his Millwall debut, had a solid game in midfield in what was to be his only appearance in the first team.

With some of the fans turning against McCarthy with the side twenty-first in the division he received backing from chairman Burr. 'I know this is the kiss of death, but I've got every confidence in him,' he said. 'Mick knows exactly where he stands with me and he is still the man in charge.'

McCarthy was desperately trying to bring in more new faces as the injury nightmare continued with Van Blerk cracking two ribs, but had been unsuccessful. He did manage to sign central defender Damian Webber from Bognor Regis.

In their present situation going to Molineux to face high-flying Wolves was not the best place to go and Ian Dawes, making his first start after long-term injury, found himself filling in in midfield.

With the score 1-1 at half-time (Goodman had scored the goal), it looked like they might hold on for a draw but the Lions found themselves two goals down with ten minutes left. When Richard Cadette came off of the bench to score his first goal for the club it looked like a consolation but Goodman scored again to earn a thrilling 3-3 draw.

That may have been the fillip the team needed and goals from Cadette and Kennedy took the Lions through to the next round of the Coca-Cola Cup with a 2-0 away win over Mansfield. The Stags though had Boothroyd sent off near the end but it had no effect on the result. The same pair scored again in the 2-1 home win over Sheffield United; Kennedy with a penalty and Cadette scored in injury time at the end of the game. With Keith Stevens returning to the first team after a lengthy lay off due to injury, things started to look better.

All of this prompted McCarthy to sign Cadette permanently for a fee of £125,000 and to extend Witter's loan period. He also brought in on loan midfield player Tony Kelly from Bolton and let James Saddington go to Kettering on a free transfer without him playing a single first-team game. Goalkeeper Dave Wietecha went on loan to Brighton.

Having snatched all the points in the dying seconds against Sheffield United it was disappointing to throw two points away in similar circumstances in the home game with Portsmouth.

Having taken the lead in just two minutes with a Goodman header and then retaken the lead through a Rae twenty-five-yard special, they gave away an injury-time penalty and the game ended 2-2.

Millwall's first away win of the season came next, 2-1 against Swindon. In fact it was their 350th away win in the Football League but it came with a price. Keith Stevens was sent off for two bookable offences. His second booking produced the penalty from which Swindon scored, and the game was spoiled by a card-happy referee who also booked seven other players and sent off Swindon's Andrew Thomson in a game which did not have one malicious foul in it.

For the record Millwall's goals came from Goodman and Kennedy, and it proved to be Goodman's last for the club as he was then sold to Wimbledon along with Kenny Cunningham for a joint fee of £1.3 million. The sum of £75,000 was used to secure the permanent services of Tony Witter when his loan ended in December.

A programme from the 1994/95 season.

Chairman Burr explained that the sale was necessary for a variety of reasons and said, 'The simple fact of the matter is that the costs of the club exceed its income.' He added, 'If somebody had deeper pockets and could do a better job you would not need to push me, I'd be only too delighted to hand over.'

Losing 0-1 away to Grimsby in the next match did not help matters. Alan Kelly made his Millwall debut in the match when he replaced Mark Beard, who started the match as Cunningham's replacement. In torrential rain on a heavy pitch it looked like Mitchell had scored an equaliser but it was ruled out for pushing and the Lions returned home pointless again.

Kelly started the next game, at home to Barnsley, and was himself replaced by a debutant, Damien Webber. It was to be Kelly's last game for the club. Seeing their side lose 0-1 again, a fans' protest against Burr started and he agreed to see representative of the fanzines *No One Likes Us* and *The Lion Roars* in the hope of answering the fans' questions in an open meeting. 'I certainly want to meet the fans before the Wolves game,' explained Burr. 'I think the fanzines reflect the views of the widest range of supporters and I hope between us we can come up with the best way to approach this meeting.'

Before the televised game against Wolves there were two other games to play. The first, away at Port Vale, saw Greg Berry on the substitutes bench as the first of the long-term injured started to come back.

Mark Kennedy's goal was not enough as the Lions lost 1-2 to another injury-time winner and although Berry played a part in the game he was to make a more telling contribution in his first start of the season when the Lions took on Nottingham Forest at the County Ground in the Coca-Cola Cup. Considering the form of both clubs no one gave the Lions a chance but Berry's two goals secured a 2-0 win and put the London side into the next round.

The meeting between the fans and Reg Burr took place and after five hours Burr appeared happy with the outcome, which included holding monthly meetings with delegates from the fanzines. 'Unlike other chairmen of this club I've never been afraid to talk to Millwall fans because I actually like them,' said Burr.

The Lion Roars' editor, Paul Cassella, added, 'We've always been willing to offer constructive advice.' Then, in speaking about Burr, he said, 'I don't think there's any doubt that he's got his heart in the club, I just think it's a shame he's the only one who takes the flack.'

The televised home game against Wolves at the start of December began with the Lions twentieth in the division but their 1-0 win started a run that saw them win every game in the month. The team were good value for their win. Confidence was high after the Forest game, but maybe it hinged on the sending off of David Kelly for a foul on Mark Beard.

After consulting his linesman, referee Ian Hemley sent Kelly off and as he made his way to an early bath Dave Mitchell, who had earlier hit the bar and a post, headed home the winner.

The Lions had brought young Danish goalkeeper Jimmi Nielson to the club and had high hopes for him. They also gave trials to his compatriot Jesper Topp. The striker was quickly sent back home, as was another trialist, Joseph Odegbami, and Tony McCarthy went on loan to Crewe.

The revival continued with a 2-0 home win over Sunderland, although it took a half-time roasting from McCarthy after a dour first half to get the side going. The goals came from Kennedy and Mitchell in what was ultimately a well-deserved victory in a game where Keller introduced a new art to goalkeeping. Stranded by a poor back pass outside the area, he dropped to his knees, trapped the ball between them and waddled with it there until he could stand and clear the ball while the opposition appealed in vain.

Tony Dolby went on loan to Chesham and Jermaine Wright, once highly thought of, went to Wolves for £50,000 without playing a first-team game, although he did manage to get on the substitutes bench on one occasion. Etienne Verveer, who had tried to find a new club all season, had his contract cancelled and ended up at Bradford City and Van Den Hauwe was placed on the transfer list and eventually had his contract terminated too.

Striker Jason Beckford became an addition to the squad having been released by Stoke and he made his debut in the 1-0 away win at Southend. He supplied the cross for Cadette's winner and Jason Van Blerk made his comeback from injury.

Unfortunately Keith Stevens was sent off for the second time this season after half an hour for a tackle on Ronnie Whelan, so the Lions' win was all the more satisfying having played for so long with ten men.

Burr was back in the papers discussing a proposed Premiership Division Two and wanted to make sure that Millwall would be part of it. Insisting that it was inevitable Burr said, 'There is nothing set in stone as far as I'm aware, but I think this new league is a certainty after next season.' That certainty is still to materialise.

Richard Huxford's extended loan to Bradford City was finally made permanent when he signed for a £50,000 fee and the club also decided to move their training ground from Eltham to a new site in Bromley because the current one was prone to flooding. 'It will cost the club a substantial amount of money,' said Burr, 'but we are confident we can fund it.'

Two games in two days over Christmas is difficult for any team. Add in some travelling and it becomes harder so the 1-0 win at Notts County was particularly welcome. Dave Mitchell's goal in the pouring rain was the icing on a well-prepared Christmas cake in a game the Lions dominated.

So it was back to London and the arrival of Watford, who were convincingly beaten 2-1 the following day. The goals, a penalty from Rae and another from Cadette ten minutes later, were enough, although it needed Keller to save a Tommy Mooney penalty to make sure of all three points. Stevens celebrated his 400th Millwall League game with a win. Five games, fifteen points and ten places up the table. Not a bad way to end the year.

With a full League programme the following Saturday the fans were looking forward to a trip to The Valley and the derby game against Charlton. But it was suddenly switched to the Sunday – New Year's Day – and a midday kick-off at that. There was no convincing reason as to why it happened.

It proved to be an entertaining game that ended 1-1. Rae scored with an amazing thirty-yard strike. It was the first goal scored anywhere in 1995 and Damien Webber started in place of the suspended Stevens.

This was followed by the arrival of Oldham at The New Den two days later and another 1-1 draw but this was a game about three penalties. Lee Richardson chipped the first, a dubious

Mark Kennedy and Mark Beard, the heroes of Highbury, both scored in the FA Cup replay to knock Arsenal out of the competition.

one awarded to Oldham for a foul by Thatcher, over Keller. The second, only slightly more obvious, was scored by Rae after a foul on Kennedy and the most obvious, when Cadette was pretty much assaulted by Steve Redmond, was not given.

Bradford City striker Lee Power arrived on a month's loan but never featured in a first-team game, while Phil Barber went to Plymouth for the same amount of time.

Life can often throw up strange things and the FA Cup even more so, so when the third round draw sent Arsenal to The New Den for the second year running it was time to avenge the previous year's result. The match was fairly uneventful for the near-18,000 crowd, apart the firecracker an Arsenal fan fired into the Millwall fans. Arsenal came and got what they wanted, a 0-0 draw, although Ian Wright's pre-match comments that Millwall fans were racist inflamed many.

Having described Wright as a silly young man and declining to report his remarks to the Football Association, Burr said, 'We've just to get on with our football on the pitch and let other things take their own course.'

The replay was to be a very different affair but first there was the Coca-Cola Cup match at Swindon and a league game away at Sheffield United to contend with.

Dave Mitchell's goal against his old club was no more than a consolation as Swindon won 1-3 with Jan Aage Fjortoft running the show, although his thirty-sixth-minute opener was more of a fluke than a shot.

An injury crisis to the strikers saw the mysterious involvement of Australian international Alistair Edwards at Sheffield, where he made his debut in the 1-1 draw. Mark Beard scored his first of the season and Damien Webber was sent off by referee Ken Powell, who had taken over at half-time because Paul Harrison had gone down with flu, and the equaliser came from the free-kick that followed.

Kasey Keller saves a vital spot kick at Stamford Bridge as the Lions knock out Chelsea from the
FA Cup.

Those two games were not the ideal preparation for a trip to Highbury. Edwards again started the game and when Beard put the Lions in front after just ten minutes the 6,000 Millwall fans went berserk. The game was full of everything a cup tie should be and although the Lions had to defend well they gave a good as they got.

With Wright booked for a foul on Keller and completely losing his head, and with Adams shooting wide from a couple of feet, the Millwall fans knew it would be their night and they celebrated long into the rain-soaked Wednesday evening when Kennedy ran the length of the Arsenal half in the final seconds of the match to smash the ball past Seaman to complete a wonderful 2-0 win.

Their reward was the visit of Chelsea and this would become the next game as the league match against Swindon was called off, as were all games in London, because of a waterlogged pitch.

Although Millwall were the better side, chances were few and far between and the eventual 0-0 score was perhaps inevitable and another replay beckoned. The question was could the Lions do it again?

Still looking to increase his attacking options and with Lee Power back at Bradford City, McCarthy signed Scott Taylor for £15,000 from Staines Town as well as taking midfield player Lee McRobert from Sittingbourne for £35,000, while Michael Harle made the reverse journey on loan.

A 2-0 win over Grimsby, with goals from Kennedy and Roberts, was a good warm up for the Chelsea replay and when Dave Savage equalised Mark Stein's opener with just eleven minutes left it was no more than the Lions deserved. With the scores level after extra time the dreaded penalty shoot-out came into force.

Goals from Savage, Van Blerk, Stevens, Roberts and Rae had been countered by Stein, Wise, Burley and Lee but when Keller spectacularly saved Spencer's spot kick the Lions were through again, this time to play Queens Park Rangers. It was to be their next game, beamed back to The New Den because of the high demand for tickets.

A questionable ninetieth-minute penalty was the only goal of the game. The Lions' cup run had ended but not without some exciting times for players and fans alike.

So it was back to the League and a 1-4 away defeat by Barnsley on a pitch resembling a beach where the tide had just gone out. Damien Webber, the penalty 'culprit' at QPR, was the scorer. McRobert made his debut when replacing May. This game was followed by the televised match against Middlesbrough that ended as a 0-0 bore in which striker David Oldfield, on loan from Leicester City, made his debut.

It was a relief when the Lions won 3-1 at home to Swindon in their rescheduled match with two goals from Rae and Van Blerk's first, which was also Millwall's 7,000th goal scored in all competitions.

The injury crisis was still taking its toll so McCarthy brought in defender Roger Joseph, from Wimbledon on a month's loan, who made his debut in the 1-1 draw at Luton. Dave Mitchell scored Millwall's goal.

Mitchell scored again in the 2-0 home win over Reading, when David Oldfield also opened his Millwall account, and he scored again with a spectacular overhead kick when the Lions went down 2-3 at Derby. Rae was the other scorer and Tim Carter got a rare outing because of Keller's hip injury. It was Mitchell's last goal for the club as he left after just two more games to take up a coaching position with Malaysian club Selangor for £150,000. Tony McCarthy also left to join Colchester for free.

Oldfield and Witter, with his first for the club, scored at Portsmouth but the Fratton Park outfit won 2-3 and when former Lion John McGinlay scored the only goal in the televised game with Bolton the chase for a play-off spot was effectively gone. Losing 0-3 away to West Bromwich just confirmed it.

A bigger loss was the sale of Mark Kennedy to Liverpool. The £2 million the club received for him may have helped them out of financial problems, something denied by Burr, but none of the money found its way to reinforcing the side, although Kerry Dixon arrived on loan. Burr said, 'Selling Mark was not forced on us by financial necessity, it was something we sat down and analysed over a six-hour meeting.' Most fans failed to see how selling their best players could be a good strategy for a club claiming to aim for promotion to the Premier League.

Dixon made a dream debut in the home match against Tranmere, when he opened the scoring, and his all-round performance help the Lions secure a 2-1 win. Andy 'Pikey' Roberts was the other scorer but the fans were hoping that Dixon's goal would be the start of Millwall signing experienced strikers who would actually score for them.

Two goals from Oldfield gave the Lions a 2-1 away win over Burnley and, in the knowledge the side were safe from relegation, McCarthy began to experiment for the coming season and gave a debut to Scott Taylor when he came off the bench against Port Vale.

It was a disappointing game that the Lions lost 1-3. Oldfield scored again but the team played much better when beating Charlton 3-1 three days later. Lee McRobert celebrated his first start with his first goal with his first touch of the ball when he opened the scoring after three minutes and further goals from Thatcher – how better to score your first goal than a thirty-yard screamer?– and Dixon made it an easy win.

The Lions then lost 0-1 in a televised game at Watford and played an uninspiring 0-0 draw with Notts County. A Savage goal was the only eventful thing that happened in the 1-0 win at Oldham apart from Taylor making his first start and the twenty-two-man scuffle that referee Paul Vanes took no action over. But the final away match at Stoke was full of incidents.

A cruel last-minute winner for Stoke saw the game end 3-4 in a game that was a defensive nightmare for both sides and saw Millwall concede their 4,000th Football League goal.

Goals from Dixon and Oldfield did their chances of a close-season permanent move no harm. Webber scored the other and Dixon helped himself to another goal in the 1-1 draw against Bristol City in the final game of the season, where Steve Forbes made his debut when coming on as a substitute.

It was not the end to the season that Burr had been hoping for. Handing over the chairmanship of the club to Peter Mead he said, 'I couldn't go on for ever and now it's time for me to spend more time with my wife and family.' Then he added, 'You don't run a club for nine years without regrets but I've got to look at the stadium and how far we've come. The dream scenario was to build the stadium and then get promoted and we came so close to doing that.'

And he told the fans, 'I know you sing '"No one likes us we don't care" but I truly do like you and do care. I have enjoyed my nine years as your chairman – I wouldn't have missed it for anything. Thank you for giving me the opportunity.'

There is no doubt that Burr left his legacy for the club and the fans showed their feelings for him with a warm send off. How they would respond to Mead only time would tell but starting his tenure as chairman with the words, 'I'm not awash with money, I'm no Jack Walker,' didn't augur well.

1994/95   Football League Division One

Date		Opposition	Score	Scorers
Aug	13	SOUTHEND UNITED	3-1	Mitchell, Goodman, Opp OG
	20	Sunderland	1-1	Rae
	27	DERBY COUNTY	4-1	Kerr (3), Rae
	31	Bolton Wanderers	0-1	
Sept	3	Reading	0-0	
	10	WEST BROMWICH ALBION	2-2	Goodman (2)
	14	BURNLEY	2-3	Rae (pen), Savage
	17	Tranmere Rovers	1-3	Roberts
	24	LUTON TOWN	0-0	
Oct	1	Middlesbrough	0-3	
	8	Bristol City	0-1	
	15	STOKE CITY	1-1	Goodman
	22	Wolverhampton Wanderers	3-3	Goodman (2), Cadette
	29	SHEFFIELD UNITED	2-1	Cadette, Kennedy (pen)
Nov	2	PORTSMOUTH	2-2	Rae, Goodman
	5	Swindon Town	2-1	Goodman, Kennedy
	12	Grimsby Town	0-1	
	19	BARNSLEY	0-1	
	26	Port Vale	1-2	Kennedy
Dec	4	WOLVERHAMPTON WANDERERS	1-0	Mitchell
	10	SUNDERLAND	2-0	Mitchell, Kennedy
	17	Southend United	1-0	Cadette
	26	Notts County	1-0	Mitchell
	27	WATFORD	2-1	Rae (pen), Cadette
Jan	1	Charlton Athletic	1-1	Rae
	3	OLDHAM ATHLETIC	1-1	Rae (pen)
	14	Sheffield United	1-1	Beard
Feb	4	GRIMSBY TOWN	2-0	Roberts, Kennedy
	21	Barnsley	1-4	Webber
	26	MIDDLESBROUGH	0-0	
Mar	1	SWINDON TOWN	3-1	Rae (2), Van Blerk
	4	Luton Town	1-1	Mitchell
	8	READING	2-0	Mitchell, Oldfield
	11	Derby County	2-3	Rae, Mitchell
	15	Portsmouth	2-3	Witter, Oldfield
	19	BOLTON WANDERERS	0-1	
	22	West Bromwich Albion	0-3	
	25	TRANMERE ROVERS	2-1	Roberts, Dixon
Apr	1	Burnley	2-1	Oldfield (2)
	5	PORT VALE	1-3	Oldfield
	8	CHARLTON ATHLETIC	3-1	Thatcher, McRobert, Dixon
	14	Watford	0-1	
	19	NOTTS COUNTY	0-0	
	22	Oldham Athletic	1-0	Savage
	29	Stoke City	3-4	Webber, Dixon, Oldfield
May	7	BRISTOL CITY	1-1	Dixon

League Cup

Round	Date		Opposition	Score	Scorers
2/1	Sept	21	SUNDERLAND	2-1	Goodman, Kennedy
2/2	Oct	4	Sunderland	1-1	Goodman
3		25	Mansfield Town	2-0	Cadette, Kennedy
4	Nov	30	Nottingham Forest	2-0	Berry (2)
5	Jan	11	Swindon Town	1-3	Mitchell

FA Cup

Round	Date		Opposition	Score	Scorers
3	Jan	7	ARSENAL	0-0	
3R		18	Arsenal	2-0	Beard, Kennedy
4		28	CHELSEA	0-0	
4R	Feb	8	Chelsea	1-1*	Savage
5		18	Queen's Park Rangers	0-1	

*a.e.t Millwall won on penalties

1994/95　　　　　Football League Division One

	P	W	D	L	F	A	Pts
Middlesbrough	46	23	13	10	67	40	82
Reading	46	23	10	13	58	44	79
Bolton Wanderers	46	21	14	11	67	45	77
Wolverhampton Wanderers	46	21	13	12	77	61	76
Tranmere Rovers	46	22	10	14	67	58	76
Barnsley	46	20	12	14	63	52	72
Watford	46	19	13	14	52	46	70
Sheffield United	46	17	17	12	74	55	68
Derby County	46	18	12	16	66	51	66
Grimsby Town	46	17	14	15	62	56	65
Stoke City	46	16	15	15	50	53	63
Millwall	46	16	14	16	60	60	62
Southend United	46	18	8	20	54	73	62
Oldham Athletic	46	16	13	17	60	60	61
Charlton Athletic	46	16	11	19	58	66	59
Luton Town	46	15	13	18	61	64	58
Port Vale	46	15	13	18	58	64	58
Portsmouth	46	15	13	18	53	63	58
West Bromwich Albion	46	16	10	20	51	57	58
Sunderland	46	12	18	16	41	45	54
Swindon Town	46	12	12	22	54	73	48
Burnley	46	11	13	22	49	74	46
Bristol City	46	11	12	23	42	63	45

Disastrous Distractions 1995/96

He might not have been a Jack Walker but Peter Mead sanctioned a lot of pre-season changes that he and McCarthy felt would bring the success to the club that everyone had been looking for since their move to The New Den – now referred to without the 'new'.

Out went Oldfield and Joseph, who were not taken on after their loan periods. Dawes retired due to injury, Allen ended up at Carlisle, Beckford went to Northampton Town, Gavin Maguire went to Atlanta in the USA, Danny Chapman to Leyton Orient and Phil Barber to Bristol City. Tim Carter joined Oxford, Andy May went coaching in Malaysia. John Kerr also left the club, as well as youngsters Neville Gordon who went to Reading and Matthew Middleton, who joined Dulwich Hamlet. But the shock departures were those of Andy Roberts, who went to Crystal Palace for £1.8 million plus utility player Ricky Newman who was valued at £500,000, and Mark Beard, who was a £117,000 sale to Sheffield United just before the start of the season

Apart from Newman, in came midfielder Maurice Doyle from Queens Park Rangers for a nominal fee and full-back Mickey Bennett from Charlton on a free. Kerry Dixon was given a permanent contract, with Millwall paying £5,000 to Luton for his services. Midfield player Bobby Bowry was bought from Crystal Palace for £250,000 and defender Anton Rogan came from Oxford on a one-month loan. However it was the arrival of strikers Chris Malkin from Tranmere for £400,000 and Uwe Fuchs, a £750,000 buy from German club Kaiserslautern, which excited the fans, especially after the disappointment of losing Beard and Roberts. Fuchs had spent a large part of the previous season on loan at Division One champions Middlesbrough where he received a three-match ban, two of which became Millwall's opening two games.

John Plummer won the Groundsman of the Year award after his second place the previous year and Millwall picked up the Giantkillers award for their FA Cup run.

A successful pre-season saw the Lions lose only once to QPR and, with the league reverting back to two automatic promotion places plus play-off winners, promotion looked a real possibility. A change in the substitute rule meant that three outfield players could be named and used at any time in the match.

The season started on 12 August with a home match against Grimsby Town with Bennett, Doyle and Malkin all making their Lions debuts. Malkin made the perfect start by scoring in the 2-1 win after Rae had put the Lions ahead with a penalty after just nine minutes.

Dixon scored the only goal of the game at Port Vale, where Newman, starting in place of the injured Bennett, made his Millwall debut, as did Bowry and Rogan when they came on as substitutes. Keith Stevens made his 500th appearance for the club and the Lions became the early league leaders. Look at the first league table of the season and compare it with the last and the effects of the distractions that befell the club become evident.

	P	W	D	L	F	A	Pts
MILLWALL	2	2	0	0	3	1	6
Tranmere Rovers	2	1	1	0	4	2	4
Reading	2	1	1	0	4	3	4

The 0-0 home match with Southend saw them slip a place and even after just three games a pattern was emerging that was to blight the season. Uwe Fuchs made his belated debut when he replaced Dixon in the game and Millwall mascot Zampa the Lion was also seen for the first time.

Millwall's away strip of green and white halves again proved lucky at Reading, although it came at a cost when Rae was sent off after levelling the score from the penalty spot. Dixon had just put the Lions in front when Rae smashed Mick Gooding in the face. This time his short-fused temper did not bring any loss of points. Millwall won 2-1 and they were back on top again. They stayed there after another Dixon goal gave them a 1-0 away win over Portsmouth.

Having scored three times in five games Dixon said, 'I had a couple of bad years at Southampton and Luton but now I'm averaging a goal every other game again and, although my pace has slowed a bit, I can still score at this level.' When will players learn the futility of making statements like this?

There had been a lot of speculation about McCarthy being offered various managerial positions, including that of the Republic of Ireland when manager Jack Charlton retired, so to quash the rumours and show his commitment to the club he signed a new three-year deal just before the visit of Barnsley.

On the player front, Greg Berry went on loan to Brighton, hoping that it would help to build his fitness after his long injury lay-off and Rogan was signed until the end of the season.

A second-minute goal by Redfern gave Barnsley a 0-1 win at The Den and knocked the Lions from the top spot. Once again the inability to score goals was their undoing although Malkin came off the bench to snatch a last-minute winner when they beat Luton 1-0 at The Den the following Wednesday.

The lack of goals continued though with 0-0 draws away at Norwich and the home leg of the Coca-Cola Cup second round match against Everton, and when they lost the next game 1-2 at home to Sunderland it was defender Keith Stevens who scored.

The Lions certainly needed a lift for the televised away match at Derby the following Sunday. It came in the form of Kingsley Black, who signed on loan from Nottingham Forest before the game. Making his debut, he scored Millwall's second goal with a great free-kick. Rae scored the first after just six minutes, but the game ended 2-2 and it was to be Black's only start and only goal.

The result certainly lifted the Lions before their visit to Everton for the second leg of their Coca-Cola Cup match but once again the goals were coming from midfield rather than the expensive strikers who had been brought in to score them.

The Lions had built a reputation for themselves after their cup exploits the previous season but their stay in this competition looked to be over when they found themselves two goals down, having given away soft goals at the start of the second half. Yet it would become a night that the team and especially Scott Taylor would remember for a long time.

Taylor had replaced the injured Thatcher just before half-time and on sixty-three minutes scored what looked like being a consolation goal. But three minutes later he burst into the area and came tumbling down under Earl Barrett's challenge. Most referees would not have given the spot kick but Mike Reed did and a delighted Rae cracked it home.

No one gave the Lions a chance of surviving in extra time but Taylor scored again from the edge of the area and Savage wrapped it up with virtually the last kick of the match from Taylor's pass. It ended an unbelievable comeback with a 4-2 win. What a game to score your first goals for the club in!

The European Court ruling on the case brought by Jean-Marc Bosman found that it was unlawful for clubs to demand a transfer fee when a player's contract had come to an end and this was to have an effect on the transfer system when it was later implemented. However, the fee Forest wanted to make Black's move permanent was more than could be afforded at this time and he eventually went back, although goalkeeper Nick Colgan did arrive from Chelsea.

Supersub Scott Taylor slides in Millwall's first goal in the 4-2 extra-time win over Everton.

Taylor was in the starting line up for the away match against Watford but it was Alex Rae who stole the limelight this time with a stunning twenty-five-yard shot to win the game 1-0. 'If we can keep this going I think we've got a very good chance, at least for promotion,' said Rae, adding, 'This club has got under my skin and I want to play in the Premiership with Millwall.'

Rumours of McCarthy, Rae, Thatcher and Keller leaving the club were rife but the only one going was Edwards, who went back to the Far East after having his contract terminated. With one striker gone and the others finding it difficult to score it was a relief when Dixon netted in the 2-2 draw with Tranmere.

It was a see-saw of a game spoilt by some strange refereeing decisions by Rob Harris. Just why Millwall seem to be playing when referees are at their most inconsistent or eccentric we will probably never know.

Dixon had replaced the injured Fuchs after half an hour and a match that had been boring in the first half came to life when Tranmere took the lead on fifty-seven minutes. Dixon was then denied a penalty when he was manhandled in the box. Gary Stevens would have been arrested for GBH had he committed the offence in the streets around the stadium but got away with it on the pitch. He then scored from the spot when Malkin was brought down.

It looked all over when Keith Stevens scored with a simple tap in but in the dying seconds Rob Harris intervened for the umpteenth time to award a penalty against the outstanding Tony Witter.

At last the two strikers started to earn their keep when both Malkin, after just three minutes, and Fuchs scored in the televised 2-1 win at Crystal Palace. Fuchs' first goal for the club was more of a fluke than anything else. Palace goalkeeper Nigel Martyn punched the ball only for it to hit Fuchs and rebound into the net. No matter, it was a goal and the Millwall fans went home happy.

They both repeated the trick again in the home 2-1 win over third-placed West Bromwich Albion. Fuchs' effort was a more legitimate goal when he scored the winner that sent Millwall back to the top of the table, after Malkin had opened the scoring with an excellent goal when he burst past three players to score. They were to stay there until the beginning of December.

In between these two games the Lions lost 0-2 to Sheffield Wednesday in the Coca-Cola Cup. Once more a bitter taste was left in the mouth after two more idiots invaded the pitch. They were

Alex Rae hits the winner at Watford.

quickly dealt with, arrested and banned from the club but again the club were suffering poor publicity because of the mindless few.

Some ugly crowd scenes marred a 2-2 away draw against Birmingham, where Dixon and Rae scored. But this time the Birmingham fans were to blame. City's managing director, Karen Brady, thought otherwise but Birmingham's police superintendent laid the blame squarely on the home fans who had attacked the team and fans' coaches and one of whom had punched Dave Savage in the warm up before the game. Policemen and police horses were also injured.

Putting Millwall fans in a stand below the tier occupied by Birmingham fans was just crass stupidity and asking for trouble. It also highlighted that other clubs had their hooligan problems too and that all clubs must continue to be vigilant and work to eradicate the problem.

Back to life on the pitch and a 2-1 home win over Ipswich kept the ball rolling. Tony Witter scored the winner, his first goal for the club, after Malkin had put the Lions in front after just eighty seconds. Once again the goal-shy forwards missed a hatful of chances.

The speculation started about McCarthy leaving the club to take over the international reins of the Republic of Ireland refused to die down. 'If it happens it happens, it's down to the club and Ireland, not me,' said McCarthy. 'Everybody is making a lot of presumptions, including that I would want the job if offered.' He promptly signed Australian Under-18 international Lucas Neill, perhaps to prove a point.

A disappointing 0-0 draw at home to Huddersfield was followed by a 2-2 draw at Oldham that showed the old Millwall never-say-die spirit. Two goals down with just six minutes left and the excellent Witter, who had hit a post, injured in the dressing room, Alex Rae headed home his seventh goal of the season. Sensing the chance of a point they continued to attack and with just two minutes to go Thatcher's cross was met by Malkin, who headed home the equaliser. They were unquestionably outplayed for most of the game but their determination certainly made them championship contenders.

The 'who's leaving for where?' speculation started again but chairman Peter Mead insisted that no one was leaving and then spent £500,000 to bring Watford full-back Gerard Lavin to the club. 'This does not mean we are not going to sell anyone,' insisted Mead, 'but shows how ambitious we are as a club.'

Lavin immediately took his place in the away match against Stoke but could not prevent the Lions from losing 0-1. Once more a host of chances went begging and the speculation about changes at the club started again, although the only player to go was Kingsley Black, now at the end of his loan period.

Naturally this had an unsettling effect on the players and they lost the next two home games, 1-2 against Watford when Malkin was the scorer, and 0-2 against Charlton, a game that saw Stevens sent off. 'You've got to be concerned and I am,' said McCarthy, 'but I don't think the word "panic" is the right one to use, because there isn't any panic here.' He then re-signed Tim Carter, who had been given a free transfer by Oxford and allowed Colgan to return to Chelsea.

Kerry Dixon seemed to reinforce the message when he said, 'Very soon we're going to give someone a good thumping the way we are playing.'

The thumping came in the very next match but not in the way the team were expecting as they lost 0-6 away to Sunderland. The Lions were woeful. 'We have to get back to basics and put in some hard graft,' said McCarthy and he pledged, 'We'll turn it round, starting with Derby,' but the side had started to plummet down the table and had gone from first to seventh.

Meanwhile a new television deal was done with BSkyB who paid £125 million for a five-year deal that should have helped the club's finances and save them from selling any other players. Unfortunately reality proved to be different.

Harle, still to kick a ball for the first team after his transfer from Sittingbourne, was sent on loan to Bury.

Perhaps the continuing distraction of McCarthy being touted for the Republic of Ireland job was not helping, but the uncertainty of a place in the side and whether there would soon be a new manager must have played on the players' minds because they lost to Derby 0-1.

Perhaps looking to deflect those thoughts McCarthy said, 'We need someone who can hold the ball up and stick it in the back of the net. Hopefully we can get someone in in time for our next game but it depends who we can get.' He got Brendan Markey from Irish club Bohemians. Brendan who? You might well ask, as he never played a first-team game. At least the Christmas and New Year games brought little cheer to players and fans alike.

Malkin's goal brought the run of five consecutive defeats to an end in the 1-1 Boxing Day draw at Wolves and, with the Saturday game against Sheffield United called off because of a frozen pitch at Bramall Lane, he did it again on New Year's Day in the 1-1 home draw with Leicester.

The game was tinged with sadness though with the announcement of the death from a heart attack of Millwall legend Harry Cripps. The 9,953 crowd observed a minute's silence impeccably. Affectionately known as 'Arry Boy', Cripps, who played 437 times for the Lions from 1960-1974 would have been pleased with the way they showed some of the fighting spirit he had when they came from behind and nearly grabbed a win.

The FA Cup game at home to Reading was a welcome distraction from the league although the rumours about McCarthy would not go away. Nor would the rumours of a breakaway Division One and who would be in it.

None of this helped Millwall to halt the slide down the table. But rumours could not be used as an excuse for the 3-3 draw with Oxford United. Denis Smith had assembled a well-organised and attractive side and the Division Two outfit contributed to an exciting game. Having seen their early lead equalised by Rae, who was lucky still to be on the pitch after swinging a fist at David Rush, Paul Moody put the Royals back in front, only for Malkin to equalise again. Rae put the Lions back in front with just six minutes left and that should have been that. But Oxford had other ideas and with just two minutes left they got the equaliser they deserved.

Watching from the stands were Russian internationals Vassili Kulkov and Serguei Iouran (commonly pronounced Yuran), who had both sensationally signed on loan the day before. They made their debuts in the home game against Port Vale.

With Kasey Keller away on international duty, Tim Carter took over in goal. The crowd was swelled to 14,220 with fans who, having bought their Russian hats and flags, were eager to see the players who would be the final piece in the jigsaw. With juniors coming in on another of the club's 'Kid A Quid' days and female supporters allowed in for free this might have been another reason.

Port Vale obviously had not read the script and went away with a 1-2 win. Rae's goal was nowhere near enough and although the Russians huffed and puffed they looked out of place. Maybe they just needed time to settle.

Neither played in the replayed cup game that Oxford won 0-1 with a stunning twenty-five-yard shot from Massey. It was Millwall's 100th FA Cup defeat and all that was left was to try and restore their shattered pride and fix a season that was looking worse with every game. Darren Keown will remember the game as his first-team debut when he came on as a substitute for Lee McRobert.

The arrival of the Russians heralded the departure of Kerry Dixon and he left to join Watford for £25,000. The fans were now turning on McCarthy and he received the dreaded chairman's vote of confidence when Mead said, 'I can quite understand the frustration everyone is feeling. The easy way would be to blame the manager and say "sorry your time's up and so on your bike" but I don't think it would solve anything.' However, the McCarthy for Ireland rumours persisted and the team's uncertainty about the future continued when teenage goalkeeper Neilson went back to Denmark.

Two Rae goals in the 2-1 away win over Grimsby lifted the gloom for a while. With Portsmouth also out of the cup they rearranged their evening game to take place the next Saturday. Van Blerk's goal was only enough to secure a 1-1 draw and the Lions' inability to score was highlighted once more as Portsmouth had ten men for almost an hour of the game. Losing 0-2 away to Southend in the next game was rubbing salt into an ever-widening wound.

The tension was certainly growing about McCarthy's possible departure and Peter Mead finally realised it had become an unwanted distraction. 'I think it is in everyone at this club's interests that the situation is resolved as soon as possible so we all know where we stand,' he said.

The Southend game was McCarthy's last as Millwall manager. He took the Republic of Ireland post and took Ian Evans with him. He said farewell to the team leaving them ninth in the division.

Keller was back in goal for the home match with Reading under the stewardship of new manager Jimmy Nicholl, who brought Martin Harvey with him as his assistant. The fans were hoping to improve their league position with seventeen games of the season left.

Although not officially taking over for the game, Ian Evans and Ian McDonald took charge of the team. The 1-1 draw was not the start Nicholl wanted. In fact it was only through Newman scoring his first for the club with a twenty-yard wonder goal when he came on as substitute for Connor and cancelled out Bobby Bowry's own goal, that a point was salvaged. 'The expectations of the supporters are the same everywhere and what you want to do at any club is get into the play-offs and win promotion. If we can regain our form and confidence then I think we can do it,' said Nicholl, before adding, 'The challenge is the exciting thing for me and as I've done this before then I can do it again.'

It was Nicholl's team that took the field at Sheffield United and their 0-2 defeat was followed by a 0-1 reverse at Luton, even though the Hatters had ten men for the last fifteen minutes.

The winner came from a late disputed penalty. Tony Dolby and Anton Rogan came in from the wilderness to take places on the bench. Lucas Neill made his debut in the game and showed some great touches, coming closest to scoring for the Lions, and he kept his place in the next game at home to Norwich. Nicholl celebrated his first win as manager when goals from Bowry, his first not counting own goals, and Fuchs, were enough to secure a 2-1 win.

The two Russians were starting to come to grips with the English game. Iouran hit the bar with a great dribble and shot but the Lions had looked far from convincing. They were back to their old selves in losing 1-3 at Barnsley the following Tuesday night. Fuchs scored again, although two injury time goals sealed their fate. Just where do referees get this extra time from sometimes? There were ten minutes added on to the Norwich game and Barnsley scored their last two in an added six minutes. It seemed like there was nothing more to play for than mid-table mediocrity and losing 0-1 at home to Wolves pretty much confirmed it. Whatever the frustration Iouran was suffering was not worth the stupid challenge on Andy Thompson that earned him a red card.

The team needed to put a run of good results together but once you start to free-fall it is hard to stop. Defeats away to Charlton (0-2), Leicester (1-2, Rae scoring) and WBA (0-1), plus losing at home to Crystal Palace (1-4, Rae scoring again from the penalty spot although he had another saved and Van Blerk getting his marching orders), was punctuated by a solitary 1-0 home win over Sheffield United in which Fuchs found the net and Cadette found himself on the substitutes bench.

The team were now fighting against relegation and this was despite the fact that Nicholl had brought in Dale Gordon on loan from West Ham, who made his debut against Leicester, and David Weir on loan from Hibernians. Weir made his first start against Crystal Palace because Nicholl said the team needed wingers although he had sold Scott Taylor to Bolton for £150,000 and let Greg Berry go on loan to Leyton Orient. Iouran, with that first elusive goal, and Malkin, scored in the 2-2 away draw with Tranmere but with the nerves now fraying, Lavin found his way to an early bath. So did Dolby in the next game which was lost 0-1 away to West Brom.

Now down in twentieth position they needed to do something quickly. A 2-0 home win over Birmingham with goals from Bowry and Malkin was exactly what was required. This was a very passionate and vocal match after the problems encountered at St Andrews earlier in the season and the Lions dominated the game. More like this and they would remain safe.

However the tension returned after they were beaten 0-3 away at Huddersfield and 0-1 at home to Oldham. This battle at the bottom was won with a penalty after Witter was adjudged to have fouled Lee Richardson. You could cut the tension with a knife when Rae was sent off with Oldham's Chris Makin with ten minutes left after they threw punches at each other. It need not have been the end of the world though. A win at home against Stoke would have made them safe but, although Rae scored twice, it was not enough and the Lions lost 2-3.

It was still possible to stay up and it looked like a point at Ipswich on the last Sunday of the season would give Millwall enough points to stay up. They fought for a valiant 0-0 draw and got the point they wanted. The final tally was enough to stave off relegation. Unfortunately the goals they scored were not and an unlikely 1-0 win by Portsmouth over Huddersfield gave them the same number of points and a better goal difference. Look back and compare the first league table of the season with the last one.

	P	W	D	L	F	A	Pts
Portsmouth	46	13	13	20	61	69	52
MILLWALL	46	13	13	20	43	63	52
Watford	46	10	18	18	62	70	48
Luton Town	46	11	12	23	40	64	45

Yes, there were many distractions throughout the season – injuries, suspensions and the McCarthy saga all took their toll – but without doubt a lack of goals proved to be the team's undoing. Life in Division Two would have a profound effect for all sorts of reasons, so how would Nicholl deal with it?

1995/96   Football League Division One

Date		Opposition	Score	Scorers
Aug	12	GRIMSBY TOWN	2-1	Rae (pen), Malkin
	19	Port Vale	1-0	Dixon
	26	SOUTHEND UNITED	0-0	
	29	Reading	2-1	Rae (pen), Dixon
Sept	2	Portsmouth	1-0	Dixon
	9	BARNSLEY	0-1	
	13	LUTON TOWN	1-0	Malkin
	16	Norwich City	0-0	
	23	SUNDERLAND	1-2	Stevens
Oct	1	Derby County	2-2	Rae, Black
	7	Watford	1-0	Rae
	14	TRANMERE ROVERS	2-2	Stevens, Dixon (pen)
	22	Crystal Palace	2-1	Fuchs, Malkin
	28	WEST BROMWICH ALBION	2-1	Fuchs, Malkin
Nov	4	Birmingham City	2-2	Rae, Dixon
	11	IPSWICH TOWN	2-1	Witter, Malkin
	18	HUDDERSFIELD TOWN	0-0	
	21	Oldham Athletic	2-2	Rae, Malkin
	25	Stoke City	0-1	
Dec	2	WATFORD	1-2	Malkin
	5	CHARLTON ATHLETIC	0-2	
	9	Sunderland	0-6	
	16	DERBY COUNTY	0-1	
	26	Wolverhampton Wanderers	1-1	Malkin
Jan	1	LEICESTER CITY	1-1	Malkin
	13	PORT VALE	1-2	Rae
	20	Grimsby Town	2-1	Rae (2) (1 pen)
	27	PORTSMOUTH	1-1	Van Blerk
Feb	3	Southend United	0-2	
	10	READING	1-1	Newman
	13	Sheffield United	0-2	
	17	Luton Town	0-1	
	24	NORWICH CITY	2-1	Bowry, Fuchs
	27	Barnsley	1-3	Fuchs
Mar	2	WOLVERHAMPTON WANDERERS	0-1	
	9	Charlton Athletic	0-2	
	16	SHEFFIELD UNITED	1-0	Fuchs
	23	Leicester City	1-2	Rae
	30	CRYSTAL PALACE	1-4	Rae (pen)
Apr	2	Tranmere Rovers	2-2	Iouran, Malkin
	6	West Bromwich Albion	0-1	
	10	BIRMINGHAM CITY	2-0	Bowry, Malkin
	13	Huddersfield Town	0-3	
	20	OLDHAM ATHLETIC	0-1	
	27	STOKE CITY	2-3	Rae (2) (1 pen)
May	4	Ipswich Town	0-0	

League Cup

Round	Date	Opposition	Score	Scorers
2/1	Sept 20	EVERTON	0-0	
2/2	Oct 4	Everton	4-2	Taylor (2), Savage, Rae (pen)
3	25	SHEFFIELD WEDNESDAY	0-2	

FA Cup

Round	Date	Opposition	Score	Scorers
3	Jan 6	OXFORD UNITED	3-3	Rae (2), Malkin
3R	16	Oxford United	0-1	

1995/96   Football League Division One

	P	W	D	L	F	A	Pts
Sunderland	46	22	17	7	59	33	83
Derby County	46	21	16	9	71	51	79
Crystal Palace	46	20	15	11	67	48	75
Stoke City	46	20	13	13	60	49	73
Leicester City	46	19	14	13	66	60	71
Charlton Athletic	46	17	20	9	57	45	71
Ipswich Town	46	19	12	15	79	69	69
Huddersfield Town	46	17	12	17	61	58	63
Sheffield United	46	16	14	16	57	54	62
Barnsley	46	14	18	14	60	66	60
West Bromwich Albion	46	16	12	18	60	68	60
Port Vale	46	15	15	16	59	66	60
Tranmere Rovers	46	14	17	15	64	60	59
Southend United	46	15	14	17	52	61	59
Birmingham City	46	15	13	18	61	64	58
Norwich City	46	14	15	17	59	55	57
Grimsby Town	46	14	14	18	55	69	56
Oldham Athletic	46	14	14	18	54	50	56
Reading	46	13	17	16	54	63	56
Wolverhampton Wanderers	46	13	16	17	56	62	55
Portsmouth	46	13	13	20	61	69	52
MILLWALL	46	13	13	20	43	63	52
Watford	46	10	18	18	62	70	48
Luton Town	46	11	12	23	40	64	45

Under Administration 1996/97

A new strip and new shirt sponsors – the *South London Press* – were not the only changes seen by Lions fans this season. Nicholl wanted to make an early push for promotion; indeed the Lions were amongst the early promotion favourites, but he knew there had to be changes to the squad to do this. 'We don't have any money to bring in players until we sell,' he said. 'But we've got to keep looking about.'

Just how prophetic his words would be, not just about players but also the monetary problems at the club, would soon become evident. But for now everyone was looking forward to the start of the new season.

Nicholl made some backroom staff changes, bringing back Bob Pearson, who had been away from the club since the Rioch era of 1991, as youth development officer along with Mick Beard, Les Briley and Kevin O'Callaghan, who took up coaching roles in the school of excellence.

On the playing side out went the Russians, Iouran and Kulkov, as well as Weir and Gordon, none of whom had their loan spells extended to permanent contracts. The money came from Alex Rae's transfer to Sunderland for £1 million and Ben Thatcher's to Wimbledon for £1.9 million.

Neill, Carter and Rogan were all offered new contracts and in came goalkeeper David Nurse, on a free transfer from Manchester City. Striker Steve Crawford, defender Dave Sinclair and winger Jason Dair all joined from Raith Rovers in a £1.2 million package deal and winger Paul Hartley was a £400,000 buy from Hamilton Academicals. Midfielder Graham Robertson also came from Raith Rovers, after a pre-season trial, for free.

Commenting on the changes, club chairman Peter Mead said, 'We want to be a Premiership club in two years' time and this is the beginning of a new era.' It was certainly the beginning of a new era but the rest turned out to be wishful thinking.

An unconvincing pre-season tour of Scotland was followed by a 0-0 draw with Liverpool, as promised as part of the Kennedy sale, although it took some brilliant goalkeeping from Kasey Keller to keep the score that way.

Unfortunately he never started the season for the Lions. He moved to Leicester City in a £900,000 deal just before the season started but this was only a dent in the huge financial losses the club was to publish.

The side that opened the league programme, a home game with Wrexham on 17 August, was probably not the one Nicholl would have chosen but injuries forced his hand. As expected the Scottish quartet of Steve Crawford, Jason Dair, Dave Sinclair and Paul Hartley, as a substitute for Dair, made their Lions debuts. It was Crawford's late penalty, awarded for a foul on Malkin, which saved the day in a 1-1 draw which saw the old problem of creating chances and not taking them rear its ugly head again.

The injuries were mounting up. Michael Harle finally made his Lions debut, three years after arriving at the club, in the first leg of the Coca-Cola Cup first round match at home to Peterborough the following Wednesday. Although Malkin scored after just nine minutes, once more the Lions failed to take advantage of their many chances and were lucky to escape with a 1-0 win, especially as the Posh had a goal disallowed in the dying seconds.

Harle kept his place for the next match, away at Watford, and marked his first taste of league football with the opening goal on the stroke of half-time. When Crawford added a second four minutes after the break, finishing a move that saw defender Damien Webber bring the ball from one penalty box to the other, beating player after player in the process, Lions fans were starting to see a bright future. Without doubt the 2-0 win was well deserved.

Travelling to York City three days later they were full of confidence and goals from Savage and Malkin only encouraged their belief that immediate promotion was on the cards. However, they saw a defensive horror show in the second half and the resulting 2-3 defeat deflated their hopes somewhat.

On the subject of deflation, two balls were burst in the match and the same two players, Damien Webber and Nigel Pepper, were involved. Was this a football first?

A 2-1 home win over Burnley brightened things up again, although goals from Newman and Neill, a stunning twenty-yard effort for his first senior goal, were late in coming. The Lions finished the first month of the season in fifth place.

	P	W	D	L	F	A	Pts
Plymouth Argyle	4	3	1	0	10	6	10
Brentford	4	3	1	0	9	3	10
Bury	4	3	1	0	8	2	10
Chesterfield	4	3	0	1	4	2	9
MILLWALL	4	2	1	1	7	5	7

Anton Rogan was fit enough to take his place in the Millwall line up to face Peterborough in the second leg of their Coca-Cola Cup match but an injury to Crawford sustained in the Burnley match gave Tony Dolby his first start of the season. With Peterborough leading 1-0 with just minutes to go Dair saw his penalty, awarded for a foul on Malkin, saved. With the match drifting to a penalty shoot-out a late extra-time goal gave Peterborough a 2-0 win which put them through on aggregate. The Lions' finishing had once again let them down.

Nicholl was upset with the loss, but even more so with his players. 'I was very disappointed with the penalty kick because I thought two or three other players should have taken responsibility and they've been told. I'm not trying to clear Jason Dair's name on that but I looked around and he was third or fourth choice to take that penalty,' he said and added, 'the only point I made to the players afterwards was "be honest with yourselves and if you shirked responsibility for taking the penalty, make sure you don't shirk responsibility again in the future".'

Nicholl had to do something about his goals shortage and he brought Darren Huckerby in from Newcastle on loan to rectify the problem. His impact was immediate.

Making his debut in the next match, at home to Bristol Rovers, Huckerby livened up both the forward line and the crowd with his head down, straight-for-goal running. First of all Rovers captain Andy Tilson, who was sent off for his trouble, fouled him. Then he scored the second in a 2-0 win after Rogan had put the Lions in front. Huckerby's goal was the 100th Football League goal scored by the Lions in their new home but unfortunately this game also saw skipper Keith Stevens receive a knee injury that was to put him out of action for some time.

With the injury list mounting, Nicholl named himself in the squad for the away match against Peterborough the following Tuesday. Luckily he did not need to put his boots on.

The match ended 3-3 with Millwall coming from behind each time although they left it late. Malkin's final equaliser came in the last minute. Huckerby and Neill were the other scorers and there was no doubting the courage or character of the side. However some simple defensive errors were to blame for the goals the Lions gave away. 'I think I'm happier with the point than Barry Fry,' said Nicholl after the match. Taking everything into consideration he was probably right.

The same side took the field away at Notts County and it was a hard-fought battle that produced the 2-1 win. An own goal from County's Phil Robinson, who deflected a Dair shot past his 'keeper on eighty-eight minutes, coupled with Neill's twenty-yard opener were enough to win the game. An enthusiastic Nicholl said afterwards, 'We are capable of playing a lot better than that. Watch us go in our bid for promotion.'

They would have to do it without Fuchs though. He had not featured in the side for some time and had been looking for a new club around Europe. He was given a fortnight to sort out the situation and finally went on loan to German club Bielefeld.

Crewe Alexandra were next to step into The Den and the Lions had a fairly comfortable 2-0 win that took them to second in the table behind Brentford. Huckerby was again the star of the show, scoring the first goal and making the second for Dair. It was Dair's first for the club, after Huckerby's shot at the end of a run from the halfway line had come back off the crossbar.

What was worrying was the fact that goals were coming at a very late stage in games and although the fact that they were eventually coming was encouraging, the reason for the Lions' slow start to matches needed finding. There was no doubt that there was now a spirit in the side that had been lacking at the end of the previous season. 'When we arrived here the boys never had a night out, there was no real team spirit,' explained Sinclair, 'but we're changing all that and there's a real group feel building up.'

An interesting arrival at The Den was Andy May. He played for the reserves and went to Glentoran in Ireland to get himself fit, hoping to get a recall to the Millwall side. However he never played for the first team again.

The slow start to matches contributed to the Lions losing the next two although players missing through injury and those playing with them were also a contributing factor.

The first, away to Preston, ended 1-2 and Newman's consolation strike was no more than a disappointing performance deserved. The second, a 3-4 home defeat by Stockport, may have excited the fans but there was a lack of spirit in the side. Those nights out obviously had not worked. Down 1-3 with an hour gone due to some schoolboy defending, Rogan's goal of the season contender was the only glimmer of light in a poor Millwall performance. The crossbar saved them from being 1-4 behind before Rogan pulled another back.

The introduction of substitutes Hartley and youngster Danny Hockton, making his debut, changed things dramatically. Hartley scored the equaliser and Hockton was only inches away from a dramatic possible winner, but Stockport had other ideas. They snatched the winner themselves in the closing seconds and perhaps justice was done. To add to the disappointment it was Huckerby's last game for the club. Although Millwall tried to buy him, the asking price was too high and he returned to Newcastle.

A 0-0 draw away at Plymouth followed. At least the Lions restored some pride with a battling display, but to emphasise the problems Nicholl was having, the team ended the match with Newman substituting for Rogan as a central defender while Michael Harle moved from left back to replace Webber. Dolby moved to left-back from the striker's position he started in and midfielder Graham Robertson made his debut as a striker with Hockton. All that was compounded by a penalty miss from Dave Savage.

With so many defenders out injured Nicholl brought in Scott Fitzgerald on loan from Wimbledon who made his debut in the 2-1 home win over Chesterfield. In fact he was unlucky not to score when defender Chris Parkin punched away his goalbound header and was sent off for his trouble.

The goals that counted came from the heads of Neill and Rogan, although another missed penalty, this time by Crawford, would have made the win more comfortable against an inventive Chesterfield side that always looked threatening. Just as in the previous season, rumours about the manager did not help matters. This time it was alleged that Nicholl was leaving to take up the vacant manager's role at Hibernian.

Nicholl pledged his future to the club and then sold Malkin to Blackpool for £260,000 and claimed he needed another striker. That need was emphasised in the next game, at home to Bury. Although the Lions won 1-0 it was Rogan, with a twenty-yard chip, who scored again. Once more the strikers had failed to put the finishing touches to a good all-round performance.

Anton Rogan chips the ball over the Bury goalkeeper for a sensational goal.

'I thought the first half was the best display I've seen since I came here,' said Nicholl, before adding, 'but we must learn to finish teams off.'

The Lions were back in second place in the table and stayed there with an excellent 3-2 win away at Gillingham. Two goals from Crawford and another from Hartley secured the win the team's thrilling performance deserved. Millwall's penalty takers should learn from how Steve Butler netted from the spot. Both the Gills goals came that way. Goalkeeper Tim Carter dislocated his shoulder in the match and played on in some discomfort but the result was never in doubt.

The top-of-the-table clash with Brentford ended 0-0 but the Lions should have done better against a side with only ten men after Ashby was sent off just before half-time. Again they struggled in a scrappy game and were lucky not to lose when Brentford's Taylor headed against the crossbar.

The luck stayed with them on the following Wednesday night in the 2-1 win over Blackpool. The game kicked off an hour late when the Blackpool team coach got stuck in a traffic jam on the M25, but they hit the ground running when Malkin put them in front after thirteen minutes. If only he had played like that in his time at The Den!

Once again it was Anton Rogan who saved the day. This time he scored both Millwall's goals from the penalty spot in the second half. A collective sigh of relief was heard all around the ground. 'We seem to have problems getting into our stride at home,' was Nicholl's after-match assessment but that was not the case when Walsall came to south Bermondsey on the Saturday.

Crawford's third-minute goal was enough for the 1-0 victory that took the Lions to the top of the table but again they failed to turn their dominance into goals. On the brighter side the injury crisis looked to be ending as Gerard Lavin made a substitute appearance in the match.

Crawford scored again in the 1-1 away draw with Bristol City but a broken bone in his foot put paid to Fitzgerald's proposed move to The Den and he returned to Wimbledon. With Van Blerk and Webber on the bench though, things were starting to look better.

FA Cup matches against non-League sides can always be an embarrassment, especially when they are away from home and under the spotlight of television cameras. The Friday night cup match against Woking was no exception. When Savage equalised Woking's second-minute opener and then Crawford put them in front the Lions looked on their way to the next round. But the killer third goal never came and after Woking equalised from the penalty spot only two excellent saves from Carter kept their hopes alive.

With so many players still on the injury list, it came as something of a surprise when club physio Keith Johnson left to join Derby, especially as he had only taken up the position from Peter Melville the previous season. Gerry Docherty, who also came from Raith, soon replaced him.

Depressing news was that the club made a loss of £3.471 million for the year ending May 1996. This was soon to have a devastating effect on the club.

Two goals from Crawford gave the Lions a 2-1 win over Shrewsbury the following Wednesday evening but how they got away with it is anyone's guess; in fact there were a smattering of boos to be heard at half-time. The 0-0 away draw with Rotherham increased the anxiety as only a string of fine saves from Carter kept the Lions in the match, but being beaten 0-1 at home by Woking in the FA Cup replay was more than most fans could stand.

They were left in stunned disbelief and with the televised match against second-placed Brentford just three days later there was genuine concern about the Lions' lacklustre play and their lack of goals. With Brendon Markey back in Ireland on loan to Dundalk and the rumoured arrival of Tony Hateley proving unfruitful a 0-0 draw was a welcome result.

At least the Lions put in a better performance; indeed, they controlled the match from start to finish, but again they could not find the final ball their approach work deserved. Sinclair finally played his first ninety minutes for the club.

The alarm bells rang again on the Tuesday night when the Lions went to Wycombe. You knew what sort of a night it was going to be when the floodlights failed and then the sprinklers came on, soaking the Millwall fans behind the goal. The late goal that Mickey Bell blasted past the outstanding Carter for Wycombe's 0-1 win was probably expected.

Now having gone four games without scoring, various names were touted as coming to The Den to solve the goalscoring problem. The 4-0 win over Hereford in the Auto Windscreens Shield was most welcome. This competition, the renamed Football League Trophy, had been revamped this season and was to be played as a knockout competition in two regions, north and south, with the winners of each region playing in the final at Wembley. Two goals each from Crawford and Dair flattered the Lions but at least they were scoring again. Steve Aris made his debut for the club when he replaced Lavin, although he never featured in the first team again. McRobert appeared for the first time this season.

Nicholl was not fooled by this goal burst and brought Mark Bright in on loan from Sheffield Wednesday. He scored on his debut in the 1-1 draw at Bournemouth but it was his only goal for the club.

Four consecutive home matches followed and hopes were high, but the first, against Luton, was lost 0-1, Ceri Hughes scoring in the last minute. They fared no better on Boxing Day when Peterborough left The Den 0-2 winners although the Lions were not helped when Carter injured his finger in the warm-up and was replaced by Andrew Iga to make his Millwall debut.

The fans howled their disapproval and with Saturday's game at Bristol Rovers and the New Year's Day match at Crewe cancelled due to the weather, it got even louder when Colchester won the Auto Windscreens Shield game 2-3 at The Den. The surprise at the match was not the

Mark Bright celebrates his debut goal at Bournemouth with Steve Crawford.

goals from Savage and Crawford, nor the fact that Iga kept his place in goal, but the debut of former England star Ray Wilkins.

The match itself was awful and Iga was at the centre of the fans' anger although it has to be said that he got very little help from his defence. The return of Fitzgerald to the first team, who had come back from Wimbledon for another two months, was eagerly looked forward to. Twice in the lead, the Lions tried hard to throw it all away. They finally succeeded three minutes into extra time when Paul Buckle scored his twenty-yard 'golden goal'. After the game fans demonstrated outside the club offices, their frustration and anger clear for all to see. 'This is the lowest point of my career,' said Nicholl, 'but if the fans want my resignation they're not going to get it.'

Nicholl had to do something, not just to appease the fans but also to stop the rot that had set in, so on the first Saturday home game for two months, against Preston North End, he gave debuts to youngsters Marc Bircham and Steven Roche. With Bright's unsuccessful loan coming to an end he brought Cadette back in from the wilderness for his first start in eighteen months.

The gamble paid off as Cadette opened the scoring and even though the Lions went behind they came back with goals from Crawford and Savage, on his 100th appearance for the club, to win 3-2, just!

The fans' joy was short-lived though. The team was beaten 1-5 away at Stockport in their next game. Webber scored and Bircham was sent off for a handball offence he did not commit, which resulted in the penalty from which Stockport took the lead.

They then lost 0-3 away at Blackpool and 0-2 at home to Bristol City, in a match that saw the debut of yet another youngster from the club's youth set-up, Richard Sadlier. It also brought another injury, to Keith Stevens, which put him out until December. They also lost 1-2 away to Walsall, where Bowry scored his only goal of the season.

Thoughts of the previous season's dive from promotion challengers to relegation raised their heads, and the fans conveyed their worries to the players. This did not help a team playing well below its ability. Added to that was the fact that the club were struggling financially and the administrators had been called in on 21 January.

With the money problems that clubs have now, going into administration is almost commonplace but in 1997 it was rare. Indeed, at one stage, it looked as though the club might cease to exist. The club's shares were frozen at just 4p and trading of them was suspended on the Stock Market but Mead dismissed rumours that the club's future was in jeopardy. 'We are currently looking to refinance the club,' he said, adding, 'we asked the Stock Exchange to suspend the shares, as we are required to do by law, in order to carry this out.' It may have been a legal requirement but that did not stop everyone worrying about the future of the club and where it left them.

The day-to-day running of the club was now in the hands of the administrator, David Bulcher, and he started to look at ways to cut costs, fix up deals with major creditors and find someone willing to bail the club out of its predicament. There were plenty of rumours about who would go and of course who would help salvage the club, if indeed anyone would, but Mead went on record to say that at least Nicholl would not be leaving, saying, 'Jimmy's job is perfectly safe, and I don't want that to sound like the dreaded vote of confidence.'

So what went wrong? The move to the new stadium and the lack of entertainment events that were to provide needed finances obviously played a major part in the problems, as did the failed investment in Tavern Leisure.

Relegation to Division Two was a disaster and not just for the players and fans. For the club the lost revenue from not playing in a higher division took its toll.

Sinclair was sold to Dundee for £90,000; Ray Wilkins' loan period ended and more changes were soon to follow. No doubt all of this had an effect on the players as the results immediately after the administration order was made show. But the game must go on and although everyone was waiting for the axe to fall a creditable 2-0 win over Rotherham came next, even though they did it under new leadership.

Nicholl, his assistant Martin Harvey, reserve team manager Ian MacDonald, chief executive Graham Hortop and groundsman John Plummer, along with eighteen other staff members, were sacked, twelve players were transfer listed and everyone who stayed was asked to take a pay cut.

In came John Docherty to manage the side and he brought David Kemp in as his assistant. Keith Stevens was asked to take over management of the reserves. This all happened exactly one year after Nicholl had been appointed to replace McCarthy.

The win over Rotherham, courtesy of a Rotherham own goal and another from Crawford, lifted the hearts. Docherty had changed the playing style, going back to his long-ball roots, and he also brought back Greg Berry to the first team. Docherty urged the fans not to get too excited over one result and then brought back Alan McLeary to the club from Bristol City. He made his comeback in the 1-1 draw away at Shrewsbury in a game not without controversy.

Shrewsbury were leading with a goal scored by Lions old boy Steve Anthrobus when Doyle, on as a substitute, scored in the ninetieth minute. It was not just his first goal for Millwall but his first goal ever in the Football League. Then Shrewsbury 'scored' through Darren Currie, but referee Brian Coddington blew the whistle for full time before the ball was kicked and the goal did not count.

Was Docherty's magic working again? Was lady luck back with the Lions? Either way the old never-say-die spirit was back and a creditable draw gained. A Savage goal gave the Lions a 1-0 home win over Notts County but a new blow was soon to affect the club.

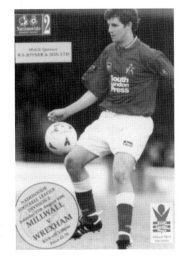

The Football League put a transfer embargo on the club to remain in force until they had settled outstanding payments to former players. This meant that the move to make Fitzgerald a permanent member of the squad was put on ice and the administrators had to find a way of overcoming yet another obstacle to the club's survival.

When Tony Dolby scored the winner in the 2-1 win over Wycombe Wanderers it was his first goal in just over four years. It came at the right time for the Lions who, having been in the lead through Hartley's fourteenth-minute strike were hanging on for a point.

That win, in what was the 100th competitive game in the new stadium, also moved the Lions back to third in the table and a 2-0 away win over Luton, with goals from the same two players, consolidated the position. Luton had played

A programme from the 1996/97 season.

with ten men after twenty-five minutes and were themselves unlucky not to score on many occasions; they hit the woodwork three times. Could promotion be back on the cards?

Things were looking up off the field as well. Lee Manning of Bulcher Phillips had put the finishing touches to the first draft of a business plan that it was hoped would save the club from extinction. He was now prepared to show it to prospective investors.

The announcement of a public meeting to be held at The Den on 11 March was followed by the confirmation that thirty-six-year-old Greek millionaire Theo Paphitis was interested in rescuing the club. The head of various business interests said, 'I have a reputation of helping to turn ventures around and I was asked if I would be interested in Millwall. The club has great potential but we are a long way from things being finalised.'

The excitement on the playing front took a knock with a 0-1 home defeat by Bournemouth. A 0-0 away draw with Crewe, where Crawford hit the bar, did not help either.

Meanwhile Steven Forbes moved to Colchester on a free transfer and Darren Keown went to Ashford Town on loan. Fitzgerald returned to Wimbledon as the personnel changes continued.

After losing 0-1 at home to Watford, where Dean Canoville made his first-team debut, the 3-3 draw away at Wrexham on Good Friday brought some excitement for the fans. The excitement started the day before when it was revealed that Docherty had resigned from the club and then changed his mind, but the game itself had many twists and turns.

Two goals down after half an hour, the Lions pulled one back through Crawford when a dubious penalty gave the Welsh side their two-goal advantage back at half-time. A goal from Newman gave Millwall a fighting chance. Then Neill was sent off but when the ball was handled in the Wrexham penalty area Anton Rogan, on as a substitute for Dolby, crashed home his spot kick for the equaliser.

The transfer deadline had come and gone. The Football League embargo had stopped Millwall buying any players and no one had come in to buy any from the club. Any thoughts that a needed cash injection from last-minute transfers come were quickly dispelled.

A 1-1 draw at home to struggling York City – a ninetieth minute Webber goal was Millwall's salvation – saw the start of a run that had the fans groaning again. Losing consecutive away matches to Burnley and Bristol Rovers, both 0-1, a 0-0 home draw with Chesterfield and another 0-1 away defeat, this time to Chesterfield saw the Lions slide down to twelfth in the table. But Docherty had done his job. 'My first job was to avoid relegation – that's been done,' he said. 'Now my next job is to assess the playing personnel.'

However the fans had grown restless, especially with Docherty's long-ball tactics. Having got used to watching some flowing football under the helm of Rioch, McCarthy and Nicholl they had forgotten that Docherty's style had given them their first ever place within the game's elite. The final home game of the season was a disastrous 0-2 loss to Gillingham. Millwall put on a poor show for their fans in what was Docherty's last game as manager.

At least they performed a lot better when they lost their final match of the season 0-2 to league champions Bury with David Kemp in charge of the team. Docherty had resigned the day before having had meetings with new chairman-elect Theo Paphitis. 'I just didn't think we would have been able to work together,' was Docherty's reason. 'I am not bitter at what's happened,' he added, 'and I enjoyed my time back at the club tremendously.'

Paphitis was to become the club's new chairman on the back of a £10 million rights issue and, along with his new board members, now had to start looking for a new manager. 'I'm looking forward to getting involved on a day-to-day basis with the club,' he said and declared, 'I've been a Millwall supporter for a long time, this hasn't come completely out of the blue.'

However the rescue package met immediate problems when Lewisham Council claimed they were owed £700,000 and threatened legal action to recover it. Fortunately the problem was solved. Paphitis certainly came into the hot seat with a warning for the players saying, 'I want players in a Millwall shirt to be prepared to die for the club. Fans pay their money week in week out and I don't want them to waste their time watching people who don't give their all. If players don't like that then I don't want them at the club. I'm determined to save the club and I'm working very hard to do that.'

Everyone waited to see what would happen next.

1996/97   **Football League Division Two**

Date		Opposition	Score	Scorers
Aug	17	WREXHAM	1-1	Crawford (pen)
	24	Watford	2-0	Harle, Crawford
	27	York City	2-3	Savage, Malkin
	31	BURNLEY	2-1	Newman, Neill
Sept	7	BRISTOL ROVERS	2-0	Rogan, Huckerby
	10	Peterborough United	3-3	Neill, Malkin, Huckerby
	14	Notts County	2-1	Neill, Opp OG
	21	CREWE ALEXANDRA	2-0	Huckerby, Dair
	28	Preston North End	1-2	Newman,
Oct	2	STOCKPORT COUNTY	3-4	Rogan (2), Hartley
	5	Plymouth Argyle	0-0	
	12	CHESTERFIELD	2-1	Rogan, Neill
	16	BURY	1-0	Rogan
	19	Gillingham	3-2	Crawford (2), Hartley
	26	Brentford	0-0	
	30	BLACKPOOL	2-1	Rogan (2) (2 pens)
Nov	2	WALSALL	1-0	Crawford
	9	Bristol City	1-1	Crawford
	20	SHREWSBURY TOWN	2-1	Crawford (2)
	23	Rotherham United	0-0	
	29	BRENTFORD	0-0	
Dec	3	Wycombe Wanderers	0-1	
	14	Bournemouth	1-1	Bright
	18	LUTON TOWN	0-1	
	26	PETERBOROUGH UNITED	0-2	
Jan	11	PRESTON NORTH END	3-2	Savage, Crawford, Cadette
	18	Stockport County	1-5	Webber
	25	Blackpool	0-3	
Feb	1	BRISTOL CITY	0-2	
	8	Walsall	1-2	Bowry
	15	ROTHERHAM UNITED	2-0	Crawford, Opp OG
	22	Shrewsbury Town	1-1	Doyle
	25	NOTTS COUNTY	1-0	Savage
Mar	1	WYCOMBE WANDERERS	2-1	Hartley, Dolby
	8	Luton Town	2-0	Hartley, Dolby
	15	BOURNEMOUTH	0-1	
	18	Crewe Alexandra	0-0	
	22	WATFORD	0-1	
	28	Wrexham	3-3	Newman, Crawford, Rogan (pen)
Apr	2	YORK CITY	1-1	Webber
	5	BURNLEY	0-1	
	8	Bristol Rovers	0-1	
	12	PLYMOUTH ARGYLE	0-0	
	19	Chesterfield	0-1	
	26	GILLINGHAM	0-2	
May	3	Bury	0-2	

Millwall FC Since 1987

League Cup

Round	Date		Opposition	Score	Scorers
1/1	Aug	21	PETERBOROUGH UNITED	1-0	Malkin
1/2	Sept	3	Peterborough United	0-2	

Associate Members Cup

Round	Date		Opposition	Score	Scorers
1	Dec	7	Hereford United	4-0	Crawford (2), Dair (2)
2	Jan	7	COLCHESTER UNITED	2-3	Savage, Crawford

FA Cup

Round	Date		Opposition	Score	Scorers
1	Nov	15	Woking	2-2	Savage, Crawford
1R		26	WOKING	0-1	

1996/97 — Football League Division Two

	P	W	D	L	F	A	Pts
Bury	46	24	12	10	62	38	84
Stockport County	46	23	13	10	59	41	82
Luton Town	46	21	15	10	71	45	78
Brentford	46	20	14	12	56	43	74
Bristol City	46	21	10	15	69	51	73
Crewe Alexandra	46	22	7	17	56	47	73
Blackpool	46	18	15	13	60	47	69
Wrexham	46	17	18	11	54	50	69
Burnley	46	19	11	16	71	55	68
Chesterfield	46	18	14	14	42	39	68
Gillingham	46	19	10	17	60	59	67
Walsall	46	19	10	17	54	53	67
Watford	46	16	19	11	45	38	67
MILLWALL	46	16	13	17	50	55	61
Preston North End	46	18	7	21	49	55	61
Bournemouth	46	15	15	16	43	45	60
Bristol Rovers	46	15	11	20	47	50	56
Wycombe Wanderers	46	15	10	21	51	56	55
Plymouth Argyle	46	12	18	16	47	58	54
York City	46	13	13	20	47	68	52
Peterborough United	46	11	14	21	55	73	47
Shrewsbury Town	46	11	13	22	49	74	46
Rotherham United	46	7	14	25	39	70	35
Notts County	46	7	14	25	33	59	35

Under New Management
1997/98

Paphitis did not officially take office until later in the summer but he needed to get to work first of all in finding new manager and then to sort out the club's finances. Having found an answer to the problem with Lewisham Council he also found the vast majority of the club's creditors backed his proposals.

He took a bold step by appointing Billy Bonds as manager and just how the fans would react to the ex-Hammer would define how the club's immediate future went. Bonds brought in Pat Holland as his assistant and David Kemp left the club, disappointed that he had not been offered the manager's job. But the league embargo on transfers was still in position so Paphitis got to work on getting that lifted.

It was not easy and, after a lot of lobbying, he finally managed to have it removed in time for Bonds to bring in players for the new season and the race was on to rebuild the team.

Paphitis also found a new shirt sponsor to go with the new shirt design, a blue shirt with white sides and a white away shirt, and it came as a bit of a surprise when the sponsor was revealed to be cable channel Live TV's *The Weather In Norwegian* along with appearances of Live TV's News Bunny and weather girl Anne Marie Foss. 'I wanted to bring the fun back into football,' was Paphitis' answer as to why, although the £200,000 sponsorship money that came with it played a part as well.

Bonds was philosophical about his new position. 'Whatever club I have gone to I have given them 100 per cent and Millwall will be no different,' he declared. 'I know the crowd will be hard but all I can say is that I will work at it. If that's not enough in the end so be it.'

It was also rumoured that Brighton & Hove Albion would share the ground and no doubt the extra cash that would have been generated would have been welcome. In the end the Seagulls went to Gillingham instead.

Having announced that there would be no pre-season tour and that all pre-season matches would be local, the time had come to sort out the playing staff. Out went young defender Lee Canoville to Arsenal for £50,000. Tony Dolby, Greg Berry, Jason Van Blerk (who went to Manchester City), Richard Cadette and Anton Rogan (who went to Blackpool) were all at the end of their contracts and were allowed to leave. Michael Harle went on a free to Barnet while Steve Crawford moved to Hibernian for £360,000. Youngsters Darren Keown and Lewis Nightingale also left the club.

Uwe Fuchs, whose contract the club still held, finally had it revoked by mutual consent. Also leaving the club, again, were backroom staff Bob Pearson and Kevin O'Callaghan. Mickey Flanagan replaced them in the youth set-up. Scott Fitzgerald finally made his move from Wimbledon a permanent one for a tribunal-fixed fee of £50,000 plus money for appearances, and joining him at the club were defenders Paul Sturgess from Charlton and Brian Law from Wolves, who both came on free transfers. Kenny Brown also arrived, from Birmingham, for £60,000.

Midfielder Paul Allen came from Bristol City, also on a free transfer, striker Kim Grant arrived just before the start of the season on loan from Luton and youngsters Tim Cahill and Paul Ifill also joined the club.

Bonds changed the playing system and opted for a five-man defence, three in midfield and two up front, although this changed to a conventional 4-4-2 fairly quickly into the season. After a fluctuating set of pre-season friendlies, including a 0-4 home defeat by Crystal Palace, the season started with a home game against Brentford on 9 August.

Bonds had a message for the fans about the coming season. 'At the moment we're not good enough, but hopefully that will change,' he warned. The fans started wondering what they had let themselves in for.

There was also an interesting rule change to contend with. Any player who had been cautioned would have a booking removed if he went five consecutive matches without being shown a yellow card but when five bookings were reached an automatic three-match ban was incurred, two from the beginning of December.

The 3-0 win over Brentford was a stroll in the sunshine. The new-look side in which Allen, Brown, Grant, Law and Sturgess all made their debuts, made it look easy. After the Lions took the lead when Allen's shot hit Jamie Bates and went in it was no contest. A goal from Sadlier and another from Grant, both of them scoring their first for the club, had the crowd wondering what Bonds was worried about. The three defeats in a row that followed showed them what he meant.

The first came in the away leg of the first round of the Coca-Cola Cup at Northampton. Although Grant put the Lions ahead they were beaten 1-2. Then came the 1-2 away defeat against Preston where once again they gave away the lead, which was given to them in the sixth minute from Sadlier's twenty-five-yard strike. Although the first of Grant's two goals gave them the lead at home to York they again threw it away, losing 2-3. Lions old boy Paul Stephenson scored the winner.

Paul Hartley moved back to Scotland, joining Raith Rovers for £110,000. Bonds made Grant's move to The Den permanent by paying Luton £185,000 for him but there were few other team changes that could be made without using some of the youngsters. Bonds knew there had to be a better result in the return leg of the Coca-Cola Cup against Northampton or the fans would turn on him. It turned out to be a bizarre match.

Two goals from Hockton gave the Lions a 2-1 win, leaving the aggregate score level and extra time failed to separate them. So it was up to the penalty shoot-out to decide a winner. Grant put Millwall in front before Sturgess and Northampton's Frain and Seal thought they were taking part in a back pass competition. Newman, Allen and Northampton's Gibb decided to quieten the crowd by knocking them out with the advertising hoardings on top of the South Stand, which they all hit, and Carter then saved Hunter's effort. Fortunately Brown was not affected by these antics and blasted home the winner.

Perhaps the Lions had started to turn the corner and the 2-0 win at Luton with goals from Law, his first for the club, and Hockton helped this belief.

With the funeral of Princess Diana taking place the following Saturday all matches were cancelled, so when the Lions beat Southend 3-1 at home a week later with goals from Newman, Sadlier and Hockton things were looking good for Bonzo's boys. Jason Dair went back to Raith Rovers on a free transfer and that meant all four of the Scots who came with Nicholl had now returned north of the border.

Paphitis vowed that nothing like that would ever happen again. 'There's going to be no more Mr Nice Guy from me, no more expensive mistakes and no more non-triers at Millwall,' he said.

To bolster his squad Bonds brought in strikers Paul Shaw from Arsenal for £500,000 and Paul Wilkinson from Barnsley for £150,000. Shaw made his debut in the away leg of the second round Coca-Cola Cup match at Wimbledon. When Savage put the Lions in front it looked like their fine run would continue but some woeful defending and some exhilarating attacking play allowed Wimbledon to run out easy 1-5 winners.

Two away League games followed, with mixed fortunes. Wilkinson made his debut at Grimsby and scored the only goal in a 1-0 win, but it all went wrong at Northampton where

Danny Hockton glides the ball past the Northampton Town goalkeeper.

the Lions lost 0-2. New signing Nigel Spink could do nothing about the goals. Bought from West Bromwich Albion for £50,000, he went straight into the side. The game produced a catalogue of strange decisions.

Newman was booked after just three seconds, a Football League record that still stands, but Northampton were chasing shadows. When Shaw hit a post in the second half it seemed only a matter of time before the Lions took the lead. Then a shot from Sampson that was going nowhere took a wicked deflection off Kenny Brown to leave Spink stranded. When Sturgess won the ball and passed to Newman, who was making a run into the centre circle, it looked like another Lions attack was about to start. However referee Steve Baines then started the strangest five minutes seen on a football pitch for some time. Seeing his linesman, Paul Barston, waving his flag he stopped the game to allow the Northampton physio on to treat Sean Parrish. He then sent off Sturgess and took the ball into the centre circle to restart the game with a drop ball. Bizarrely he then changed his mind and awarded a penalty, from which, after another delay while the Millwall players made complaints, Northampton scored. Even then Shaw hit the bar and the players and fans felt hard done by with the 0-2 defeat.

Spink was cup-tied for the return Coca-Cola Cup match with Wimbledon and David Nurse took his place in goal. It was to be his only first-team appearance, although his memory of it will be clouded by the 1-4 scoreline. Shaw scored his first for the Lions from the penalty spot in the final minute.

Ricky Newman's spectacular volley is just off-target against Chesterfield.

Winger Michael Black arrived on loan from Arsenal and found himself in the starting line-up against Blackpool. The 2-1 home win, with goals from Wilkinson and Grant, saw the Lions back in business with a thoroughly deserved win. Grant's goal came from a dreadful blunder from goalkeeper Banks when he missed a clearance from a back pass.

The Lions went behind in the home match against Oldham and the previous season would have probably lost the game, but Bonds had instilled a fighting spirit into the side and they came back to win 2-1 with goals from Law and Black in a devastating six-minute spell. They were certainly a different side from a year earlier, both in personnel, skill and attitude. It was a great way for McLeary to celebrate his 400th game for the club and the win had moved them to third in the table.

Paul 'Baldy' Shaw was quickly becoming a favourite of the fans and he enhanced his position with a goal from the edge of the box to secure a 1-0 win at Watford.

With a glut of midfield players, Bonds let McRobert go on loan to Dover although there was more bad news about Neill who, having been out with a bone injury in his foot, did the same to his other foot on his comeback.

A hard-fought 0-0 draw at Bournemouth was followed by a 1-1 draw at home with Wigan although it could have been worse. The Lions really did not play well. Having gone behind on eighty-six minutes it was Bowry's last-minute headed equaliser that saved the day.

Nothing could save them when another poor display saw them lose 0-2 to Bristol City at The Den the following Wednesday. A trip to Gillingham next was the last thing they needed especially after a row over ticket allocations; Lions fans were given just 1,405.

Those fans lucky enough to get a ticket need not have worried. The Lions were brilliant, especially McLeary and Law, and the 3-1 win, with goals from Black, Shaw and Wilkinson, sent them home happy. Although Gillingham had Statham sent off in the second half, how he had remained on the pitch that long was a mystery. A win had never been in doubt.

Bonds, though, was pleading for caution. 'We're not that good that all we have to do is turn up and win,' he claimed. He was right to do so as a poor performance in their next game, at home to Fulham, in the 100th League game played at the new ground, resulted in a 1-1 draw. A goal six minutes from time by Shaw, whose poor back pass had gifted Fulham the lead, levelled the match.

By this time Brendon Markey had gone back to Bohemians on loan, his Lions career halted. James Connor's career had also come to an end as he had to give up the game due to injury.

Another 1-1 home draw with Carlisle, Law the scorer after just two minutes, was followed by a 0-1 defeat at Bristol City. The Lions were out of the FA Cup in the first round again.

Inconsistency continued to blight the season when goals from Bowry and Savage gave them a convincing 2-1 win at Burnley, followed by a 1-1 home draw with Chesterfield, Shaw scoring. A 1-2 away defeat at Bristol Rovers followed, where Shaw scored again, Law was sent off and Neill made a welcome return to the first team by coming on as a substitute. Then there was a 0-1 loss at home to Walsall.

There was also a surprise when Pat Holland announced he was leaving the club to take up a youth team post with Tottenham, and Bonds decided to carry on without replacing him.

Up until then it was the Lions' home form that had been the problem. They were winning well away from home and a 2-0 win at Cardiff in the Auto Windscreen Shield, with goals from Shaw and Grant, kept this trend going. But fortune has a habit of changing quickly and it certainly did with a 0-3 defeat at Plymouth.

Millwall's new signing Carl Veart, a £100,000 buy from Crystal Palace, made his debut in this match. It was a strange deal that saw Millwall paying £50,000 up front and the same amount again a year later. Veart never made it that far.

The Lions struggled badly in the game and the final score could, and should, have been much worse but just to show how inconsistent they were they came home to beat Wycombe 1-0 with a goal from Shaw the following week.

A run of poor results now put a dent in the Lions' promotion bid. A 1-4 defeat at Bristol City on Boxing Day, where Veart scored his first and only goal for the club, and perhaps more importantly Neill broke his foot again, was followed by a 0-2 home defeat by Luton two days later. Both goals came in the last minute.

Keith Stevens returned to first-team action after a year out of the side but Millwall had gone from third to tenth by the end of the year. Worse was to come. Bristol City were again the victors, winning 0-1 at home in the Auto Windscreen Shield, where Bircham, making his first start of the season, was sent off. Then Brentford won 1-2 at Griffin Park.

Michael Black had gone back to Arsenal but this match saw the debut of Andy Cook, a £50,000 purchase from Portsmouth. Even though Grant gave the Lions the lead another dismal performance followed.

More signings followed. Leon Cort came from Dulwich Hamlet and Robbie Ryan came on trial from Huddersfield and was eventually signed for £10,000. When the Lions lost their next game, at home to Wrexham, 0-1, the fans, who had shown a lot of patience, started to get restless. The problems Bonds had with players did not help the situation.

Carter had returned in goal, replacing Spink who had gone down with glandular fever, and Fitzgerald, Grant, Wilkinson, (Grant's replacement) and Cook all had to leave the field at some point. The added injuries to an already decimated squad made things look bleak.

The trip to York was certainly worth the effort and not just for the 3-2 win, courtesy of two goals from Shaw and another from Grant. The change in the team brought about by two new additions both making their debuts was marked. Stuart Nethercott, brought in on loan from Spurs, strengthened the defence but Andy Gray, bought for a nominal fee from Bury, added a new dimension to the midfield with his skill on the ball and incredibly long throw-ins. Lee McRobert made his first appearance of the season.

Robbie Ryan made his debut in the 0-0 draw at Southend and the fans were hoping that this was now the turning point in the season. How wrong they were.

Losing 0-1 at home to Grimsby would not have been too much of a disaster if the game had not have been followed by defeat at Blackpool, 0-3, and a succession of draws. The first of these was a 0-0 home draw with Northampton, a game in which Mark Crossley made his debut in goal having arrived on loan from Nottingham Forest. The club also gave its support to the 'Kick Out Racism' campaign and the Northampton match was their focus match for it.

After the Northampton game there was a 1-1 home draw with Watford, with Shaw scoring, and an away one at Oldham by the same score. Millwall's goal in the latter came via a late own goal.

Losing 0-1 at Carlisle meant that the Lions were now seventeenth in the table and relegation worries were starting to haunt the fans again. They had given Bonds more than a fair crack of the whip and now they were beginning to show their restlessness with him in charge.

Bonds decided he now needed an assistant, perhaps to take some of the pressure off him, and appointed Steve Gritt to the position. Nethercott signed on a permanent basis until the end of the season for a nominal fee.

Law's goal for the 1-0 home win over Gillingham gave Bonds some respite, as did the 2-1 away win against Fulham. What a game that was. A goal down at half-time and without the defensive assurance of Nethercott who had left the field after just seven minutes with a dislocated shoulder, Millwall equalised through Shaw. It seemed that disaster had struck when Witter, Nethercott's replacement, was harshly sent off.

Bonds reshuffled his pack and when Gray scored his one and only goal for the Lions to put them in front perhaps justice had been done. It still needed a wonder save from Crossley right at the end to keep it that way in time added on, shown by the fourth official for the very first time in English football.

How different it was the following Friday at Wrexham. A patched-up side got little reward for all of their possession and lost 0-1 to an early goal. Kim Grant's goal, which was enough for a 1-0 home win over Burnley, moved the Lions back up to within touching distance of the play-offs. Even though they stayed there after they lost 0-1 at The Den to Preston four days later, they were about to slide down the table again.

Transfer deadline day came and went with few changes in the Millwall area of south-east London. Stuart Nethercott, who had previously signed only to the end of the season, put pen to paper on a three-year deal and two strikers arrived. Graeme Tomlinson came on loan from Manchester United until the end of the season, Neil Harris arrived from Cambridge City for £30,000 and Russell Watkinson signed from Southampton until the end of the season. Lee Holsgrove moved to Wycombe Wanderers and David Nurse went on loan to Brentford. Tomlinson made his debut away at Chesterfield and scored but it was not enough to prevent the Lions losing 1-3.

Gerard Lavin played for the first time in over a year when he came on as substitute with thirty minutes of the game left and he started the next match, a 1-1 home draw with Bristol Rovers when Harris made his debut. Shaw's late equaliser secured a share of the spoils but it was a dreadful game and one that will quickly be consigned to the 'forgotten' bin. Brian Law was sent off on the stroke of full time. They must surely be his personal bogey team!

The rest of the season just came to a quiet end although points were needed to make sure that the relegation trap door did not open right at the end of the season. A 0-2 defeat at Walsall was followed by a 1-1 home draw with Plymouth on Easter Monday. Hockton scored after just four minutes in what was to be Crossley's last game for the club.

Successive 0-0 away draws against Wycombe Wanderers and Wigan followed and the final game of the season, at home to Bournemouth, was lost 1-2, with Grant scoring from the penalty spot. It was a shame really when the match had begun with Witter receiving recognition of playing 100 games for the club and then scoring an own goal to give Bournemouth the lead. Mo Doyle captained the side in what was the last appearance for the club for both players.

Two bright spots in an otherwise dull afternoon were the debuts of Tim Cahill and Steven Reid, which were spoiled by a few idiots who ran onto the pitch forcing the match to end a couple of minutes early. They perhaps stopped the Lions from scoring an equaliser. Millwall had kept their Division Two status, just. It had been close at times.

'Thankfully we're safe now and I'm already looking forward to next year,' said Bonds and he added, 'We've got to make sure that next season is a better one for the club, and particularly for our fans.' It proved to be an interesting close season for everyone.

1997/98   Football League Division Two

Date		Opposition	Score	Scorers
Aug	9	BRENTFORD	3-0	Sadlier, Grant, Opp OG
	16	Preston North End	1-2	Sadlier
	23	YORK CITY	2-3	Grant (2)
Sept	2	Luton Town	2-0	Law, Hockton
	13	SOUTHEND UNITED	3-1	Newman, Hockton, Sadlier
	20	Grimsby Town	1-0	Wilkinson
	27	Northampton Town	0-2	
Oct	4	BLACKPOOL	2-1	Wilkinson, Grant
	11	OLDHAM ATHLETIC	2-1	Law, Black
	18	Watford	1-0	Shaw
	21	Bournemouth	0-0	
	25	WIGAN ATHLETIC	1-1	Bowry
	29	BRISTOL CITY	0-2	
Nov	1	Gillingham	3-1	Black, Shaw, Wilkinson
	4	FULHAM	1-1	Shaw
	8	CARLISLE UNITED	1-1	Law
	18	Burnley	2-1	Bowry, Savage
	22	CHESTERFIELD	1-1	Shaw
	29	Bristol Rovers	1-2	Shaw
Dec	3	WALSALL	0-1	
	13	Plymouth Argyle	0-3	
	20	WYCOMBE WANDERERS	1-0	Shaw
	26	Bristol City	1-4	Veart
	28	LUTON TOWN	0-2	
Jan	10	Brentford	1-2	Grant
	17	WREXHAM	0-1	
	24	York City	3-2	Shaw (2), Grant
	31	Southend United	0-0	
Feb	7	GRIMSBY TOWN	0-1	
	14	Blackpool	0-3	
	21	NORTHAMPTON TOWN	0-0	
	25	WATFORD	1-1	Shaw
	28	Oldham Athletic	1-1	Opp OG
Mar	3	Carlisle United	0-1	
	7	GILLINGHAM	1-0	Law
	14	Fulham	2-1	Shaw, Gray
	17	Wrexham	0-1	
	21	BURNLEY	1-0	Grant
	25	PRESTON NORTH END	0-1	
	28	Chesterfield	1-3	Tomlinson
Apr	4	BRISTOL ROVERS	1-1	Shaw
	11	Walsall	0-2	
	13	PLYMOUTH ARGYLE	1-1	Hockton
	18	Wycombe Wanderers	0-0	
	24	Wigan Athletic	0-0	
May	2	BOURNEMOUTH	1-2	Grant (pen)

League Cup

Round	Date		Opposition	Score	Scorers
1/1	Aug	12	Northampton Town	1-2	Grant
1/2		27	NORTHAMPTON TOWN	2-1*	Hockton (2)
2/1	Sept	16	Wimbledon	1-5	Savage
2/2	Oct	1	WIMBLEDON	1-4	Shaw (pen)

*a.e.t Millwall won on penalties

Associate Members Cup

Round	Date		Opposition	Score	Scorers
1	Dec	9	Cardiff City	2-0	Grant, Shaw
2	Jan	6	Bristol City	0-1	

FA Cup

Round	Date		Opposition	Score	Scorers
1	Nov	15	Bristol City	0-1	

1997/98   Football League Division Two

	P	W	D	L	F	A	Pts
Watford	46	24	16	6	67	41	88
Bristol City	46	25	10	11	69	39	85
Grimsby Town	46	19	15	12	55	37	72
Northampton Town	46	18	17	11	52	37	71
Bristol Rovers	46	20	10	16	70	64	70
Fulham	46	20	10	16	60	43	70
Wrexham	46	18	16	12	55	51	70
Gillingham	46	19	13	14	52	47	70
Bournemouth	46	18	12	16	57	52	66
Chesterfield	46	16	17	13	46	44	65
Wigan Athletic	46	17	11	18	64	66	62
Blackpool	46	17	11	18	59	67	62
Oldham Athletic	46	15	16	15	62	54	61
Wycombe Wanderers	46	14	18	14	51	53	60
Preston North End	46	15	14	17	56	56	59
York City	46	14	17	15	52	58	59
Luton Town	46	14	15	17	60	64	57
MILLWALL	46	14	13	19	43	54	55
Walsall	46	14	12	20	43	52	54
Burnley	46	13	13	20	55	65	52
Brentford	46	11	17	18	50	71	50
Plymouth Argyle	46	12	13	21	55	70	49
Carlisle United	46	12	8	26	57	73	44
Southend United	46	11	10	25	47	79	43

We're Going to Wembley
1998/99

Making all the right noises, Bonds went looking for players to add to the squad, so that a concerted challenge for promotion could be made. To make way for this new influx Bonds let nine players leave the club. It was eight really as Damian Webber never overcame his injury and was forced to retire. 'Cutting the squad back has given me the opportunity to give the kids a go,' said Bonds. 'I think the fans want to see bright young kids coming through the ranks and making it into the first team.'

Out went Tim Carter to Halifax, Maurice Doyle to Shrewsbury, Paul Allen, Tony Witter (to Northampton), Lee McRobert, David Nurse and Steve Aris (to Fisher Athletic). Graeme Tomlinson's loan contract was never extended and before the season started Paul Wilkinson, who went to Northampton for free and Carl Veart, who had gone back to Australia for personal reasons at the end of the season, joined the exodus. Brendon Markey went to Stockport County, having never played a first-team game and Graham Robinson had his contract cancelled.

The shock departure though, was Bonds himself. Paphitis claimed he was sacked while Bonds said that he had resigned three times during the season but had been talked out of leaving. Explaining this bolt out of the blue, Paphitis said, 'I had to make a decision, popular or not, that I felt would benefit this club in the long run and that's why I let Billy go. I've supported him all season and we've been straight with each other right the way through,' he added.

Bonds said, 'I can't complain about the support he has given. I just wish he'd given me a bit more time. This was something I didn't expect to be honest.'

Whatever the reasons behind Bonds' dismissal, and there were many rumoured, the players found themselves under the management of fans' favourite Keith Stevens, with Alan McLeary as his assistant. Stevens said, 'We're both putting our heads on the block here because there are going to be people out there ready to knock us at the first opportunity.' Then echoing the fans' anthem he added, 'If players don't want to come to the club for the right reasons then we don't want them. If they don't like us because of it we don't care.'

The first player to arrive for the new season was defender Jamie Stuart, who had been sacked by Charlton, and he was followed by the return of Jimmy Carter, now at Portsmouth, on a free transfer. Striker Junior McDougald, who had had spells with several clubs, followed him and was given a three-month contract. Goalkeeper Tony Roberts also joined on a free transfer from QPR under the Bosman rules. Various trialists were looked at but discarded.

Stevens announced that the team were reverting to 4-4-2 and using a long-ball style. Everyone looked forward to seeing how things would develop. News that the club were still in financial trouble came as no surprise and Paphitis told everyone that running costs had to be brought down.

A new third strip, gold with a blue and black vertical stripe, was introduced, and it had incorporated in it the old seventies badge of two lions. A new supporters club was launched. Costing £10 per season and £5 for juniors, it allowed for discounts on match tickets and purchases in the club shop and also priority when buying tickets for high-profile fixtures.

Richard Sadlier shoots narrowly wide against Wigan Athletic.

A change in the substitutes rule for cup competitions meant that five players could be named on the bench but only three of them could be used. Pre-season seemed to go well although the friendly matches they played did not really give an indication as to the sort of season the team would have. 'Don't expect a miracle but do expect a totally different type of Millwall this season,' was Stevens' message as the season kicked off with an away game at Wigan on 8 August.

Stuart and McDougald, who came on as a substitute, made their debuts in the game and a Shaw goal gave the Lions their first victory under Stevens' leadership. The last five minutes – always a Millwall shortcoming – were nail-biting but the impressive Fitzgerald and Spink were always in command and it was a good way to start the campaign.

Two late goals were their undoing in the first leg of the Worthington Cup (the renamed Coca-Cola Cup), as they lost 0-2 to Birmingham at St Andrews but they were back to winning ways in their first home game of the season, beating Wycombe Wanderers 2-1. They may have been a tad lucky here. Fitzgerald's first goal for the club came in the dying seconds to add to Sadlier's opener, but a win is a win and the three points were most welcome.

Paul Shaw's goal in the 1-1 home leg of the Worthington Cup was not enough to keep the Lions in the competition but some inconsistent decisions from referee George Cain, including an infuriating amount of time added to the first half during which Birmingham equalised, did not help. Once more though Spink had an outstanding game and there were impressive performances from youngsters Cahill and Reid when they were both introduced to the match as substitutes.

Reid made his first start at Dean Court but some woeful defending saw Bournemouth win 0-3. It would have been worse if Stein had not hit the bar with his penalty kick. True, two of those goals came in injury time and the Lions could have scored a few themselves but it really was a sloppy performance from them. 'I wanted to make them watch the video on the coach coming home to spoil their Saturday night because they certainly spoiled mine,' said Stevens. 'Unfortunately I couldn't get hold of a copy.'

There were a few changes to the side against Macclesfield. Tony Roberts made his debut in place of virus victim Spink, but did not really improve things. The Lions were pleased that the woodwork twice came to their rescue in the 0-0 home draw but losing 1-2 at Burnley, with Shaw scoring a late consolation goal, continued the misery.

This match was a personal nightmare for Brian Law, who injured his knee. It was an injury that ended his season and ultimately his career. At the same time Andy Gray underwent an operation for a similar injury that also ended his career.

With international matches forcing the cancellation of the weekend match against Manchester City, the Lions next played the following Wednesday at home to Lincoln City. Shaw and Neill, back after nearly a year out with injury, were the second-half goal-scorers in this 2-0 win but it was a first-half penalty save from Spink, back in goal after his illness, which proved to be the turning point.

Paul Sturgess was sent on loan to Brighton, and the Lions went to the Potteries to play Stoke. Losing 0-1, to another injury time goal, did not do the Lions justice. It was only some wayward finishing that failed to give them the three points long before the end of the game. 'They put on a performance worthy of a Millwall shirt,' said Stevens and nobody would disagree with him.

Mike Flanagan now left the backroom staff and Kevin O'Callaghan returned yet again to coach the youngsters. It was two youngsters that got their names on the scoresheet for the very first time in the 2-1 home win over Northampton. A goal down at half-time to Northampton's only shot of the half, Harris' curling shot and Cahill's thumping header gave the Lions the win their display deserved.

Lucas Neill's second-minute goal looked like keeping the momentum going at Notts County but they were behind seven minutes later. A poor penalty miss by Paul Shaw was probably the Lions' undoing and they went on to lose 1-3.

They redeemed themselves in the 1-1 draw with Manchester City although it was another goal in added time that was their downfall after Harris had given them the lead at the beginning of the second half. The game though made headlines for all the wrong reasons. It was Shaw's 50th appearance for the club, but he and Vaughan were sent off for fighting. About thirty youngsters came onto the pitch when they thought Harris had scored a second after he had run from almost the halfway line to score. Referee Matt Messias disallowed the goal for an infringement somewhere in midfield. Just where the transgression had been was impossible to have known. He also disallowed another goal scored by Kim Grant, this time for offside. No wonder Millwall felt robbed.

While not condoning what happened, the press and Manchester City manager Joe Royle blew the incidents out of proportion. But damage to the club's reputation had been done yet again by a mindless few and club chairman Paphitis urged genuine supporters to help move the club forward. 'We cannot and will not tolerate anyone trying to damage Millwall, that's why it is important to make it clear that anyone going on the pitch will be banned,' he stated.

After all the exertions, excitements and big-match atmosphere, perhaps it was inevitable that the game against Chesterfield four days later would produce a 0-0 draw. Meanwhile, Dave Savage left to join Northampton for a £100,000 fee and Junior McDougald moved to Leyton Orient; his short contract had not been renewed.

It was thrill-a-minute stuff though with the trip to Blackpool being an entertaining 3-2 win. Paul Shaw, eager to put in a good performance before his ban, made Cahill's opener and then scored two himself. The second was a twenty-five-yard screamer in an impressive Millwall performance. But those old defensive frailties came back to haunt them at times.

Losing 0-1 at home to free-spending Fulham was disappointing in more ways than one. An injury time winner – yes another one – was bad enough but having Stuart sent off for two bookable offences in the first half made it difficult for the Lions, who did more than enough to earn at least a point.

It was business as usual the next Saturday when York City came to The Den. Goals from Sadlier, Harris and Neill gave the home side a comfortable win. Even though York had a player sent off with just five minutes left it had no effect on the outcome. It might have been a bit patchy in parts but Harris was outstanding and the result helped to put the disappointment of the previous Tuesday night out of everyone's mind.

Conditions at the Racecourse Ground were not good. A swirling wind and pouring rain made it difficult for both sides and the resulting 0-0 draw was a fair result, even if thoughts of a late Wrexham winner crossed many minds.

Torrential rain did not help the home match against Oldham either. An appalling back pass from Nethercott, in which the rain-soaked pitch played its part, gave Lions old boy

John McGinlay the chance to score. The Lions played poorly though. You could not blame the pitch for that and they struggled even after Oldham were reduced to ten men. It was a relief when Shaw, back from suspension, came off the bench to equalise.

Even so, Oldham could have taken all three points. Having dominated the second half without getting any reward, Millwall eased off and let their opponents back into the game. 'I didn't like the way we started and I didn't like the way we finished. This game gave me the raving hump,' was Stevens' verdict.

An even worse display followed in the 0-3 defeat at Walsall. But they followed it with their best performance of the season so far when beating Preston 1-0 at Deepdale. Shaw's goal was enough to win the match but whether or not it was the fact that Stevens put himself on the bench – he even played for the last twelve minutes – that galvanised the players we will never know.

It certainly did not work for the FA Cup match at Swansea, which had been switched to a Friday night by the Football Association. Just because it was Friday the thirteenth did not excuse the dismal display. The Lions were back to their inconsistent worst and even though three away matches and a lot of travelling over six days may have taken its toll only a brilliant goalkeeping display by Spink kept the score down to 0-3. The FA Cup first round hoodoo had struck again. The squad needed strengthening but with no money to buy players the club had either to sell first or persist with the youngsters.

The Lions let two more points slip away with the 1-1 home draw with Bristol Rovers, although Stuart's second red card of the season had a lot to do with it. Leading from a Harris goal after eleven minutes a stupid tackle from Stuart saw him have another early bath. Rovers equalised four minutes later.

Even then the Lions had more than enough chances to win and there were signs that things could only get better from here. Because of problems with defensive players, McLeary made a long-awaited comeback.

Those problems got worse at Layer Road when a 0-0 draw with Colchester saw Nethercott sent off for retaliating to a stamp on him by Tony Lock. Somehow, though, the officials seemed to have missed the Colchester player's misdemeanour. It was another good display all the same and Harris was a constant threat and was unlucky not to have scored.

The FA had decided to charge the club over the Manchester City incident. After asking for a personal hearing the club were relieved when, having been found guilty of failing to control its fans, they avoided any punishment. 'It's absolutely essential now that we keep our nose clean because heaven forbid that there is a next time, they will come down on us like a ton of bricks,' commented Paphitis.

A cup run had been hard to find at The Den so winning 2-0 against Cardiff in the Auto Windscreens Shield, with Shaw and Harris scoring, meant a lot. Although they rode their luck at the beginning of the game they ended worthy winners. Another of the club's youngsters, Leke Odunsi, made his debut when he came on as a substitute.

They lacked the killer touch against Reading though and the 1-1 draw (Neill scored) was disappointing after they created so many chances. They also had two decent penalty appeals turned down. The only thing missing from an exciting match was more goals but surely they would soon come?

Two came at Kenilworth Road and the 2-1 win over Luton was well deserved, even though they left it until the eighty-second minute before Neill added to Harris' opener to win the match. It set them up nicely for the Christmas and New Year games.

Well, that was the plan, but another late goal gave Bournemouth a deserved 1-2 victory at The Den on Boxing Day, Harris being the Millwall scorer. Then disaster struck for the away match with Gillingham three days later.

When the Lions turned up at the Priestfield Stadium, it was without goalkeeper Spink, who had rushed to the hospital to be with his wife who was seriously ill, so youngster Phil Smith made his debut. Smith played well in the 1-1 draw, where a late Neill goal earned a share of the points but it could have been much worse; the Lions had both Gerard Lavin and Scott Fitzgerald sent off.

An elegant lob by Danny Hockton puts Millwall 5-1 in front against Brighton. The game was played at Gillingham in the FLT/AWS competition.

Meanwhile Stephen Roach, who had played three times for the club in November, was released, having never really fulfilled the promise he showed. Kim Grant went on loan to Notts County, a permanent move having never materialised and the year came to an end with the team in mid-table.

Back at the same ground to play Brighton in the Auto Windscreen Shield a week later the goals came. A 5-1 win might have flattered the Lions – Brighton even took the lead through Jamie Moralee – but two from Harris and one each from Lavin (his one and only goal for the club), Shaw and Hockton gave the scoreline a look that, but for some dreadful goalkeeping by Ormerod, would have been much closer.

The goals kept coming with a 3-1 home win over Wigan. Nethercott netted his first for the club, while Sadlier and Shaw were the other scorers. It was three points well won. 'We've set our standards, now we have to keep them,' said Stevens. Cahill's goal was enough to ensure a 1-0 win at Wycombe kept the standard going. It was not the best of displays but it was another win and the play-offs started to beckon.

The team came back down to earth with a bang in the next match losing 2-1 at home to Burnley. Sadlier was the scorer but hope was restored with a 2-0 win at Macclesfield in the pouring rain, where Harris scored both goals.

A six-goal thriller against Gillingham followed where the points were shared. The fans leaving The Den had a lot to talk about. Behind at half-time, the Lions had gone in front thanks to Cahill and Harris. After Gillingham levelled the score a Harris penalty put Millwall back in front. But, after Cahill had been sent off, Gillingham drew level again. Anything could and did happen in the last fifteen minutes and a thoroughly entertaining game ended all square, leaving the fans breathless.

Another draw followed, 1-1 with Bournemouth, where a poor first half saw the Lions go in level thanks to Shaw's goal. In the second half they dominated but could not score. It demonstrated that football really is a funny old game. This game, however, had to go on. There has to be a winner in the Auto Windscreen Shield and with extra time failing to produce a goal it was down to penalties. Shaw scored for Millwall, Bowry missed and Bournemouth were 2-1 ahead. Reid, Ryan and Sadlier all scored while Bournemouth had missed one. It was 4-3 to the Lions and up stepped Mark Stein who, just like in the league match earlier in the season, smacked his shot against the crossbar. Millwall were through, just!

Losing 0-3 at Maine Road in their next match says more for how a score can disguise the facts. The Lions were unlucky not to get something out of the game and the result was cruel after the effort they had put in. They even had a goal disallowed. It was cruel for the fans too, who were taunted throughout and then blamed for trouble that was ultimately shown to have been caused by Manchester City fans. The game was a lesson for everyone to learn from.

Two new faces made their debut at Lincoln. Youngster Paul Ifill, who had been on the bench at Manchester City, started the match, as did goalkeeper Ben Roberts. Roberts had signed on loan from Middlesbrough due to Spink suffering from a hernia and Tony Roberts, who had injured a finger back in November, being told to retire from the game. This left only youngster Phil Smith to keep goal.

Maybe the players had their minds on the cup quarter-final the following Tuesday but without doubt the 0-2 defeat was their worst performance of the season. Fitzgerald picked up an injury to his cartilage that needed an operation. 'I find it difficult to find any crumbs of comfort from that display,' said Stevens, 'and we will certainly need to be better against Gillingham.'

With so many players unavailable it was difficult to see where a win over Gillingham would come from. The shock debut of another youngster, central defender Joe Dolan, had the fans worried before the game. They need not have been worried; Dolan was outstanding. He inspired the rest of the team and Sadlier's 'golden goal' took them into the semi-final.

It was a dramatic end to an enthralling cup-tie even if it should never had reached that far. A goal from Neill had been cruelly disallowed after Bartram had dropped the ball. Still, Millwall thoroughly deserved the win and a Wembley appearance was getting nearer.

The 2-0 win over Stoke the following Saturday concealed the facts of the match. Already exhausted after the game against Gillingham, Millwall had to battle against some diabolical refereeing from Rob Styles, who quite frankly was not up to the job. Many fans were not even in their seats when Bowry was sent off as he and Wallace jumped for the ball. The embarrassment on the Stoke players' faces was increased with bookings for Harris and Cahill before six minutes had even been played. Add to that the fact that Roberts injured himself in the warm up and was replaced by Smith and the fans held out little hope of a win. But after goals from Harris and Cahill had put the Lions in front, Mr Styles decided things needed evening up. As Sadlier put the ball in the net for a third Millwall goal, he blew for a foul, booked Sadlier for kicking the ball away and, as he had already been cautioned, sent him off.

The final twenty minutes seemed like the longest ever played but the Lions held out and might even have scored again. You could not ask for a better performance. As a team they were simply superb. To think there were six teenagers in the side.

Away from the pitch £300,000 was raised from some additional shares and that eased the financial commitments to a youth academy that was producing such promising youngsters and would continue to do so in the future.

Back on the playing front, the Lions won again next time out, 2-1 away to Northampton, but not without cost. Goals from Nethercott and Sadlier gave them victory but a rash tackle from Reid gave him the present of an early bath eight minutes from time. Millwall rode their luck though, as Northampton hit the woodwork three times and had twice put the ball in the net only to see them ruled out. Sometimes fortune really does favour the brave.

Speaking of the red cards shown to his players – there had been ten so far this season as well as numerous bookings – Stevens said, 'I'm asking my players to go out with a bit of pride and passion, but there is not one player in my side who would go out with the intent to hurt anyone.'

Maybe the players' minds were on the cup semi-final games due to be played against Walsall because they lost the next two league matches. First came a 1-2 defeat away at Chesterfield, with Dolan registering his first for the club, and then 1-3 at home to Notts County. Hockton this time was the scorer. It was not that the Lions played badly in either game but a few momentary lapses and having minds elsewhere when decisive tackles needed to be made were their undoing.

And so to the matches against Walsall; there were three of them in a row as a home league game was sandwiched between the two cup ties. The first leg of the Auto Windscreen Shield semi-final, played at The Den, came first and it was nail-biting stuff. A goal from Cahill after just three minutes was enough to give the Lions a 1-0 win but would a one-goal advantage be enough for the return leg? Everyone played their part but none more so than Ben Roberts, who was back in the side after a four-match layoff with a groin injury and a possible return to Middlesbrough. He made some crucial saves, particularly the fifty-eighth-minute penalty save from Neil Pointon. The return of Stevens in the injury-hit defence also helped when the boat started rocking.

How different the league match, also at The Den and this season's Anti-Racism Focus Match, was. Whereas the win on the previous Tuesday had been down to some stout defending, two defensive blunders gave Walsall the lead. Roberts was unable to stop a penalty this time and Harris' goal was no more than a consolation, although he also hit a post. The Lions had been in complete control of the match, however, so just how would this result affect the game at the Bescot Stadium three days later?

The answer was that they totally dominated the game yet again. Walsall's last-gasp goal was only enough to equalise Sadlier's opener. Although the Lions had enough chances to win the game – Harris hit the bar – the 1-1 score was enough to take them to Wembley for only the second time in their history. The first was in 1945 when they played a War Cup final against Chelsea, where both sides played a lot of 'guest' players.

There was no doubt that the Lions deserved their place in the final but it looked like the player who had scored the goal that got them there, Richard Sadlier, would suffer the heartache of not being with his teammates as he had been selected to play for the Republic of Ireland in an Under-20 World Championship competition in Nigeria, which ran from April 3-24. With the Wembley appearance due on 18 April it looked like his chance of a playing visit to the Twin Towers had gone.

There were two other possible absentees from Wembley. Steve Gritt was running in the London Marathon that day but postponed his appearance and Ben Roberts was due back at Middlesbrough but had his loan extended to cover the match.

There were still league points to be won though and an outside chance of clinching a play-off spot. So a Cahill goal and three points at Oldham were more than welcome, as were the wins over Wrexham and Blackpool, both at The Den.

A goal from Kim Grant and two from Harris gave the Lions a comfortable 3-0 win over Wrexham, in a match that saw the return of Andy Cook from injury. It was a Harris goal that was enough to beat Blackpool where both Fitzgerald and Shaw overcame their injury problems to take their places on the bench. Funny what can happen when Wembley places are up for grabs. There was heartbreak though for Lucas Neill, who injured his knee in the Blackpool game and was out for the rest of the season. With the transfer deadline day approaching Kenny Brown left the club, as did Dean Canoville.

Were the players' minds on Wembley when they played York? Most probably and the 1-2 win for the home side (Shaw scoring for Millwall), came with two goals in the last three minutes. But York could and should have had many more as the Lions did not put any effort into the game despite Roberts saving another penalty.

Perhaps it was with the cup final in mind that Stevens chose a side for their next match, at home to Colchester, which did not contain a single player who would start at Wembley the following week.

Debuts were given to Byron Bubb, Ronnie Bull and Mark Hicks, while youngsters Tommy Tyne and Billy Mead were on the bench. Stevens even played himself and gave Andy Cook his only start of the season. He need not have worried about the result though. Two goals from Grant, the first after just one minute and the second a fifteenth-minute penalty, gave the Lions an easy 2-0 win in a one-sided contest. Spink even saved a penalty, the third in a row saved by a Millwall goalkeeper.

And so to Wembley. With painted faces, strange hair-dos and costumes, some in lion suits and in a party mood, over 46,000 Lions supporters made the walk along Wembley Way.

Richard Sadlier had returned from Nigeria to take his place in the side; the Republic of Ireland had been knocked out. Just for the record the team was, Roberts, Lavin, Stuart, Cahill, Nethercott, Dolan, Ifill, Newman, Harris, Sadlier, Reid with Shaw, Bowry and Bircham on the bench.

The first half was almost shot-less but the second came to life after Harris had a shot kicked off the line and Roberts saved well from Balmer. There were chances for either side to win, penalty claims denied and it looked like an extra-time 'golden goal' or penalties would be the only way to find a winner when, in injury time, Paul Rogers scored for Wigan. The final whistle came twenty seconds later.

The sad faces of 46,000 fans made their way back along Wembley Way but they could be proud of their team and of the wonderful atmosphere that they had created. Hearts had been broken but the disappointed fans and players knew they had a great future to look forward to. 'However disappointed we all are the main thing is that all the players can hold their heads up high,' said Stevens. And the fans could too. They had been behind their team with songs and roars of encouragement for the whole of the match and left the stadium in the same, if subdued, party mood that they had arrived in. Speaking to the fans, Stevens said, 'You were superb, a great

Supporters at Wembley Stadium for the FLT/AWS final against Wigan Athletic, April 1999.

Millwall fans on Wembley Way, April 1999.

credit to the club and you created a marvellous atmosphere.' Millwall chairman, Theo Paphitis, summed them up by simply saying, 'You are the best.'

However, the rest of the season was an anti-climax. Dolan broke his jaw and Lavin turned an ankle when the Lions lost 1-4 to Fulham at Craven Cottage, with Shaw scoring late in the game. Very late goals from Cahill and Ifill (his first for the club) secured a 2-2 home draw with Preston that was followed by away defeats at Bristol Rovers, 0-3, all three goals being scored past stand-in goalkeeper Scott Fitzgerald after Roberts was sent off for deliberate handball, and Reading, 0-2.

And so the final game of an extraordinary season came on Saturday 8 May with a 0-1 home defeat by Luton. Before the match the fans had been shown the new kit for the following season. It was all white, with the two lions rampant badge and the new shirt sponsors Giorgio. The only way for the Lions to go now was upward. All the signs were there, so just what would a season that would end in a new millennium bring?

1998/99   Football League Division Two

Date		Opposition	Score	Scorers
Aug	8	Wigan Athletic	1-0	Shaw
	15	WYCOMBE WANDERERS	2-1	Fitzgerald, Sadlier
	22	Bournemouth	0-3	
	29	MACCLESFIELD TOWN	0-0	
Sept	1	Burnley	1-2	Shaw
	9	LINCOLN CITY	2-0	Shaw, Neill
	12	Stoke City	0-1	
	19	NORTHAMPTON TOWN	2-1	Harris, Cahill
	26	Notts County	1-3	Neill
	29	MANCHESTER CITY	1-1	Harris
Oct	3	CHESTERFIELD	0-0	
	10	Blackpool	3-2	Shaw (2), Cahill
	17	FULHAM	0-1	
	21	YORK CITY	3-1	Sadlier, Harris, Neill
	24	Wrexham	0-0	
	31	OLDHAM ATHLETIC	1-1	Shaw
Nov	7	Walsall	0-3	
	10	Preston North End	1-0	Shaw
	21	BRISTOL ROVERS	1-1	Harris
	28	Colchester United	0-0	
Dec	12	READING	1-1	Neill
	19	Luton Town	2-1	Neill, Harris
	26	BOURNEMOUTH	1-2	Harris
	29	Gillingham	1-1	Neill
Jan	9	WIGAN ATHLETIC	3-1	Nethercott, Sadlier, Shaw
	16	Wycombe Wanderers	1-0	Cahill
	23	BURNLEY	1-2	Sadlier
	26	Macclesfield Town	2-0	Harris (2)
	30	GILLINGHAM	3-3	Harris (2) (1 pen), Cahill
Feb	6	Manchester City	0-3	
	13	Lincoln City	0-2	
	20	STOKE CITY	2-0	Harris, Cahill
	27	Northampton Town	2-1	Nethercott, Sadlier
Mar	2	Chesterfield	1-2	Dolan
	6	NOTTS COUNTY	1-3	Hockton
	13	WALSALL	1-2	Harris
	20	Oldham Athletic	1-0	Cahill
	27	WREXHAM	3-0	Harris (2), Grant
Apr	5	BLACKPOOL	1-0	Harris
	10	York City	1-2	Shaw
	14	COLCHESTER UNITED	2-0	Grant (2) (1 pen)
	21	Fulham	1-4	Shaw
	24	PRESTON NORTH END	2-2	Cahill, Ifill
	27	Bristol Rovers	0-3	
May	1	READING	0-2	
	8	LUTON TOWN	0-1	

League Cup

Round	Date		Opposition	Score	Scorers
1/1	Aug	11	Birmingham City	0-2	
1/2		19	BIRMINGHAM CITY	1-1	Shaw

Associate Members Cup

Round	Date		Opposition	Score	Scorers
1	Dec	9	CARDIFF CITY	2-0	Harris, Shaw
2	Jan	5	Brighton & Hove Albion	5-1	Harris (2), Lavin, Shaw, Hockton
QF	Feb	2	Bournemouth	1-1*	Shaw
SF		16	GILLINGHAM	1-0	Sadlier
F/1	Mar	9	WALSALL	1-0	Cahill
F/2		16	Walsall	1-1	Sadlier
F	Apr	18	WIGAN ATHLETIC	0-1	

*a.e.t Millwall won on penalties

FA Cup

Round	Date		Opposition	Score	Scorers
1	Nov	13	Swansea City	0-3	

1998/99   Football League Division Two

	P	W	D	L	F	A	Pts
Fulham	46	31	8	7	79	32	101
Walsall	46	26	9	11	63	47	87
Manchester City	46	22	16	8	69	33	82
Gillingham	46	22	14	10	75	44	80
Preston North End	46	22	13	11	78	50	79
Wigan Athletic	46	22	10	14	75	48	76
Bournemouth	46	21	13	12	63	41	76
Stoke City	46	21	6	19	59	63	69
Chesterfield	46	17	13	16	46	44	64
MILLWALL	46	17	11	18	52	59	62
Reading	46	16	13	17	54	63	61
Luton Town	46	16	10	20	51	60	58
Bristol Rovers	46	13	17	16	65	56	56
Blackpool	46	14	14	18	44	54	56
Burnley	46	13	16	17	54	73	55
Notts County	46	14	12	20	52	61	54
Wrexham	46	13	14	19	43	62	53
Colchester United	46	12	16	18	52	70	52
Wycombe Wanderers	46	13	12	21	52	58	51
Oldham Athletic	46	14	9	23	48	66	51
York City	46	13	11	22	56	80	50
Northampton Town	46	10	18	18	43	57	48
Lincoln City	46	13	7	26	42	74	46
Macclesfield Town	46	11	10	25	43	63	43

Building for the Future
1999/00

Wearing white shirts for the season that would move into the new millennium was not a sign of surrender but rather one of advancement. Paphitis wanted to modernise things about the club although there was a big debate as to whether the club should abandon their traditional blue or not.

There were the usual comings and goings. Going were Andy Gray, forced to retire due to injury, Gerard Lavin, who went to Bristol City under the Bosman rules, Jimmy Carter, who was out of contract and did not have it renewed due to injury and Kim Grant, who went to Belgium club KFC Lommelse for £65,000 after a protracted deal.

New arrivals at The Den were striker Paul Moody, a £150,000 buy from Fulham and defender Sean Dyche, who came from Bristol City for the same amount. Unfortunately he injured himself in a pre-season match against Crystal Palace and did not figure in the first team until March. Goalkeeper Tony Warner came from Liverpool for free as did Michael Gilkes from Wolves, both under the Bosman ruling, and midfielder David Livermore arrived on a three-month loan from Arsenal. In what appeared a strange move it was announced that Stevens and McLeary would now be joint managers, although this had actually happened before the Wembley appearance the previous season.

Discussing the fact that they had been working that way throughout the previous season anyway, McLeary said, 'Our roles are going to be exactly the same and our work will be exactly the same.'

There were also changes to the rules, which now saw squad numbers on shirts and shorts. The Lions numbered their shirts alphabetically, with the exception of the goalkeepers who wore numbers one and thirteen, and there was the addition of players' names on their shirts.

The five-substitute rule that was used in the Worthington Cup now became a permanent feature for all games as Nationwide clubs became a copy of Premiership sides. A copy in everything except, of course, the money, which was coming fast and furiously into the game mainly through television rights and merchandising.

Money was the talk of the club again when a £3 million loss for the year 1998 was announced but a cash boost of £2.3 million from new shares softened the blow.

Paphitis also took the unusual step of writing to every club in the division and asking that they make their home match against Millwall an all-ticket affair in a bid to stop the hooligan faction that attaches itself to the club. They would find it difficult to attend away matches as these tickets would only be sold to season ticket holders and members of the official Millwall Supporters Club. Not many clubs responded in a positive way, although there was a positive reaction to the new family enclosure at The Den, which now extended to the whole of the lower section of the East Stand. With prices that encouraged families it was no wonder that a staggering seventy per cent increase in season tickets for this part of the ground was made.

The club also held their matches with the Khalsa Football Federation, started the previous season, to promote and develop football in the Asian community.

A tough pre-season had been a good workout and the season proper started on 7 August with an away match at newly promoted Cardiff City. Moody, Warner and Livermore, who came on as a substitute for Odunsi, made their debuts in a 1-1 draw that was the story of two penalties. Harris scored for Millwall and Boland for Cardiff. The Welsh side also hit the bar and had Jason Fowler sent off.

Unfortunately the headlines were for off-the-field activities on an opening day that saw violence up and down the country. Lions fans were more sinned against than sinful in the Welsh capital, although it took a long time and various inquiries to find the answer as to what happened and why.

The Lions stayed in Wales and travelled to Swansea for the first leg of the first round of the Worthington Cup. They were beaten 0-2 with Harris missing a penalty. Poor defending allowed Swansea too much time and room. Indeed the score would have been worse but for the woodwork, which was hit twice.

The first league match at The Den was against Wigan and the Lions were looking to avenge their Wembley defeat. It certainly did not look as if they would manage it when Millwall found themselves 0-3 down with just twenty-five minutes left to play. The whole team and especially goalkeeper Warner looking very embarrassed. When Shaw scored twelve minutes from the end it looked no more than a consolation but when Cahill hit home Ifill's cross seconds later the impossible looked on. A Harris penalty in the last minute, after Shaw had been fouled, made the score 3-3. No one could really believe what they had witnessed.

The Sunday televised match at Stoke was a lively encounter that the Lions dominated from start to finish, yet they lost 1-3 with Bircham scoring his first Millwall goal. A harsh penalty decision put an end to any comeback here but poor defending had cost them dearly.

It was the same story in the 1-1 draw in the return game with Swansea. There was plenty of possession but no end result. A missed penalty by Harris would have given the Lions a level aggregate score when Sadlier scored and the result might have been different. Even the introduction of Michael Gilkes for his debut did not help.

Neither did the 1-1 draw with Chesterfield. Maybe it was the new 4-3-1-2 system that was the problem but they should have gone on to win after Cahill had put them in front. The frustration of all – fans, players and management – was plain to see.

The performances of David Livermore persuaded the club to sign him on a permanent basis and £30,000 was enough to convince Arsenal to let him go. The nineteen-year-old signed a three-year deal.

A behind-closed-doors game with Charlton, where the Lions played a 4-4-2 formation, gave the management something to think about and they employed it in the 0-0 away draw with Bristol City. It was the first game for the Lions for two weeks because of international call-ups.

The match itself was backs-to-the-wall stuff for Millwall as only a string of fine saves from Warner kept the score at 0-0 and the Lions contrived to give the ball away every time they had it. There was even an amazing thirteen minutes' injury time added on to the second half. But the team survived for a hard-earned point.

David Kemp, dismissed with Docherty at the start of the Bonds era, was brought back to freshen up training. His influence was apparent by the way the Lions played. Danny Hockton went out on loan to Leyton Orient and so did Phil Smith to Ashford Town.

Whatever the reasons, the Lions finally won their first game of the season, 2-1 at home to a Cambridge United side that employed an offside trap just inside their own half. Nevertheless they had to come from behind to do it, after Butler had scored from the penalty spot. The goals came from Harris and Cahill and Millwall survived a late goal when the referee blew for a foul on Stuart.

It was a late Ifill goal that gave them the 1-0 victory at home to Colchester, when he came off the bench to run past the Colchester defence and thump the ball into the net. But the Lions' overall performance was not impressive.

Paul Ifill fires an unstoppable shot into the Colchester United net.

To keep the rich vein of youngsters with which the club were having success coming, Dave Mehmet was brought back to the club as the assistant academy director with responsibility for nine to sixteen-year-olds.

Losing 0-2 away to Gillingham was disappointing, not just because of the defeat but in the manner it happened. The team started sluggishly and that sluggishness, seen in most games so far this season, continued throughout most of the game. They came to life when they were two down but a post, twice, bad luck and a lack of time added to their misery.

Perhaps the fact that the joint managers were not sure what their best side was, especially up front, added to the problems and decisions needed to be made quickly before a relegation dogfight became a priority, even as early as October.

Captain Stuart Nethercott admitted they were playing badly. 'We're not playing well,' he stated, 'but at the end of the day we've only lost two games. We're not gelling.' Not gelling was an understatement but changes in the side for the away match against Oxford gave them a 3-1 win. With players away on international duty they could have called the game off but the decision to play it was vindicated by the score.

Two goals from Shaw, his first a cracker from the edge of the area, and another from Cahill meant that Murphy's penalty was no more than a consolation. It was not a disaster when the same side only managed a 1-1 draw at home to Burnley, Cahill equalising late in the game. After all, Burnley were among the promotion favourites and doing well in the league and their goalkeeper Paul Crichton made some fine saves. But losing the next game, also at home and with just one change to the side, 0-2 to Preston meant the fans started to moan. Yes it was a defensive mix-up that gave Preston the first goal and a Nethercott own goal the other, but the Lions' play was not convincing.

Andy Cook found that he no longer had a part to play and had his contract cancelled by mutual consent. He had made only 5 appearances for the club since joining in January 1998.

It was next off to Layer Road and in the pouring rain Millwall won 2-1 against Colchester. It could have been so different though. A goal behind early on, the Lions were on level terms after Moody opened his Millwall account. Then Ifill scored a 'goal' of the season contender. Beating two players wide on the right, he cut inside and let fly from the edge of the box. The ball flew into the net and as he went off to celebrate. Cahill slammed the ball back into the net. Up went the linesman's flag and after a long discussion with referee Rob Harris, the goal was disallowed. It transpired that both officials thought that the ball had hit the post and not gone in, perhaps a good case for the introduction of goal line technology. Fortunately Ifill managed to score again and save the officials' blushes.

The police switched the first round FA Cup match against Hartlepool to a midday Sunday kick-off. The Millwall first round hoodoo continued when they lost 0-1, with another last-minute goal being their undoing.

Back to league action and the 1-0 home win over Luton. Three points came thanks to Cahill's scrambled effort, yet in truth this was a dour game. Neil Harris started in the game at Scunthorpe, replacing the injured Shaw, and scored twice, as did Ifill, in a 4-1 win. The team was unrecognisable to the one that played against Luton, which probably shows what a funny old game football really is.

Ahead after just two minutes, the Lions were in complete control and never looked like they were in any danger of losing the match. The score could have been a lot higher but for a post, a disallowed goal and some wayward finishing. A goal from Harris gave them hope of a point at Oldham but that old 'give a goal away at the end of the game' problem reappeared and they lost 1-2. A 0-0 draw on a Friday night at The Den, with ten men after Shaw was sent off, did nothing for their confidence, even though they had enough chances to have won the game comfortably against Wrexham.

The 5-0 win over Reading the following Tuesday night was not expected after the previous two games but Paul Moody justified his selection over Shaw with a hat-trick, and two more goals from Harris completed the demolition. McLeary was anxious that the result carried nobody away. 'I don't think we played any better or any worse than in some other games recently. Tonight we just took our chances,' he said.

A cold Tuesday night in Blackpool followed and so did two more Moody goals, which clinched the 2-1 win. They had to cling on after Newman was sent off and Blackpool threw everything at them trying to score an equaliser.

It was Harris' turn to score twice with the 2-1 win at Bournemouth. In truth it was an easy win and, even though Bournemouth's goal was punched into the net by Jorgensen and missed by the officials, the Lions were never in any real danger of losing a match that they dominated throughout.

After the problems during the opening game of the season, stringent measures were taken when Cardiff came to The Den. Only the upper tiers of the ground were opened, with the exception of the family enclosure, which itself was restricted, and the match was strictly all-ticket. A massive police presence failed to stop some skirmishes before and after the game and there was some £15,000 of damage done to the ground by Cardiff fans, but the game itself was over after half an hour when two more impressive Harris goals sealed victory.

A quick return to Wembley was not to be as the Lions lost 0-1 to Brighton at the Withdean Stadium in the first round of the Auto Windscreens Shield. Once again it was a last-minute goal that was their undoing.

This tournament was also used as an experiment for a new rule at free-kicks. What became known as the ten-yard rule involved the ball being moved forward ten yards from where the free-kick was to be taken if dissent, delaying the restart by kicking, carrying or throwing the ball away, failing to retreat ten yards or any other form of unsporting behaviour was committed. A penalty was not to be given if moving the ball put it into the penalty area.

Back to league action and a 2-1 win at Wycombe. Goals from Ifill and Moody helped the Lions continue their impressive move up the table. A late Sadlier goal, scored when he replaced Moody, kept it going with a 1-0 win over Notts County at The Den.

A 1 p.m. kick-off on a Sunday is not everyone's cup of tea and when the Sunday happens to be Boxing Day and the kick-off is in Bristol against the blue half of the city, who can blame you for staying in bed? Yet 452 Lions fans made the trip and the reward for their efforts was to see Reid sent off after just six minutes, a host of chances created and missed and Rovers snatching a 0-1 win with a goal in the last five minutes.

The last game of the year, at home to Brentford just two days later, proved to be a cracker. A goal-less first half was spoilt by some controversial refereeing decisions but it came to life in the

An injury-time equaliser on 28 December by Paul Shaw, but there was still time for David Livermore to score the winner and the last Football League goal of the twentieth century.

second half when Mahon's screamer put Brentford in front. Ten minutes later and Harris had equalised. Then Reid hit the bar but with just five minutes left Brentford were back in front. It looked like another late defeat for the Lions.

Nobody had reckoned with cavalrymen Shaw and Livermore, who were sent on to try and salvage something. With a minute left Shaw scored the equaliser and then, with the clock running down added-on time, Warner threw the ball to Shaw on the right. His pass from the halfway line missed Harris but Livermore, who had run the length of the pitch, was at the back post to thump the ball home for the winner.

Not only was it his first goal for the club but, due to the delayed start to the match, it proved to be the last goal scored anywhere in the country. Therefore it was the final goal of the millennium. What a way to win!

The Lions, who had seen themselves in twenty-third position in the table in August, were now fourth at the end of the year. Three consecutive draws kept them there. First came a 2-2 draw at Bury where this time they were on the receiving end of a last-gasp goal after Harris and Ifill had given them the lead.

Next came a 1-1 home draw with ten-man Wycombe – Harris the scorer – and another 1-1 draw away at Wigan, where once again the kick-off time was changed to 1 p.m. causing problems for the fans. Despite the results there were enough chances to win both games.

At least they had a Livermore goal to cheer. Spink, playing his only game of the season for the injured Warner, had a fairly quiet game. But once again a late goal saw another two points slip away and that was after Wigan had to play with ten men when Balmer was sent off for handling the ball on the line. Moody had the resulting penalty saved.

Meanwhile, Danny Hockton left to join Stevenage Borough and the club raised another £600,000 from a new share issue.

Scoring your first goal for your club is always something special and when it turns out that it is also the 200th league goal to be scored on a ground it is something extra special. So Michael Gilkes must be pleased that it was also the winning goal in Millwall's 1-0 win over Stoke. It does not tell the whole story of course. Stoke must have been glad to leave The Den having conceded only one goal, as the Lions laid siege to their goal without adding to the score. The only mystery is how they failed to get any more goals.

Proof of the club's intention to get out of the division was seen when they brought in Ray Harford to coach the first team in place of Kemp, who had gone to Portsmouth just before Christmas. Harford had quite a pedigree in the game and his appointment was seen as a major coup.

A programme from
the 1999/00 season.

Three points from the bottom club Chesterfield seemed a certainty, especially as the home team were having trouble scoring goals. But losing 0-2 was not what Millwall fans had expected to see. A swirling wind upset matters but if the Lions did not leave the field embarrassed by their endeavours then their fans certainly did. 'That ranks as our poorest display of the season,' said McLeary to wholehearted agreement.

Five changes to the starting line-up at home to Oldham proved that the management were not happy with what they had been seeing and yet it took a last-minute Shaw penalty to secure the points. Harris had been sent off in the first half and Oldham were also reduced to ten men just five minutes later in this hot-headed encounter. But the 50ft by 25ft flag that was unfurled in the family enclosure for the first time before the match might just have been the omen they were looking for.

Injuries and pending suspensions looked like they may sabotage the Lions' season so they moved to sign Christophe Kinet, who they had been trying to sign since just before Christmas, for £75,000 from Strasbourg. He made his debut when coming on as a substitute in the home match against Bournemouth.

Before that there was a trip to Reading. Although the Lions huffed and puffed they never looked happy – they lost the game 0-2. Again the goals came late in the game.

Beating Bournemouth 3-1 was just what the doctor ordered, especially as they went behind after just three minutes. Two goals from Sadlier and another from Ifill were enough to restore some confidence in the side, especially with first-choice strikers Moody and Harris missing.

Moody replaced Sadlier for the trip to Cambridge and showed that anything his stand-in could do so could he. He scored both goals in the 2-0 win but Sadlier was back for the home match against Bristol City, scoring in the 4-1 win. The other scorers were Cahill (2) and Ifill and the game featured the debut of David Tuttle, who had been bought from Barnsley for £200,000 to help shore up the defence.

When the Lions played Scunthorpe the following Tuesday, The Den faithful were looking forward to another three points, especially after Cahill had given them the lead. But the Jekyll and Hyde season took another twist as they conspired to throw the game away. They lost 1-2 so perhaps it was no surprise when they travelled to Luton and won 2-0.

There were some surprises though. But the game was not one of them with another two goals from Cahill. The first surprise was that Sean Dyche played, making his Millwall debut, and the second that he was given the captain's armband. The third, perhaps not so much of a surprise given Millwall's record of buying central defenders who get injured, was that he did not play again all season.

Life with the Lions is never dull. The Blackpool game, which was this season's Anti-Racism Focus match, had been preceded by an exhibition on black footballers and not just those who had worn the Millwall shirt. The exhibition had run for the previous ten days and had proved to be a successful venture. The match itself though was not. Neil Harris' penalty proved to be Millwall's get out of jail free card in a 1-1 draw. The fact that Millwall dominated yet another match without taking all three points should have worried the management and a 1-1 draw at Wrexham where a Gilkes goal with only seconds left on the clock salvaged a point from another game where all three should have travelled south.

The Wrexham game had seen the debut of Matt Lawrence, bought from Wycombe for £250,000, and the defender's arrival was timely with Neill being away on international duty. Harris Sadlier and Ifill were all on target as Millwall ran out easy 3-0 winners against Bristol Rovers, especially satisfying as their West Country opponents held second place in the table.

There was no stopping Harris now that the bit was between his teeth and he scored in five of the last seven League matches. First came the only goal in a 1-1 draw at Notts County. Then came another (he should have had two but he missed a penalty) when the Lions beat Bury 3-0. Moody and Dolan were the other scorers. He got all three when Millwall beat Brentford 3-1, two when they lost 3-4 to Burnley (Cahill the other scorer) and the only goal when they beat Oxford 1-0 in the final league game of the season. The games he missed out in were the 2-2 draw with Gillingham, where Moody and Ifill were the scorers, and the 2-3 defeat at Preston where Neill and Ifill again netted.

The Bury and Brentford games were as easy as the score suggests. In fact only the woodwork, twice, stopped Brentford losing by more. The Burnley game was almost a great comeback. At 0-4 up, Burnley were coasting when the Lions started to play. But for a blatant penalty denied them and time running out they could have snatch at least a point, if not all three.

There was a similar fight-back in the Gillingham game but this time it was Gillingham who came back to share the points. It was not to be when the Lions failed to pull back the three goals against champions Preston, even though they were denied another very obvious penalty that would have given them a share of the points.

So a nervous Lions clinched fifth place after playing Oxford and found themselves up against their old sparring partners, Wigan, in the play-offs. A 0-0 draw at The Den was never going to be enough but there had not been much between the sides all season. Wigan finally broke the draw sequence by winning the second leg 0-1 at the JJB Stadium.

Millwall were confined to another season in Division Two and disappointment descended over the blue section of south-east London again. It was made even worse by the fact that Charlton had won promotion to the Premiership. Just how crucial those dropped points were could now be seen but they would be stronger for it and, with the reserve side winning the Combination League, they were ready to make another assault on the Division Two title. The Lions had started to growl again.

1999/2000   **Football League Division Two**

Date		Opposition	Score	Scorers
Aug	7	Cardiff City	1-1	Harris (pen)
	14	WIGAN ATHLETIC	3-3	Shaw, Cahill, Harris (pen)
	22	Stoke City	1-3	Bircham
	28	CHESTERFIELD	1-1	Cahill
Sept	11	Bristol City	0-0	
	18	CAMBRIDGE UNITED	2-1	Harris, Cahill
	25	COLCHESTER UNITED	1-0	Ifill
Oct	2	Gillingham	0-2	
	9	Oxford United	3-1	Shaw (2), Cahill
	16	BURNLEY	1-1	Cahill
	19	PRESTON NORTH END	0-2	
	23	Colchester United	2-1	Moody, Ifill
Nov	2	LUTON TOWN	1-0	Cahill
	6	Scunthorpe United	4-1	Harris (2), Ifill (2)
	9	Oldham Athletic	1-2	Harris
	12	WREXHAM	0-0	
	16	READING	5-0	Moody (3), Harris (2)
	23	Blackpool	2-1	Moody (2)
	27	Bournemouth	2-1	Harris (2)
Dec	4	CARDIFF CITY	2-0	Harris (2)
	11	Wycombe Wanderers	2-1	Ifill, Moody
	18	NOTTS COUNTY	1-0	Sadlier
	26	Bristol Rovers	0-1	
	28	BRENTFORD	3-2	Harris, Shaw, Livermore
Jan	4	Bury	2-2	Harris, Ifill
	8	WYCOMBE WANDERERS	1-1	Harris
	15	Wigan Athletic	1-1	Livermore
	22	STOKE CITY	1-0	Gilkes
	29	Chesterfield	0-2	
Feb	5	OLDHAM ATHLETIC	1-0	Shaw (pen)
	12	Reading	0-2	
	19	BOURNEMOUTH	3-1	Sadlier (2), Ifill
	26	Cambridge United	2-0	Moody (2)
Mar	4	BRISTOL CITY	4-1	Cahill (2), Ifill, Sadlier
	7	SCUNTHORPE UNITED	1-2	Cahill
	11	Luton Town	2-0	Cahill (2)
	18	BLACKPOOL	1-1	Harris (pen)
	21	Wrexham	1-1	Gilkes
	25	BRISTOL ROVERS	3-0	Harris, Sadlier, Ifill
Apr	1	Notts County	1-1	Harris
	8	BURY	3-0	Moody, Harris, Dolan
	15	Brentford	3-1	Harris (3)
	22	Burnley	3-4	Harris (2), Cahill
	24	GILLINGHAM	2-2	Moody, Ifill
	29	Preston North End	2-3	Ifill, Neill
May	6	OXFORD UNITED	1-0	Harris
May	13	WIGAN ATHLETIC	0-0	
	17	Wigan Athletic	0-1	

League Cup

Round	Date		Opposition	Score	Scorers
1/1	Aug	11	Swansea City	0-2	
1/2		24	SWANSEA CITY	1-1	Sadlier

Associate Members Cup

Round	Date		Opposition	Score	Scorers
1	Dec	7	Brighton & Hove Albion	0-1	

FA Cup

Round	Date		Opposition	Score	Scorers
1	Oct	31	Hartlepool United	0-1	

1999/2000   Football League Division Two

	P	W	D	L	F	A	Pts
Preston North End	46	28	11	7	74	37	95
Burnley	46	25	13	8	69	47	88
Gillingham	46	25	10	11	79	48	85
Wigan Athletic	46	22	17	7	72	38	83
MILLWALL	46	23	13	10	76	50	82
Stoke City	46	23	13	10	68	42	82
Bristol Rovers	46	23	11	12	69	45	80
Notts County	46	18	11	17	61	55	65
Bristol City	46	15	19	12	59	57	64
Reading	46	16	14	16	57	63	62
Wrexham	46	17	11	18	52	61	62
Wycombe Wanderers	46	16	13	17	56	53	61
Luton Town	46	17	10	19	61	65	61
Oldham Athletic	46	16	12	18	50	55	60
Bury	46	13	18	15	61	64	57
Bournemouth	46	16	9	21	59	62	57
Brentford	46	13	13	20	47	61	52
Colchester United	46	14	10	22	59	82	52
Cambridge United	46	12	12	22	64	65	48
Oxford United	46	12	9	25	43	73	45
Cardiff City	46	9	17	20	45	67	44
Blackpool	46	8	17	21	49	77	41
Scunthorpe United	46	9	12	25	40	74	39
Chesterfield	46	7	15	24	34	63	36

Daydream Believers
2000/01

Having started to growl again, the Lions needed to start roaring. The young Millwall squad needed a boost from somewhere to get that roar started. It came initially from the fans, when it was announced that an increase in ticket sales and merchandising had boosted the club's coffers and chairman Paphitis was delighted. 'We do have the fans to thank for a lot of our financial success,' he said, adding, 'If the fans carry on the way they have done next season it would be a huge boost for us.'

Another boost came when leading goalscorer, Neil Harris, signed a new four-year contract and the joint management of Stevens and McLeary was confirmed for the future.

There were some departures from the club but Stevens and McLeary felt that they could continue without the purchase of anyone before the season started although they did sign goalkeeper Willy Gueret. Gueret was signed for free from French club Le Mans after a brilliant display of goalkeeping in pre-season and, with Nigel Spink not having his contract renewed, was brought in to challenge Warner for the goalkeeper's jersey. Also leaving with Spink was Brian Law, who also failed to have his contract renewed and who had not played since his injury and was forced to retire because of it.

Ricky Newman, who had been on loan at Reading since the end of the previous season, joined them for free on a permanent basis and Paul Shaw, who had seemed surplus to the management's requirements, left to join Gillingham in a £500,000 deal.

As well as the money from Shaw's transfer and the pre-season ticket sales there was another financial boost when just under £2 million was raised from a third share issue, although it was pointed out that the money was there not to buy players but mainly to keep the existing squad together.

The club brought back their blue shirts but strangely this was only as a change second strip and there were some changes to the laws that the players had to get used to. Although most of these were minor changes, the ten-yard rule, experimented with in the Auto Windscreens Shield, now became law in all matches.

The Lions were unbeaten in their pre-season matches that included playing two Division One sides. Norwich ended with a 1-1 draw and Crystal Palace were humiliated by a 6-0 drubbing; yet McLeary was not happy. 'We thought that the lads were over playing and the quality of crosses and shots were not good enough,' he stated. This was somewhat at odds to Stevens who said, 'I'm not really bothered about the results but the performances have been of a good quality.'

Of course it was the performances in the league that would matter and the first match on 12 August, at home to promotion rivals Reading, was just the tonic Millwall needed.

They started without Sadlier, who had broken his arm in pre-season training, Ifill, with a torn hamstring and Dyche, who was still unavailable. Tuttle started as captain. The 2-0 victory was a stroll in the sunshine and with Cahill scoring both goals (he could have had three but another was ruled out for a push) and without placing too much judgement on the first game of the season, things were going according to plan.

There was one change to the starting line up for the away match at Notts County; Gilkes came in for the injured Kinet, but what a game it was. Moody had opened the scoring after fourteen minutes and seen another shot hit the crossbar, before County equalised. Then Reid, with his first goal for the club on his 50th League appearance, and Harris gave the Lions a two-goal half-time lead. Two goals from County levelled the game until Bircham, on as a substitute, scored in the ninetieth minute. Two games, six goals, six points and sitting top of the table; what more could anyone ask?

Three times in as many years Millwall had drawn Brighton in a cup competition and this time they were playing the first leg of the Worthington Cup at the Withdean Stadium. With Moody injured and Harris forced to leave the field after just twenty-three minutes the Lions had a young strike force in Braniff and Tyne, both making their debuts. Little wonder that everyone was pleased with the 2-1 win. Braniff and Livermore scored from outside the box.

They fell foul to a goal attributed to the ten-yard rule. A free-kick, perhaps harshly given, was argued over by Tuttle who received a yellow card and the ball was moved forward ten yards and into the penalty area. Millwall assumed the kick was now indirect. It was not, and Watson crashed it into the net with the Millwall defence complaining.

Harris and Moody were back for the next game, at home to Wycombe, and Harris scored to give Millwall the lead on ten minutes. But from there on things started to go wrong. Braniff had already replaced Moody when, just after half-time, Tuttle was stretchered off with concussion trying to stop Wycombe's equaliser. It got worse as Harris also left the pitch still suffering from his stomach problem. A clear penalty claim had been ignored, when Wycombe took the lead and Livermore was sent off. Braniff had a goal disallowed because Tyne was in an offside position and then Reid was also sent off.

With the Wigan and Bristol Rovers matches cancelled, which helped in getting some of the injured players fit again, the second leg of the Worthington Cup against Brighton saw an amazing chip from Kinet for his first goal for the Lions. Millwall went through to the next round with a 1-1 draw, although Brighton were unlucky not to have forced extra time.

Worried about the loss of their strikers, Leon Constantine was signed from Edgware for a nominal fee and he made his debut as a substitute in the away match at Peterborough. They also signed Sam Parkin on loan from Chelsea but he did not feature until the match against Oxford.

Before that there were other matches to play. Harris was back and scored in the 1-0 home win over Swansea with a goal in the last minute. A defeat at The Den, 0-1 to Northampton, saw the team sliding down the table and they were now in twelfth place after being in top spot.

There was obviously something wrong and it was not just that some players were injured. The team was not playing with the same conviction as they had been at the start of the season. The fans knew it and had started to barrack some of the players and David Tuttle in particular. When they took the field against Brentford at Griffin Park with an obviously unfit Paul Ifill as Harris' striking partner there was a feeling of despair in the air.

A 1-1 draw against a side finding a win hard to come by, and the goal a scrappy one from Harris, was nothing to get excited about. The boos from the Lions fans showed that. Something had to change and soon. It changed the following day when the sacking of Stevens and McLeary was announced. The question now was who would take over and how would the team respond when they had to play high-flying Premiership side Ipswich in just two days time in the next round of the Worthington Cup. All was soon to be revealed.

It was difficult for the management duo to leave, especially for Stevens who had been with the club since the age of ten, but they had left behind a legacy of some young talented footballers. The new man in charge would be the recipient of a squad that could be moulded into a championship-winning side.

Explaining the sacking Paphitis said, 'It was a hard decision but once the board had made up their mind at the board meeting on Friday I said I wanted to tell them myself personally and the only opportunity was to do it on Sunday morning.' Then he added the reason why they went, saying, 'It is critical that we go up this season but we felt because of the inconsistency we are suffering at the moment we were in danger of not making it.'

'My heart will always be at The Den,' said a departing Stevens and his words were echoed by McLeary, who said, 'I won't be away from The Den completely. I will still go to a few games just to see how the lads are getting on.'

They got on pretty well in the first leg against Ipswich, with Ray Harford temporarily in charge of the team. It might have been backs-to-the-wall stuff at times – Tony Warner produced some heroic saves – but goals from Ifill and Cahill gave the Lions a 2-0 win that showed what they were made of. They left the fans with something to cheer and gave Ipswich something to think about before the return leg.

Before that there was a league game to play and if the Lions wanted to make a statement about themselves they certainly did it in this game. Beating Oxford 5-0 was not just a win, it was a symbolic demolition of the side at the bottom of the table. The minnows were not going to be Millwall's banana skin anymore.

The match itself saw the debut of on-loan striker Sam Parkin and he put the Lions in front after just two minutes. He scored another and Harris helped himself to a hat-trick, but it was the quality of an all-round team performance that lifted the fans and put the team into the right frame of mind for a piece of giant-killing at Portman Road the following Tuesday. Three decisions from referee Andy Hall and some very tired legs prevented it from happening.

There had been many names rumoured to be the new manager but although he was at the Ipswich game he did not take charge of the team until the game at Peterborough. It was not any of the people who had been touted for the position; it was Mark McGhee.

The match itself had been mainly one-way traffic as Ipswich threw everything at the Millwall goal. The Lions cause was not helped when Harris left the field injured after just thirteen minutes. Then the referee took a hand. Dolan brought down Reuser in the box. It was a penalty, perhaps, but a booking never. But Mr Hall decided that a yellow card was necessary. Having already been given a yellow card earlier, Dolan was sent off.

Warner saved Magilton's spot kick and the fans began to think that the impossible could happen, even though the ten men of Millwall were practically entrenched around their own penalty area. So when Reid tacked Bramble, a reckless tackle and worthy of a yellow card, Mr Hall decided it was worth red. Reid received a four-match ban that was later rescinded on appeal. Being down to nine men made life very difficult and a minute later Ipswich had scored. It was not enough and with just three minutes left they equalised, although Johnson's punch on the ball that helped it hit the bar and rebound into play was missed by the officials.

Cahill could still have won the tie for the Lions and it took a great save from Richard Wright to keep the ball out of the net. And so into extra time where tired legs from being two players short were never going to withstand the onslaught.

There was still time for the bizarre sight of Cahill just standing on the halfway line when the referee deemed that he could not leave the pitch as eight men were needed to complete the game. A 0-5 score did not really tell the tale but that is how the statistics will show it. Sean Dyche had made a welcome return to the side, if only as a substitute, but he, along with the others in the team that night, had played heroically. Now they had to pick themselves up for the trip to Peterborough and McGhee's first game in charge. With the exertions of the cup-tie and the resulting despondency of the result it could have proved difficult, especially without all three of the team's first-choice strikers, but that was not how things turned out.

Nobody needed to have worried; Peterborough were well beaten 4-1 with goals from Dolan, Parkin, Cahill and Neill, who was back from representing Australia in the Olympic Games. In fact, his goal would be a contender for goal of the season and he had a hand in the other three. 'The squad is everything I thought it would be,' said McGhee, adding, 'I admit that I have a lot to prove to the fans. I hope I can win the confidence of the fans and players by getting the right results.' He had certainly started the right way.

It would be hard to continue in that type of winning form and a midday kick-off at Luton the following Sunday was proof that the season was to be no walkover. The team would have to put in the effort to get anything they got and they were grateful for the 1-0 win courtesy of a late own goal.

Next came Bury, who were second in the table and the Lions made short shrift of them with a 4-0 win. Two goals from Harris and one each from Neill and Livermore capped a fine display. Now having set themselves a high standard the players had to keep it up. The match also saw the return of Sadlier and Fitzgerald who both played a part as substitutes. Unfortunately Fitzgerald's display was not good enough to win him a regular place in the side so he moved to Colchester on a free to gain a regular first-team spot just three days later.

On the same day the Lions entertained Bristol City at The Den. Although it was an entertaining match – Parkin had put them in front after just three minutes – Millwall found it hard going against a side that packed the midfield. They conceded a late goal for a 1-1 draw.

Disappointed but not despondent they travelled to Stoke but once again a last-minute defensive lapse saw the Lions defeated 2-3. They had taken a first-minute lead through Harris and were behind before fifteen minutes were on the clock. Harris levelled the scoring before half-time but that old last-minute problem saw the point disappear.

Two goals from Richard Sadlier were enough to secure a 2-0 win at Swindon and the promotion push was back on track. It was not easy, especially after the referee had sent off Swindon striker Andy Williams – booked for diving – but it was a welcome return to winning ways. Meanwhile young goalkeeper Phil Smith was sent on loan to Walton & Hersham to gain more experience.

Sadlier scored two more and Harris one in the 3-1 win over Cambridge, but it could have been closer if Warner had not saved a penalty awarded after Alex Russell went down in the box having been touched by nothing more than a puff of air. If Andy Williams had seen it he would be wondering about the inconsistency of referees, but that really is another book.

Now they needed to make a strike for the top although it would have to be done the hard way as five of their next six league matches were away from home. They could do it though, with Steve Gritt now appointed as assistant manager to McGhee. A 1-1 draw at Port Vale, Livermore the scorer, and a 0-1 defeat at table-topping Wigan had left the Lions sitting comfortably in the play-off zone. Next up were Wrexham; it was the only game in this sequence at The Den. It may have taken Paul Moody to come off the bench to head home the winner in this 1-0 game but the Lions were sheer class. How the scoreline stayed that way is anyone's guess.

Having been on the bench himself for the last five games, Sam Parkin returned to Chelsea. Even though he had fulfilled his purpose of cover while Sadlier and Moody were regaining fitness it would have been good to have retained him.

The FA Cup first round had been a stumbling block for some time and being drawn away to Conference side Leigh RMI could have been another tie to fall at, but the non-League outfit asked for the game to be played at The Den. The Manchester outfit came to London and showed some grit and determination but after Harris had put the Lions in front from the penalty spot after one minute it was no contest. Further goals from Bircham and Moody wound up the 3-0 scoreline, which perhaps flattered Millwall. But at least they had laid to rest the ghost of first round defeats.

Back to league action and next was a trip to Bristol Rovers, a game put back twenty-four hours because of the cup fixtures. It was good to get a 2-1 win here with another early goal from Harris and the other from Reid. But without the sacrifice made by Nethercott, sent off for a professional foul, it could have been two points lost. Winning ways continued with a 1-0 win at Oldham, where Cahill was the scorer and Millwall had steadily climbed to the top of the table, even if two denied penalty claims would have made the game safer.

They came off the run when they went to Rotherham but the 2-3 defeat again hides the story behind the game. It was another late goal that gave the Millers all three points but how that goal came about was a matter of contention. Having gone behind, the Lions had taken the lead with two Reid goals and then given away a poor goal for the equaliser. Defending a Rotherham attack, the referee failed to give a free-kick when Nethercott was clearly pulled back

Richard Sadlier slots home the only goal against Port Vale.

by the neck. As the ball went out of play he also gave the throw in to Rotherham, even though it was clear that the ball had come off of Rotherham's Paul Hurst. Still complaining about both incidents they failed to clear the ball and the game was lost.

There were now two home cup-ties to play. The first was the LDV Vans Trophy, which had succeeded the Auto Windscreen Shield. Northampton were the visitors when Willy Gueret finally made his Millwall debut and the Cobblers were seen off 4-1 with goals from Sadlier and a hat-trick from Kinet. It was the first cup-tie hat-trick since 1980 when John Lyons scored one.

The second was an FA Cup match against Wycombe Wanderers the following Sunday. The pitch was in an awful state and the rainstorm just before the game made it worse. Referee Uriah Rennie was at his pickiest, and two teams that looked as though they did not want to be there compounded the problem. The result was always going to be 0-0, although a Moody shot that hit the post and a Sadlier effort that hit the bar would have changed things.

Back to league action and the visit to The Den of Walsall, who had to wear Millwall's away kit having left theirs behind. They were swiftly dispatched 2-0 with goals from Bircham and Reid, who had now answered his critics with plenty of goals and the teams swapped places in the table. The Lions were not going to give up the number one position without a fight.

Two disallowed goals and one from Dolan in the 1-2 cup reply defeat at Wycombe hurt but it was the league title that Millwall wanted and they demonstrated it with a classic 2-1 win at Bournemouth. Kinet and Harris supplied the goals but it was a good all-round performance.

There was a seven-goal thriller when Colchester came to The Den on Boxing Day and the Essex club scored only one of them, courtesy of a Robbie Ryan own goal. Neil Harris scored a hat-trick and made two more for Moody and another for Ifill but the whole team were awesome.

When they lost 2-3 to Notts County in the last game of the year they were twice a goal down, coming back through Ifill and Moody. A show of stupidity from Kinet brought him a red card and it finally became too much for the Lions to hold on for a point. They lost to a last-minute goal.

So at the end of the year they were where they started the season, in first place, even if they had taken a dip down in between. The question now was could they stay there?

The first match of the New Year was at Reading. The New Year's Day game at Wycombe had been called off because of the weather and the Royals had promised to make life difficult for their old manager and his new side. Millwall answered them in the best way possible by taking a four-goal lead, three from Harris and an own goal from Newman. Though the final score was 4-3 Millwall were never in any real danger of losing the game.

The Lions lost 2-3 on penalties after a goal-less home game against Swindon in the second round of the LDV Vans Trophy but the competition had become a distraction to their league efforts that continued with three home games in a row. This was made possible because the away match at Colchester had been called off because of a frozen pitch.

Neil Harris unleashes a typical curling shot for the only goal of the game against Swindon Town.

The first was against Wigan but there were concerns over the state of The Den pitch, which was looking like a bog, particularly in front of the West Stand. 'The pitch is a concern for us,' admitted McGhee. 'We might need to adapt our game and simplify things but whatever state it turns out to be in at kick-off it will be the same for Wigan and we are going to have to deal with it.' They dealt with it well and ran out worthy 3-1 winners with a Moody hat-trick, although the sending off of Haworth after half an hour helped.

Next came Bournemouth but the 0-1 reverse knocked the Lions off top spot. They were back there again though after beating Bristol Rovers 3-0 in the next game. The goals came from Cahill, Moody and Harris but the Lions had to play with ten men after Cahill had been sent off after half an hour.

This match also saw Willy Gueret play his first league game, not because McGhee had lost faith in Warner but because he was worried that should something happen to his number one stopper Gueret would not be ready to take over. So he remained in goal for the next seven games and proved a more than an adequate replacement. However, you cannot legislate for injuries and it was Joe Dolan who suffered a broken leg when his studs caught in the pitch in a collision with Robbie Ryan after just ten minutes that needed replacing.

McGhee was feeling upbeat about the promotion possibilities of the team. 'I strongly believe that if you took this team as it stands and transferred them into Division One they would not be out of place,' he said, and they were soon to be tested as to their qualifications for a place in that division.

Ifill's goal was enough for a 1-0 win at Colchester and a 0-0 draw at Swansea was followed by a 1-0 win over Brentford at The Den, with Cahill scoring in his last game before his ban. It was backs-to-the-wall stuff at times in all three games but the points were what mattered and the march to Division One continued.

Was it nerves or was the strain starting to tell when the Lions threw away a two-goal lead to draw 3-3 at Northampton? It had started so well when Moody and Harris had put Millwall in front but with just three minutes to go they found themselves 2-3 behind. Ex-Lion Dave Savage scored twice from the penalty spot. It was Kinet who, having been on the pitch for just three minutes, grabbed a point with a diving header and saved the night.

Goals from Moody and Livermore provided a 2-0 win at Oxford but a 0-0 draw at home to Peterborough and a 1-2 defeat at Bury, Harris scoring and the dreaded last-minute goal making a comeback, started the nerves shaking again.

Nethercott's goal was enough to give the Lions a 1-0 win over Luton but then disaster struck. It was not just losing 1-2 (Harris scoring again) that was the main problem, although losing three points at this stage of the season was bad enough, but after City had Thorpe sent off Moody

Division Two championship celebrations at the New Den in May 2001.

along with City's Beadle and then Harris were also condemned to an early bath. How would the team respond and what would McGhee do now having lost the first-choice strike force at such a critical time? He brought Steve Claridge in on loan from Portsmouth and Tony Cottee from Barnet until the end of the season and appealed against Moody's red card. Fortunately the ban was overturned.

A 0-0 draw at Wycombe, where Cottee made his debut and became the first striker to play in all four English divisions in the same season, and another at Walsall meant the Lions had won only one game in March. They were now second in the table. Who said the manager of the month award, won by McGhee in April, is not cursed?

Four home games in eleven days followed, two of them against fellow promotion contenders. The first was against Stoke, with Claridge making his debut, and goals from Sadlier and Cahill secured a 2-0 win.

The Rotherham game was this season's Anti-Racism Focus match, the fourth to be held. The Millers left the top-of-the-table clash wondering what had hit them as they were torn apart with goals from Cahill, Reid and two from Claridge, his first for the club. A 4-0 win was a let off for Rotherham. It could easily have been many more and they had Alan Moore sent off as well.

It was a tense night but Sadlier's goal was enough for the 1-0 win over Port Vale and Harris came off the bench to curl a wonder goal into the corner of a stubborn Swindon's net for a 1-0 win. An Ifill hat-trick along with goals from Nethercott and Claridge saw off Cambridge 5-1 at the Abbey and so to Wrexham.

Colchester 2, Reading 1. When that result came through everyone knew that Tim Cahill's goal in the 1-1 draw at Wrexham was enough to get promotion. Now there was only one thing left, the championship. It came in style, against Oldham at The Den.

Two goals each from Moody and Harris and another from Reid capped a great performance and the 5-0 victory was no more than the Lions deserved. Harris' second goal, a last-minute penalty, made him joint top scorer in the division with Reading's Jamie Cureton and the champagne flowed. McGhee was sure that the squad were good enough to perform well in Division One and now they had the opportunity to prove it.

2000/01   Football League Division Two

Date		Opposition	Score	Scorers
Aug	12	READING	2-0	Cahill (2)
	19	Notts County	4-3	Moody, Reid, Harris, Bircham
	26	WYCOMBE WANDERERS	1-2	Harris
Sept	9	SWANSEA CITY	1-0	Harris
	12	NORTHAMPTON TOWN	0-1	
	16	Brentford	1-1	Harris
	23	OXFORD UNITED	5-0	Harris (3), Parkin (2)
	30	Peterborough United	4-1	Dolan, Neill, Parkin, Cahill
Oct	8	Luton Town	1-0	Opp OG
	14	BURY	4-0	Harris (2), Neill, Livermore
	17	BRISTOL CITY	1-1	Parkin
	21	Stoke City	2-3	Harris (2)
	24	Swindon Town	2-0	Sadlier (2)
	28	CAMBRIDGE UNITED	3-1	Sadlier (2), Harris
Nov	4	Port Vale	1-1	Livermore
	7	Wigan Athletic	0-1	
	11	WREXHAM	1-0	Moody
	22	Bristol Rovers	2-1	Harris, Reid
	25	Oldham Athletic	1-0	Cahill
Dec	2	Rotherham United	2-3	Reid (2)
	16	WALSALL	2-0	Bircham, Reid
	23	Bournemouth	2-1	Kinet, Harris
	26	COLCHESTER UNITED	6-1	Harris (3) (1 pen), Moody (2), Ifill
	30	NOTTS COUNTY	2-3	Ifill, Moody
Jan	6	Reading	4-3	Harris (3) (1 pen), Opp OG
	13	WIGAN ATHLETIC	3-1	Moody (3)
	27	BOURNEMOUTH	0-1	
Feb	3	BRISTOL ROVERS	3-0	Cahill, Moody, Harris (pen)
	6	Colchester United	1-0	Ifill
	11	Swansea City	0-0	
	16	BRENTFORD	1-0	Cahill
	20	Northampton Town	3-3	Harris, Moody, Kinet
	24	Oxford United	2-0	Moody, Livermore
Mar	3	PETERBOROUGH UNITED	0-0	
	6	Bury	1-2	Harris
	10	LUTON TOWN	1-0	Nethercott
	16	Bristol City	1-2	Harris (pen)
	27	Wycombe Wanderers	0-0	
	31	Walsall	0-0	
Apr	3	STOKE CITY	2-0	Sadlier, Cahill
	7	ROTHERHAM UNITED	4-0	Claridge (2), Cahill, Reid
	11	PORT VALE	1-0	Sadlier
	14	SWINDON TOWN	1-0	Harris
	17	Cambridge United	5-1	Ifill (3), Nethercott, Claridge
	28	WREXHAM	1-1	Cahill
May	5	OLDHAM ATHLETIC	5-0	Moody (2), Harris (2) (1 pen), Reid

League Cup

Round	Date		Opposition	Score	Scorers
1/1	Aug	22	Brighton & Hove Albion	2-1	Braniff, Livermore
1/2	Sept	5	BRIGHTON & HOVE ALBION	1-1	Kinet
2/1		19	IPSWICH TOWN	2-0	Ifill, Cahill
2/2		26	Ipswich Town	0-5	

Associate Members Cup

Round	Date		Opposition	Score	Scorers
1	Dec	5	NORTHAMPTON TOWN	4-1	Kinet 3 (1 pen), Sadlier
2	Jan	9	SWINDON TOWN	0-0*	

*a.e.t Millwall lost on penalties

FA Cup

Round	Date		Opposition	Score	Scorers
1	Nov	19	Leigh RMI	3-0	Harris (pen), Bircham, Moody
2	Dec	10	WYCOMBE WANDERERS	0-0	
2R		19	Wycombe Wanderers	1-2	Dolan

2000/01　　　　Football League Division Two

	P	W	D	L	F	A	Pts
MILLWALL	46	28	9	9	89	38	93
Rotherham United	46	27	10	9	79	55	91
Reading	46	25	11	10	86	52	86
Walsall	46	23	12	11	79	50	81
Stoke City	46	21	14	11	74	49	77
Wigan Athletic	46	19	18	9	53	42	75
Bournemouth	46	20	13	13	79	55	73
Notts County	46	19	12	15	62	66	69
Bristol City	46	18	14	14	70	56	68
Wrexham	46	17	12	17	65	71	63
Port Vale	46	16	14	16	55	49	62
Peterborough United	46	15	14	17	61	66	59
Wycombe Wanderers	46	15	14	17	46	53	59
Brentford	46	14	17	15	56	70	59
Oldham Athletic	46	15	13	18	53	65	58
Bury	46	16	10	20	45	59	58
Colchester United	46	15	12	19	55	59	57
Northampton Town	46	15	12	19	46	59	57
Cambridge United	46	14	11	21	61	77	53
Swindon Town	46	13	13	20	47	65	52
Bristol Rovers	46	12	15	19	53	57	51
Luton Town	46	9	13	24	52	80	40
Swansea City	46	8	13	25	47	73	37
Oxford United	46	7	6	33	53	100	27

Triumphs and Disasters 2001/02

The question on everyone's lips as the season started was how would the Lions fare now they were back in Division One? Opinion was divided. Some thought that the side would do well and even more thought that they would hold their own, maybe managing a mid-table position. But perhaps the majority thought that it would be an exciting adventure that should be enjoyed, as the team would be relegated at the end of the season. This group grew with the knowledge that they would be taking on Division One defences without Neil Harris, who had been diagnosed as having testicular cancer and would be out of contention for the entire season. This diagnosis had been announced just after Harris had signed a new five-year contract and was a devastating blow to the player as well as all associated with the club.

The Neil Harris Everyman Cancer Appeal was set up to promote awareness of testicular cancer and fund-raising events were held throughout the season. It did not stop the fans coming though as advance season ticket sales smashed through the £1 million barrier by the beginning of July.

The new shirt sponsors were the electrical company 24seven. The home shirt reverted to blue, the away went green and a white third strip was revealed while the team was on the tour bus that took them around the area in celebration of their championship win on 7 July.

Leaving the club were Jamie Stuart to Bury, Bobby Bowry to Colchester United, Leon Cort to Southend United, Tommy Tyne, Phil Smith, Byron Bubb and Michael Gilkes all for free while Tony Cottee retired and took up media work. Steve Claridge had problems with Portsmouth about letting him go but he finally arrived on a one-year contract before the season started along with Giovanni Savarese, who was released by Swansea, on three-month contract. Nethercott, Ifill, Ryan, Reid, Livermore, Dolan, Warner, Gueret, Lawrence, Bull, Cahill and Sadlier all signed new improved deals throughout the season. Joe McLaughlin was appointed reserve team manager and Alan McLeary returned as Under-17 coach. The Millwall Museum went to the Cumming Museum, SE17 and the exhibition of memorabilia was well supported during its time there.

It was hoped that the new ITV Digital sport channel would bring more money into the game as it had bought the rights to show live matches in the Nationwide Leagues. An important rule change was made that allowed players who were shown a red card, with the exception of one shown for violent conduct, in a non-first-team game not to have it counted for first team purposes.

Millwall had a good pre-season, even though a trip to Germany had two games called off, which disrupted the schedule. The last of which, and their only home pre-season game, was a benefit match against Spurs for Keith Stevens. A crowd of over 16,000 showed the high esteem in which he was held by the Millwall faithful.

The season opened with a home game against Norwich on 11 August and was preceded by The Walk of Awareness, a fund-raising event for Harris' cancer appeal. Almost 300 fans raised around £10,000 with some walking more than sixty miles. Goals from Claridge, Reid – a goal of the season contender if ever there was one – Cahill and Neill gave the Lions a comfortable 4-0 win and made all that walking worthwhile. If this was Division One then more please.

The next match, at St Andrews and put back a day on police advice, had the same score but this time it was the Lions on the end of a beating by Birmingham. It included a penalty miss by Sadlier. The learning curve had to start now and quickly.

Fortunately, a break from league action followed with the tie against Cardiff in the first round of the Worthington Cup, this season played with just single legs. Goals from Sadlier and Claridge took the Lions through to the next round with a 2-1 win, but it was not easy and they soon found out that life in the league would not be a bed of roses either.

Their next match was at home to Burnley, which they lost 0-2, but they had at least four good penalty appeals turned down and hit the woodwork twice. The most contentious decision of referee David Pugh came at the end of the match. A handball by Burnley's Lee Briscoe saw Mr Pugh award a penalty, change his mind and make it a free-kick outside the box and then send off Steven Reid when the players argued with the assistant referee about the decision. Savarese, making his Division One debut, would have been as disappointed as the rest of the team.

They lost the next game 0-1 away to Crewe. That late-goal syndrome was still not vanquished and a mini disaster loomed. A good performance was needed at Crystal Palace and that was just what the team gave, although the eleven-day break they had when the home game with Watford was cancelled due to international call-ups helped. Goals from Sadlier and two from Claridge gave the Lions a 3-1 win over their south-east London rivals, much to the delight of Millwall's fans. Midfielder Phil Stamp, who had joined Millwall on loan from Middlesbrough, made his debut in the match while striker Leon Constantine was going out on loan to Leyton Orient. Lucas Neill, who had gone on a three-day trial with Blackburn, signed for them for a £1 million fee.

The performance was not as good at Priestfield and Moody's goal was not enough to keep the Lions in the Worthington Cup. Gillingham went through 1-2 with yet another late goal being Millwall's undoing. A 0-1 league defeat at Preston, where young defender Mark Phillips made his debut, gave the merchants of doom something to crow about, especially as Stamp, who had injured himself in the Gillingham match, went back to Middlesbrough for treatment and never returned.

It was good to get back to The Den after four matches away from home. It was a bonus to have Neil Harris on the bench for the Barnsley game, having played a few reserve games. His just sitting there inspired the Lions, who came from behind to win 3-1. The goals came from Claridge (2) and Cahill. Harris received a standing ovation when he took to the field on sixty-one minutes when replacing Sadlier. 'It's just a great feeling to be back again,' he said.

Harris stayed on the bench when goals from Nethercott and Kinet gave Millwall an impressive 2-0 home win over Sheffield United but he played a part in the 2-2 draw at Wimbledon. Cahill and a twenty-yard free-kick from Reid, which was now becoming his trademark, gave the Lions a creditable draw.

A 0-0 draw with Walsall, where Charlie Hearn made his first team debut, followed and then came Millwall's first outing on ITV Digital when they travelled to West Bromwich Albion.

Again the Lions had extra time to prepare for the match as the home game with Manchester City had been called off. Once more this was because of players being away on international duty. They used this extra time well, getting to know new central defender Darren Ward, who had been brought in from Watford at a cost of £500,000 and who made his debut in the match. The extra rest helped them to a 2-0 win, with two Sadlier goals in the first half securing the win.

Strangely they got another break from playing as the rearranged Watford match was called off due to a fire in nearby Bolina Road, when some gas cylinders exploded in a coach workshop on the afternoon of the match. This meant that it was Nottingham Forest who next came to The Den. What a game it was.

Cahill had put the Lions in front and things stayed that way until the hour mark when Stern John put Forest ahead. Paul Ifill, on his twenty-second birthday, scored the equaliser with just four minutes left, but two minutes later John had completed his hat-trick. It looked all over but you can never count a side out when Steve Claridge is in it. Forest's goalkeeper, Ward, fumbled his cross and Sadlier was on hand to poke the ball home. Debutant Ryan Green, signed from Wolves on a free, must have been gasping for breath like the 14,154 crowd after that finish and on his twenty-first birthday as well.

The 3-1 win over Bradford City that followed looked like an easy game but it was far from that. The score could have been different as both teams hit the woodwork and had goals disallowed. Claridge also had a penalty saved but a Sadlier goal and another two from Cahill were enough to win it.

The trip to Stockport was as easy as the 4-0 scoreline suggests and the goals from Cahill, Reid – another long-range free-kick – and two from Claridge (one a penalty), could easily have been added to. It was also the last time that Savarese would feature for the Lions, as the option on his contract was not taken up.

Losing to a last-minute goal at Wolves the following Wednesday was bad enough; that the score was 0-1 and it was a header from ex-Lion Alex Rae made it even more galling. But the Lions picked themselves up to beat second-placed Coventry 3-2 at The Den the following Saturday but again they had to come from behind. They had taken the lead through Claridge, equalised through Kinet ten minutes from time and this time were grateful for a last-minute goal, which was scored by Sadlier after Coventry's David Thompson had been sent off just two minutes earlier.

Willy Gueret got a piece of league action against Rotherham although it came in an unexpected way when referee Paul Alcock insisted Tony Warner and Rotherham's Chris Swailes leave the pitch after a clash left them both bleeding. The game, brought forward to Friday night due to weekend internationals, ended 1-0 with Cahill scoring in a hard-fought game.

Even though it took a last-minute goal from Claridge and he had another disallowed, added to one scored earlier by Sadlier that earned a 2-2 draw at Grimsby, the players knew they had thrown away two points having missed numerous chances. They did so again at home to Gillingham when, after taking the lead through Cahill, they lost 1-2. A late goal once more was the problem. Perhaps it was playing against a side wearing your own away strip that did it. Gillingham had packed the wrong colour shirts, which confused them.

Late goals had started to become a habit, both conceding and scoring them, and never was this more clearly shown than in the 2-1 win at Bradford. Having led until the last minute through a Claridge goal they gave away an equaliser only for Dyche to win the game, with his first goal for the club, just seconds later.

Young goalkeeper Chad Harpur signed from Leeds following a short trial and watched a controversial rescheduled match with Manchester City. City had none of their fans allowed in the stadium due to the problems between the clubs the last time that they met. Bircham had already had a goal disallowed when City took the lead, which they held until the stroke of half-time when Sadlier equalised. The visitors took the lead again, through Huckerby, who then applauded an empty stand where the City fans would have been. Millwall equalised when they were awarded a penalty, given by the referee's assistant and perhaps dubiously, which Claridge scored. Kevin Keegan was sent from the dugout for complaining about the decision. Losing the match 2-3 you can live with but again it was a late goal and this time it was brought about because of Millwall's own lack of thought.

Searching for the winning goal they took a quick corner that failed to come off and with most of the team in the opposing penalty area there was only ever going to be one outcome. Huckerby raced away with the ball and passed to Sean Wright-Phillips. 'I didn't think they were better than us and we let ourselves down by taking a free-kick too quickly when we were not set up for it,' said McGhee. 'Until that third goal went in I thought we were the only team left in it and if anyone was going to score it would have been us.'

It was perhaps not a tragedy yet, but the Lions had slipped out of the play-off positions into ninth place, giving rise to thoughts of a complete collapse to some. Neil Harris had not been used since the Wimbledon game back in September. He had not properly recovered from his

A programme cover from
the 2001/02 season.

illness and was used sparingly throughout the season, but he was on the bench again for the trip to Sheffield Wednesday and played his part in the 1-1 draw. But it took a late goal from Sadlier and a penalty save from Warner to get a point.

He was on the bench again for the televised home game with Portsmouth and once more Sadlier scored a late goal. This time it secured a 1-0 win but neither of them could do anything in the 0-0 draw at Burnley.

Harris was in the starting line-up for the Boxing Day match at home to Crystal Palace as McGhee tried a three-man strike force, with scintillating results. Three goals in a five-minute second-half spell, two from Sadlier, the other from Claridge, gave the Lions a stroll for the rest of the afternoon and a 3-0 win. It was certainly a triumph for the Lions' followers, who could not have been given a better Christmas present.

With Cahill and Reid supplying the goals in the 2-0 win over Crewe that followed, the Lions finished the year in fifth place in the table. This was beyond the wildest dreams of most of their fans, who now began to believe that they were seeing something special and praying that it was not all going to crumble before their eyes.

New Year's Day at Watford is not many people's idea of a good time but a 4-1 win made it worthwhile for Lions fans. Harris was back on the bench for this match. McGhee was gradually easing him back to the high standards he had set himself, and he was looking on as the Lions took a three-goal lead courtesy of Cahill, Sadlier and Reid. Watford had pulled one back and had Vega sent off, when with three minutes left Harris was introduced to the fray.

Picking up the ball on the halfway line he feinted inside and outside of his marker and then curled the ball into the top corner of the goal. The entire team came to celebrate, lifting him high on their shoulders. The Millwall fans sang their delight and it was certainly Harris' own personal

Neil Harris has just scored his best goal for Millwall at Watford on New Year's Day 2002 and proved, much to the delight of his teammates, that he has recovered from serious illness.

triumph. 'It was one of my better goals,' said Harris, 'and because of the circumstances the best goal I've ever scored. It was just ecstasy. I'll never forget it.' Neither will anyone else connected with the club. What a way to celebrate your 150th appearance!

Now it was time to take a break from league action and take on Scunthorpe in the FA Cup. The Division Three side put up a strong challenge before losing 2-1, the Lions scoring both of their goals through Sadlier. At least being in Division One there were no worries about being knocked out in the first two rounds this time. This was the first time Millwall had beaten Scunthorpe in the competition – it was the sixth attempt.

The money was pouring in for the Neil Harris Everyman Appeal and on the pitch activities were going well too. Birmingham arrived at The Den for the Thursday night televised match and the goal that Dyche scored in the 1-1 draw moved the Lions into third place. The game itself was full of incidents both on and off of the pitch, including Birmingham's Woodhouse being sent off, both managers being sent from the dugouts and the intrusion of a meat pie onto the pitch.

The team moved a place higher when Watford arrived in SE16 the following Tuesday. The visitors were not in the mood to let the Lions have things their own way as they had done on New Year's Day. The sending off of Glass for handball after half an hour and Helguson in the last minute for a terrible tackle on Green only increased their determination and it took a Claridge penalty to gain a 1-0 win in a scrappy game.

In the next game, for the third match in a row the Lions had an opponent sent off. This time it was Russell, when they played Norwich at Carrow Road in yet another televised fixture. It did not help them though as the match ended 0-0. Once more the Lions were not able to turn their dominance into victory.

Lucas Neill was back at The Den when Blackburn Rovers came in the next round of the FA Cup. Willy Gueret made a rare start because of Warner's suspension but he could do nothing about Cole's late winner. Losing 0-1 to the Premiership side was no disgrace and the Lions had proven that they could live with the big boys if given the opportunity.

With his strike force depleted through injury, McGhee signed Richard Naylor on loan from Ipswich. He made his debut in the 0-2 defeat at Manchester City. The match was beamed back to The Den because Lions fans were banned from attending Maine Road. Millwall lost despite City having Benarbia sent off after just seven minutes; it was the fourth League match in a row that they had played against ten men. Warner saved a penalty but neither he nor the sending off could inspire the Lions.

Naylor only started one more game and warmed the bench for three more before returning to the East Anglia side. The match he started was at home to Walsall and it took a dubious late penalty from Harris, who had come off the bench, to give the Lions a share of the points in a 2-2 draw. Walsall had gone ahead in a similar way three minutes earlier, after Sadlier had put Millwall in front. Harris' goal was the 300th League goal scored in the 200th League game at the Lions' new home.

A 2-1 away win at Nottingham Forest, where Ifill and Cahill had given the Lions the lead, was only made possible by a terrific performance from Tony Warner. Millwall had one of those days when you play poorly but come away with all three points.

With the home game against West Bromwich put back to the Tuesday because the Baggies were involved in the FA Cup, Millwall took the opportunity to take a trip to Spain. The break did them some good as they returned to beat the Midlands club 1-0. Cahill's goal and Warner's penalty save kept the Lions in third place.

A side of the Millwall fans not often reported was seen before the Wimbledon match when they played a game against Middlesbrough supporters to raise money for the church where ex-player Colin Cooper's son Finlay had been buried. Finlay had tragically died after choking on a toy a few weeks earlier and the fans raised £3,000 towards the rebuilding of the church roof and then another £700 for the Lewisham Victim Support Scheme on the same day.

The Lions lost the match 0-1 but that was tempered by the announcement that financially the club were in a strong position although the hooligan element had started to raise its ugly head again. This was later to have a disastrous effect on the club.

Kinet's headed goal gave the Lions a 1-1 draw at Barnsley but the Tykes' penalty equaliser was one of a few contentious decisions from referee Mike Riley who, having quite correctly given the spot kick, then booked Warner for the legal action of cleaning his boots before the kick was taken. It looked like the Millwall custodian had saved the kick when the ball bounced back to almost the halfway line. The Barnsley fans did not cheer a goal and the assistant referee waved play on but Mr Riley signalled for a goal. The Barnsley fans cheered, the Millwall players protested but to no avail. Then with just a few seconds of the match remaining Matt Lawrence and Barnsley's Rankin were sent off for no more than pushing each other while waiting for a free-kick to be taken. It was a decision that brought Lawrence a four-match ban. 'The sending off was plain stupid,' said McGhee. 'We have got a great disciplinary record this year.' That was to change over the next three weeks.

Two Claridge goals gave Millwall a 2-1 win over Preston but they then went on a four-game losing streak that was almost a disaster for their promotion ambitions. First they lost 0-3 at Portsmouth, where Claridge missed a penalty, Kinet had a goal disallowed and no action was taken when Beasant handled a Harris chip shot outside the area. Then they lost 1-2 at home to Sheffield Wednesday where Sean Dyche scored a late consolation goal and midfielder Stephen McPhail, brought in on loan from Leeds, made his debut and was sent off. He played in only two more games.

Three days later they travelled to Sheffield United and were beaten 2-3 by the Blades, where defender Alan Dunne made his debut. Ifill and Nethercott scored the goals but once more the last-minute blues had descended on the Millwall defence as United scored twice in the last three minutes.

The televised game at Gillingham was lost 0-1 and the sending off of Kinet may well have played a part in the Lions losing a match that could have gone either way. The promotion dream was disappearing, for now Millwall had moved from third to sixth place. Something had to be done quickly to redress the situation. It was!

Whether it was inspiration or luck, McGhee brought in Dion Dublin on loan from Aston Villa and he promptly opened the scoring on his debut against Stockport. It was Millwall's fifth Anti-Racism match and he inspired the Lions to a 3-0 win. Nethercott and Ifill added late goals to clinch this victory that also saw the debut of Peter Sweeney. But Dublin could not inspire them to more than a 0-0 draw at Rotherham on April Fools day.

A disaster, not just for Millwall but all clubs outside of the Premiership, had been the announcement that ITV Digital was to be put into administration. Its subsequent closure and the loss of revenue – some £2 million in Millwall's case – was a devastating blow.

Television money did find its way into the Millwall coffers for the next two matches as they were both televised on a Friday night. Both games, at home to Wolves and then away to Coventry, were won 1-0. Steve Claridge scored on each occasion.

Needing just a point to guarantee a play-off place the Lions took all three by beating Grimsby 3-1 in the final league game of the season. A goal from Dublin sent them on their way and two more from Harris, taking his league tally to 70, gave the Lions fourth place in the table and a play-off against Birmingham. Whatever the outcome of the two-legged affair, the Lions had had a triumphant season, one well beyond the beliefs of all but their most ardent supporters and certainly the sceptics.

Both of the play-off matches were televised and both were hard fought, with no quarter asked or given. The Lions gave themselves every chance of progressing when a Dublin goal gave them a 1-1 draw to bring back to The Den.

Just like the first leg, this was an enthralling game that could have gone either way but just as everyone was getting ready for extra time and the possibility of the dreaded penalty shoot-out, disaster struck as Stern John fired home from a couple of yards. This took Birmingham through to the play-off final and eventually their place in the Premiership.

Yet a bigger disaster was waiting for the home fans among the 16,391 crowd that had stayed behind to applaud their heroes on a lap of honour. Indeed many of those fans would know nothing about what had happened outside the ground until they reached home later that night or in the morning when they read their newspapers.

Violence had erupted in the streets around the ground. About 100 police officers and 26 police horses were injured, cars were set on fire and property damaged. Whatever the reasons and whoever the perpetrators, the name of Millwall Football Club had again been dragged through the mire.

Just what the cost would be to the club financially, and how the players and fans would react to any sanctions that would be brought in because of the conduct of a mindless few, only time would tell, starting from now.

2001/02   Football League Division One

Date		Opposition	Score	Scorers
Aug	11	NORWICH CITY	4-0	Claridge, Reid, Cahill, Neill
	19	Birmingham City	0-4	
	25	BURNLEY	0-2	
	28	Crewe Alexandra	0-1	
Sept	8	Crystal Palace	3-1	Claridge (2), Sadlier
	15	Preston North End	0-1	
	18	BARNSLEY	3-2	Claridge (2), Cahill
	22	SHEFFIELD UNITED	2-0	Nethercott, Kinet
	25	Wimbledon	2-2	Cahill, Reid
	29	Walsall	0-0	
Oct	11	West Bromwich Albion	2-0	Sadlier (2)
	20	NOTTINGHAM FOREST	3-3	Cahill, Ifill, Sadlier
	23	BRADFORD CITY	3-1	Cahill (2), Sadlier
	27	Stockport County	4-0	Claridge (2) (1 pen), Cahill, Reid
	31	Wolverhampton Wanderers	0-1	
Nov	3	COVENTRY CITY	3-2	Claridge, Kinet, Sadlier
	9	ROTHERHAM UNITED	1-0	Cahill
	17	Grimsby Town	2-2	Sadlier, Claridge
	24	GILLINGHAM	1-2	Cahill
Dec	1	Bradford City	2-1	Claridge, Dyche
	4	MANCHESTER CITY	2-3	Sadlier, Claridge (pen)
	8	Sheffield Wednesday	1-1	Sadlier
	13	PORTSMOUTH	1-0	Sadlier
	22	Burnley	0-0	
	26	CRYSTAL PALACE	3-0	Sadlier (2), Claridge
	29	CREWE ALEXANDRA	2-0	Cahill, Reid
Jan	1	Watford	4-1	Cahill, Sadlier, Reid, Harris
	10	BIRMINGHAM CITY	1-1	Dyche
	15	WATFORD	1-0	Claridge (pen)
	20	Norwich City	0-0	
	30	Manchester City	0-2	
Feb	2	WALSALL	2-2	Sadlier, Harris (pen)
	9	Nottingham Forest	2-1	Ifill, Cahill
	19	WEST BROMWICH ALBION	1-0	Cahill
	23	WIMBLEDON	0-1	
Mar	2	Barnsley	1-1	Kinet
	5	PRESTON NORTH END	2-1	Claridge (2)
	9	Portsmouth	0-3	
	16	SHEFFIELD WEDNESDAY	1-2	Dyche
	19	Sheffield United	2-3	Ifill, Nethercott
	24	Gillingham	0-1	
	30	STOCKPORT COUNTY	3-0	Dublin, Nethercott, Ifill
Apr	1	Rotherham United	0-0	
	5	WOLVERHAMPTON WANDERERS	1-0	Claridge (pen)
	12	Coventry City	1-0	Claridge
	21	GRIMSBY TOWN	3-1	Harris (2), Dublin
Apr	28	Birmingham City	1-1	Dublin
May	2	BIRMINGHAM CITY	0-1	

League Cup

Round	Date	Opposition	Score	Scorers
1	Aug 21	CARDIFF CITY	2-1	Sadlier, Claridge (pen)
2	Sept 11	Gillingham	1-2	Moody

FA Cup

Round	Date	Opposition	Score	Scorers
3	Jan 5	SCUNTHORPE UNITED	2-1	Sadlier 2
4	26	BLACKBURN ROVERS	0-1	

2001/02   Football League Division One

	P	W	D	L	F	A	Pts
Manchester City	46	31	6	9	108	52	99
West Bromwich Albion	46	27	8	11	61	29	89
Wolverhampton Wanderers	46	25	11	10	76	43	86
MILLWALL	46	22	11	13	69	48	77
Birmingham City	46	21	13	12	70	49	76
Norwich City	46	22	9	15	60	51	75
Burnley	46	21	12	13	70	62	75
Preston North End	46	20	12	14	71	59	72
Wimbledon	46	18	13	15	63	57	67
Crystal Palace	46	20	6	20	70	62	66
Coventry City	46	20	6	20	59	53	66
Gillingham	46	18	10	18	64	67	64
Sheffield United	46	15	15	16	53	54	60
Watford	46	16	11	19	62	56	59
Bradford City	46	15	10	21	69	76	55
Nottingham Forest	46	12	18	16	50	51	54
Portsmouth	46	13	14	19	60	72	53
Walsall	46	13	12	21	51	71	51
Grimsby Town	46	12	14	20	50	72	50
Sheffield Wednesday	46	12	14	20	49	71	50
Rotherham United	46	10	19	17	52	66	49
Crewe Alexandra	46	12	13	21	47	76	49
Barnsley	46	11	15	20	59	86	48
Stockport County	46	6	8	32	42	102	26

Injurious Things
2002/03

The aftermath of the violence on 2 May was injurious to both the club and its true supporters. Threats of ground closure and police fines had an unsettling effect and the financial implications when added to the loss of income from the now defunct ITV Digital sports channel would have been devastating for the club. Thankfully these threats were never implemented but the club took action to try and rid itself of the perennial hooligan problem.

First it introduced a membership scheme that, although free of charge, meant fans had to produce photographic identification and proof of address in order not only to obtain a ticket, including ones to away matches, but also to enter the ground on match days.

Then it banned away fans from home matches that were known to attract trouble. These were Nottingham Forest, Leicester City, Wolverhampton Wanderers, Portsmouth, Stoke City and Burnley, although by the time Burnley came to The Den the club allowed their fans to attend and 209 did. There was a reciprocal arrangement made with these clubs although Portsmouth allowed Lions fans to attend and 872 took the opportunity of travelling to the South Coast club.

Of course all of this had an effect on the club as the cost of implementing the scheme, the loss of away revenue, fans who for whatever reason did not join the scheme and the loss of the casual supporter all took its toll.

However it was not just financially that the club suffered. Playing without travelling support affected the team and visiting sides in a similar situation seemed to respond well to it.

Nevertheless, finances play a part in any football club and this meant that some players' contracts were not renewed and the purchase of new players stopped, at least initially. The first to find themselves at new clubs were Sean Dyche, who went to Watford, Marc Bircham, who left to join Queens Park Rangers and Christophe Kinet, who was re-signed when the season started. Also leaving were Leon Constantine for Brentford, Leke Odunsi, who went on loan to Colchester for the season and eventually had his contract cancelled and Ryan Green. Dion Dublin returned to Aston Villa, his successful loan period over.

The only players coming into the club at this time were trialists Kevin Grogan, a midfield player from Manchester United, Australian full-back Kevin Edds and Arsenal midfielder Michael Smith. Grogan was the only one who was taken on.

Transfers were also hampered by a change in the rules, which meant that clubs could not buy or sell players except before the end of August, and in January of the following year. This rule was appealed against and in practice it remained in force for Premiership clubs only.

The club had also introduced a silver shirt that they wore as an away strip when there was a colour clash, with the white shirt being used as a third strip. The pre-season tour that had been arranged in Scotland was cancelled, not because of money problems but for fear for violence as both Birmingham and Cardiff had arranged similar tours and one in Sweden took its place.

This tour and other pre-season matches that took place in England left a good impression on those who saw them and the coming season looked like being an extension of the previous one. But things have a habit of not going to plan and injuries were about to take their toll. Of course,

working round the clock   keeping your electricity switched on   our team's working r

The 2002/03 squad.

all clubs have players injured throughout a season but this was one that was like no other in living memory. However, in times of adversity strange things happen and this injury-strewn season threw up some young stars of the future.

The season opened on 10 August with a home game against Rotherham. The Lions were without the injured Reid. Sadlier, who had struggled with a hip problem for most of the previous season that caused him to miss the last four matches, was on the bench while Harris, although in the side, was still struggling to regain form after his illness. No matter, as Millwall were expected to win comfortably against the side most experts expected to struggle against relegation. There were many reasons put forward as to why Millwall did not perform that day but whatever the truth, losing the opening game of the season 0-6 in front of your own fans is not a good way to start and Rotherham's Darren Byfield, scorer of four of their goals, was awarded the player of the match trophy by Millwall supporters. 'To score four goals, get applauded off by the Millwall fans and then get voted their Man of the Match was a brilliant gesture,' said Byfield afterwards. Sadlier had not looked happy when he came on as a substitute and was subsequently missing from the team after that game until the beginning of March.

A little bit of tinkering with the side earned the first point of the season with a 0-0 draw at Watford, where Livermore was sent off and Ben May made his debut. Watching in the crowd was Andy Roberts, brought back to the club on a free transfer, who took his place in the team in the 0-1 defeat at Gillingham.

The first goal of the season came courtesy of Ben May who scored after just four minutes – his first goal in just his second start – in the game against Ipswich. Unfortunately Millwall could not add to his effort and the game ended in a 1-1 draw.

Paul Ifill, at Sheffield United, scored the second goal of the season, the 7,500th Millwall goal in all competitions, but it came in another defeat, this time 1-3. Even though the Lions did not play badly they just could not take their chances. The first win of the season came in the last game of the month, at home to Grimsby. Both goals came from Claridge and it looked like the Lions had finally started their season, even though they were twentieth in the table.

Waiting for that first win was like waiting for a bus, suddenly two came along together. This time it was a 1-0 win over Brighton, the goal coming from Darren Ward, his first for the club. Brighton's Pethick was sent off three minutes after Ward scored but the sad sight of Tim Cahill being taken off with a cruciate knee ligament injury that kept him out of the team until the end of the season hampered the side.

A 0-0 draw at Rushden & Diamonds in the Worthington Cup followed but the Lions went out of the competition on penalties. Hearn missed Millwall's first attempt and Rushden scored all of theirs.

So it was back to league action and the trip to Fratton Park, where leaders Portsmouth won 0-1. Loan signing from Southampton Kevin Davies made his debut in the match where the Lions could easily have come away with at least a point.

Sky Sports had taken up the mantle of showing live Nationwide League football, paying a fraction of what had previously been on offer from ITV Digital. They would never have believed that Burnley v. Millwall would have seen both teams languishing at the foot of the table when they decided to show it. It was, however, a boon for Lions fans as this was the first match that they had been banned from attending.

Goals from Livermore and a club first from Davies had given the Lions the lead but the match ended in a 2-2 draw. Maybe those missing fans could have helped Millwall to keep out the Burnley equaliser. It came in the eighty-fourth minute and it was another two valuable points dropped. It looked as if Millwall had turned the corner but they were beaten 0-3 at home by Walsall in their next match and all that hard work was undone. 'I'm at a loss to explain that performance,' said McGhee. 'We lacked energy, looked lethargic and didn't seem to have much of an idea at all about what to do. It was very disappointing.' Nobody who witnessed it would argue with his assessment.

McGhee's reaction was to try and find somebody to galvanise the side and that somebody arrived in the shape of Dennis Wise, who made his debut at Highfield Road. Wise was booked after just two minutes of his first game but he seemed to have an immediate effect as goals from Davies, Kinet and Harris clinched a 3-2 win after the Lions were behind at half-time.

Unfortunately the rejuvenation did not last long and Nottingham Forest stole a 1-2 win at The Den. Davies again scored for the Lions. Referee Andy Hall booked seven players, five from Millwall and sent off Matt Lawrence, while missing Forest's Johnson clearly handling the ball for his first goal.

With both clubs near the foot of the table the 1-1 home draw with Wimbledon perhaps came as no surprise. Skipper Stuart Nethercott's late equaliser, which cancelled out an own goal by himself, was a relief to the home fans who had little to cheer. The eighty-four Wimbledon supporters in attendance did not have much to cheer either in a scrappy game.

Struggling to find some consistency and the right formation for the side, McGhee also had to contend with the loss of Lawrence through suspension and, with no natural cover for him available, brought in promising youngster Glen Johnson on loan from West Ham. He went straight into the team in the match at Norwich where, although Claridge's goal levelled the match, the Lions lost 1-3.

Looking to shore up the defence, McGhee brought in youngster Mark Phillips in place of Ward and he looked as if he had been playing there for years. His assured play was only part of a fine 3-0 win against Derby. Wise opened the scoring with his first for the club and Harris, now slowly regaining his form, scored the other two. Even though Derby had goalkeeper Mart Poom sent off the result was never in doubt.

The mini revival continued with a 1-0 away win at struggling Sheffield Wednesday. Claridge's goal was enough to take the points, leading to Wednesday manager Terry Yorath resigning the following day.

Unfortunately the Lions lost the next match, away at Reading, 0-2 and they also lost Mark Phillips with a hamstring injury after just four minutes. It was Kevin Davies' last match for the Lions. His loan period was over and he returned home to Southampton. It was not to be the last time he would feature prominently in a Millwall game.

Tony Warner's great last-minute penalty save against Leicester City ensures a point for the Lions after having been 2-0 behind.

Preston were next to visit The Den and Ifill's twenty-five-yard screamer after nine minutes set up a 2-1 win. Wise was the other scorer, but in truth the Lions had an inordinate amount of luck as Preston hit the woodwork no fewer than four times. The Lions too had plenty of goal-scoring opportunities in a very open match. Darren Ward suffered a knee injury in this match and was replaced by another youngster, Paul Robinson, who took to his place like a duck to water.

There was much written about the visit of Leicester to The Den and most of it was about Dennis Wise, who had been receiving death threats. With none of their fans allowed into the game the Leicester players certainly tried to goad him at every opportunity. Thankfully he did not rise to the bait.

Leicester were certainly having the early laughs as they took a two-goal lead inside the first three minutes and looked as if they would run up a cricket score. Somehow the Lions defence held out but when Deane was booked for yet another rash tackle on Wise and then did exactly the same just thirty seconds later he was on his way to an early bath after just twelve minutes.

McGhee took a chance by taking off defender Robbie Ryan ten minutes later and replacing him with Steven Reid for his first game of the season after injury. He repaid that decision by scoring just five minutes after his introduction after a free-kick had been awarded for yet another foul on Wise, this time by Davidson, The culprit was then replaced before he had to follow his teammate down the tunnel.

The high-octane match moved up a notch in the second half and it was now Leicester's turn to withstand Millwall's constant attacks. When Wise scored the equaliser with less than ten minutes left he celebrated by taking off at high speed and blowing kisses to his former teammates. The stadium erupted but not as much as it did with just seconds of the match left. Lawrence and Benjamin contested a high ball in the Millwall area and the referee awarded a penalty. Wise went to speak to goalkeeper Warner. Whatever he said did the trick as Warner saved Izzet's spot kick. As they say, 'He who laughs last'.

Russian players had left a sour taste in the mouths of Millwall fans so when Sergei Baltacha started training with the club a few eyebrows were raised. He had a sporting pedigree though. As he had been brought up in Britain, held a British passport and had played for Scotland at

Under-21 level, perhaps that would make a difference. He could not sign for the Lions until the January transfer window opened, having played for Scottish side St Mirren who had paid up his contract. Everyone waited to see what would happen.

Next it was the Lions' turn to play away without fans. The game was beamed back to The Den from Stoke, who were beaten 1-0 when Reid scored after just two minutes with his first ever headed goal, in his first start of the season. But it was Warner's saves, and the woodwork twice, that earned the Lions the points.

Those at The Den were also able to witness the successful return of Joe Dolan to the side after having been out injured for twenty-one months. Alas his comeback only lasted until the seventy-ninth minute of the next game, at home to Bradford, when he was stretchered off with damaged knee ligaments and missed the rest of the season. Perhaps the key moments in the game came when Bradford had Wayne Jacobs sent off and Neil Harris was introduced, who scored with his chest in the 1-0 win.

King penalty saver Tony Warner was at it again when he saved Tommy Black's spot kick in the derby match at Crystal Palace, but he could do nothing about Granville's free-kick that won the match 0-1 in what was a flat Millwall performance. Mark Phillips had returned from injury to take his place in the team for this match, which was also the last one for Glen Johnson who was recalled by West Ham.

An ankle injury to Ben May, who had played a bit part for the Lions for most of the early part of the season, forced him out of the return match against Leicester. This game did not have the same excitement as the first, not for Millwall fans anyway, even though they saw their side take the lead after sixteen seconds through Claridge. It was watched back at The Den as Lions fans were again banned from attending. The match ended 1-4 to the Foxes and the Lions could have no cause for complaint about the result.

There were no away fans at the next game either but as it was played at The Den it was the turn of Wolves to be without supporters. It looked as if it would make no difference to their performance when they took the lead through Millwall old boy Mark Kennedy after just five minutes. A Roberts blast from the edge of the box just before half-time, his first since returning to the club, made sure the game ended with a point each. The Lions had played some of their best football of the season so far.

Kevin Grogan, who had not featured all season, except in two pre-season friendlies, because of a pelvic injury, had his contract cancelled after six months with the club.

Boxing Day brought Gillingham to The Den and there was no doubt that the pantomime season had started with referee Paul Rejer at centre stage. His poor refereeing had a lot to do with the end result. Mark Phillips had just gone off injured to be replaced by a fit-again Darren Ward when Gillingham took the lead. But just before the interval Robbie Ryan, having played 195 times without scoring, popped up to blast home from twenty-five inches.

The introduction of Neil Harris after the break brightened up a game that was noticeable only for the referee's decisions. When Harris put the Lions in front it was about to become no contest, except Mr Rejer had other ideas. When Rod Wallace fell to the floor after cleanly tackled by Nethercott Mr Rejer pointed to the spot. There had clearly been no contact though.

Try as they might Millwall could not score again. But it would not have remained 2-2 if the arm that pushed the ball away from crossing the Gillingham goal line had been spotted.

There was to be no humiliating defeat when the reverse match against Rotherham was played. A comfortable 3-1 win, with goals from Harris, Reid and Claridge, gave the Lions a winning end to the year. They had only managed to move up to fifteenth in the table but, having already used twenty-six different players and having seen seven of them out injured, some of them long term, it was, perhaps, only to be expected. But things were to get worse not better. The trip to Ipswich on New Year's Day was not a good one. The teams were level with just fifteen minutes left, Reid the scorer, and both sides had struggled with the wet, bumpy pitch. But three goals in eleven minutes put paid to any thoughts of a Millwall victory. Although Millwall did not deserve to be on the wrong end of a 1-4 scoreline that is what the statistics say.

The FA Cup brought little solace. Drawn away to Cambridge United, they were grateful for Claridge's equaliser that earned them a 1-1 draw and a replay at The Den. However, they lost Stuart Nethercott to injury after just five minutes, which brought to an end a run of 100 consecutive games in all competitions for him. He was out of the team for another twelve games and an injured Andy Roberts also missed the match and was not seen for another eleven games.

Neil Harris had gradually seen his form return. Although he had found scoring difficult by his own standards, his all-round play was certainly contributing to the team. So it was a blow when a training ground injury before the home game with Watford put him out for eight games.

The result of the match was never in doubt after Claridge had opened the scoring inside of ten minutes. Ryan, who now had the taste for scoring, added a second just before half-time on his 200th appearance for the club, which prompted calls from the crowd of 'shoot, shoot' every time he received the ball for the rest of the season. A goal from Ifill and a wonder goal from Sweeney, after he had replaced Reid, completed the 4-0 rout.

The FA Cup replay against Cambridge was everything a cup tie should be and was a great advertisement for the competition at a time when many were saying that its value had diminished. After a goal-less but interesting first half the Lions hit the woodwork twice before finding themselves behind to a Dave Kitson header, although there was more than a hit of a foul on Warner. Millwall levelled with a Claridge penalty after he was fouled but Cambridge went ahead again immediately. A first goal from Robinson equalled the scoring and Ifill finally gave the Lions the lead and a fourth round tie against Southampton. It was the first time Millwall had won an FA Cup match after being behind twice.

A trip to struggling Grimsby could have been a banana skin to a Millwall side who looked like they were starting to make something of the season despite their injury problems. But after Reid had hit the post, two goals from Claridge (the second a penalty after Reid had been fouled) made sure it was not. In fact, the 2-0 win could have been three but for an overhead kick from Claridge hitting the bar. Sergei Baltacha finally made his debut when he replaced Braniff as a makeshift striker.

A tactical move by McGhee, leaving out Braniff and bringing in Hearn in a five-man midfield, almost paid dividends at Southampton. After twenty-one minutes Claridge put the Lions in front and it stayed that way until the ninetieth minute. When Kevin Davies was sent on as a substitute with just twelve minutes left in the match every Millwall fan knew what was likely to happen and of course it did. When Warner brilliantly saved a shot from Tessem it fell kindly to Davies, who broke every Lion's heart. Of course, if offered a 1-1 draw before the match everyone would have been glad of it but after such a tremendous display it seemed that justice had once again deserted the south London side.

David Tuttle had suffered all season with an ankle injury and finally gave up the struggle, having his contract terminated by mutual consent. However he took on a scouting role for the club.

Pleased with the performance at St Mary's McGhee kept the same formation when the Lions took on high-flying Sheffield United at The Den. Sweeney made his first start in place of the suspended Reid. A splendid twenty-yard shot from Ifill was enough to secure a 1-0 win and move the Lions into tenth place in the table.

Were things now starting to look up? The arrival of Southampton for the FA Cup replay was the start of a dismal time for the Lions with just two wins and a draw coming in their next ten matches.

The first of these was the Southampton replay and once again McGhee kept the same formation and side, with the exception of Reid returning from suspension in place of Sweeney. Southampton took the lead through Oakley but when Reid equalised it looked like anything could happen, especially when play went into extra time.

The Lions though were looking tired and when Oakley scored again they began to look jaded. Baltacha, on for the injured Lawrence who, incidentally missed the next six matches, nearly snatched an equaliser in injury time but it was not to be. Losing 1-2 to a side that eventually became the losing finalists was no disgrace and showed that they could live with the Premiership teams. But it hit them hard both mentally and physically as the 1-2 defeat at Preston showed, with Kinet's late goal only a consolation. Baltacha made his first start for the club at Deepdale but it was to be his only full game as injury put an end to his season.

Youngster Alan Dunne now became the fourth player to fill the right-back berth for the home match with Reading. He looked comfortable there. Ronnie Bull made a rare start, replacing an ill Dennis Wise, while Kinet replaced the suspended Ifill for the only game he missed. In truth, Millwall were lucky to lose 0-2 as Reading and Luke Chadwick in particular were rampant.

Ifill was back to play against his home town club, Brighton, as was Harris, but there must have been something of the Reading hoodoo still hanging over the team. Not in the way they played though because, although they were not back to their best, they were better. It was because Tony Rougier, on loan from Reading, scored the only goal of the game after coming on as a substitute.

An historic event took place in the game when Moses Ashikodi, at 15 years and 240 days, became the youngest Millwall player by over a year to take part in a Football League match when he came on for a tiring Harris. Ashikodi may not be the youngest player of all time, however, as some early players' births were unknown.

Trying to find a formation that would work, McGhee made a number of changes for the home match against Portsmouth. Reid played at right-back, Wise was back in the centre of midfield and Kinet took over on the left of midfield with Dunne and Hearne dropping to the bench along with Matthew Rees who had been there for the last two games. Richard Sadlier made a welcome return for the last fifteen minutes.

It did not matter though as the eventual champions won 0-5 and the architect of their win, Paul Merson, received a standing ovation from the Millwall faithful. With the Portsmouth fans banned from the game it showed appreciation for his contribution to the game.

Burnley were next to visit The Den and the original ban on their fans had been lifted to allow a maximum of 500 to the game. Just over 200 of them took advantage of it. Sadlier came off the bench again to score a late equaliser in the 1-1 draw. Alan Dunne had returned to the right-back spot. Reid's strength in midfield had been sorely missed, but he fell awkwardly in a tackle and broke his wrist and his season was now over.

Sadlier made his first start of the season in the match at Walsall. Roberts, returning from injury, took over from Wise, who was still feeling the effects of a virus, in midfield. Reid was once again at right-back. Goals from Harris, looking more like his old self, and Ifill secured a 2-1 win but it was back to the drawing board after losing 0-2 at Wimbledon.

The Lions were not helped when Sadlier went off just before half-time, with his hip still causing problems that saw him miss the rest of the season. Harris, suffering from a stomach bug that had already claimed Reid, was also replaced at the start of the second half. Matt Lawrence had returned after his injury but hurt his ankle and it was another three games before he started a match again. Had a Claridge goal that was cancelled out for a debatable offside decision been allowed to stand and Neil Shipperley's goal been disallowed for a clear offside the result might have been different. But there is no denying that Millwall were poor on the day and the Dons deserved their victory.

A 0-2 defeat at home to Norwich followed but it was the visit of Sheffield Wednesday that provided the turning point for the season. Reid's midfield attacking ability had been sorely missed, so Roberts took over the right-back slot, the fifth player there this season, and Reid moved into midfield. The move was justified when he scored twice in four minutes just before the interval. When Ifill added a third just after the break it was all over. Still the victory had a touch of pain when Robinson injured his ankle and took no more part in the campaign. Fortunately Nethercott had recovered from his injury and took Robinson's place.

Transfer deadline day followed two days later and Ben May went on loan to Colchester, but the big news was the arrival of striker Mark McCammon, signed on a free until the end of the season, from Brentford. He joined fellow striker Daniel Severino, who also signed until the end of the season on a free from Italian club Piacenza. With the Derby match called off because of international call-ups it gave the team time to get to know their new teammates as well as some of the injuries to heal.

McCammon made his debut in the 1-0 win at Bradford. Harris' late goal was perhaps daylight robbery and the Lions had Warner to thank for keeping them in the game yet again. Unfortunately, the injury hoodoo struck again and Reid was stretchered off with knee ligament damage, his season now ended. Stoke came to The Den and left 3-1 losers and their banned fans were fortunate not to see their dismal performance in Millwall's fifth annual Anti-Racism Focus match.

Lawrence, recovered from his injury, took his place at right-back, allowing Roberts to move into midfield in place of the injured Reid. After making Harris' opening goal, Roberts scored the second from just outside the box and then set up Livermore to do the same for the third in his 150th Millwall League appearance.

The 2-1 win in the rearranged Derby game gave McCammon his first Millwall goal. It proved to be the winner after Kinkladze had equalised Harris' early opener. The Lions were good value for their win even if they did have some scary moments.

Millwall fans were banned from seeing their side lose 0-3 at Wolves and they missed the return of Tim Cahill. He played for ten minutes of the game. But the fans were pleased to see him make his first home appearance of the season in the next game, just after the start of the second half, and score the winner in the 3-2 win over Crystal Palace. Palace had taken the lead after twenty minutes but a Harris penalty and a McCammon header (he was given a two-year contract after the game) put the Lions in front at half-time but a bizarre Ryan own goal had levelled the match before Cahill's appearance changed things.

There were no Millwall fans at Nottingham Forest and they missed the debuts of two more youngsters, defender Tony Craig and midfielder Marvin Elliott, as well as Cahill's first start of the season. They also missed seeing the Lions come from behind twice when goals from Nethercott, Cahill and Harris secured a thrilling 3-3 draw.

Before the final game of the season, at home to Coventry, Kinet, Baltacha, Severino and Harpur were told they would not be kept for the following season. An early injury to McCammon did not stop a 2-0 win, which saw Tony Craig score his first for the club and Cahill his third in four appearances, proving how much he had been missed. The win took the Lions' finishing position to ninth. It was very creditable considering the injury problems they had faced throughout the season. Apart from the usual niggles they had Lawrence, Cahill, Nethercott, Dolan, Harris, Sadlier, Reid, Ward, Tuttle, Roberts, Sweeney, Dunne, Phillips, Hearne, Baltacha and Robinson all missing through injury for long periods.

Tony Warner, on the other hand, had completed 100 consecutive Football League appearances and was the first player to complete two full consecutive seasons in the Football League since Alf Wood did it in 1972-4.

Just what the next season would bring was anyone's guess as financial restraints bit; a pre-season trip had already been ruled out, with only local matches being arranged. The blooding of youngsters Ashikodi, Elliott, Sweeney, Dunne, Phillips, Hearne, Rees, May, Robinson and Craig meant the future looked promising. The Lions were ready to roar once more.

2002/03   Football League Division One

Date		Opposition	Score	Scorers
Aug	10	ROTHERHAM UNITED	0-6	
	13	Watford	0-0	
	17	Gillingham	0-1	
	24	IPSWICH TOWN	1-1	May
	27	Sheffield United	1-3	Ifill
	31	GRIMSBY TOWN	2-0	Claridge (2)
Sept	7	BRIGHTON & HOVE ALBION	1-0	Ward
	14	Portsmouth	0-1	
	17	Burnley	2-2	Livermore, Davies
	21	WALSALL	0-3	
	28	Coventry City	3-2	Davies, Kinet, Harris
Oct	5	NOTTINGHAM FOREST	1-2	Davies
	12	WIMBLEDON	1-1	Nethercott
	19	Norwich City	1-3	Claridge
	26	DERBY COUNTY	3-0	Harris (2) (1 pen), Wise
	30	Sheffield Wednesday	1-0	Claridge
Nov	2	Reading	0-2	
	9	PRESTON NORTH END	2-1	Ifill, Wise
	16	LEICESTER CITY	2-2	Reid, Wise
	23	Stoke City	1-0	Reid
	30	BRADFORD CITY	1-0	Harris
Dec	7	Crystal Palace	0-1	
	14	Leicester City	1-4	Claridge
	21	WOLVERHAMPTON WANDERERS	1-1	Roberts
	26	GILLINGHAM	2-2	Ryan, Harris
	28	Rotherham United	3-1	Harris, Reid, Claridge
Jan	1	Ipswich Town	1-4	Reid
	11	WATFORD	4-0	Claridge, Ryan, Ifill, Sweeney
	18	Grimsby Town	2-0	Claridge (2) (1 pen)
Feb	1	SHEFFIELD UNITED	1-0	Ifill
	8	Preston North End	1-2	Kinet
	15	READING	0-2	
	22	Brighton & Hove Albion	0-1	
Mar	1	PORTSMOUTH	0-5	
	4	BURNLEY	1-1	Sadlier
	8	Walsall	2-1	Harris, Ifill
	15	Wimbledon	0-2	
	18	NORWICH CITY	0-2	
	22	SHEFFIELD WEDNESDAY	3-1	Reid (2), Ifill
Apr	5	Bradford City	1-0	Harris
	12	STOKE CITY	3-1	Harris, Roberts, Livermore
	16	Derby County	2-1	Harris, McCammon
	19	Wolverhampton Wanderers	0-3	
	21	CRYSTAL PALACE	3-2	Harris (pen), McCammon, Cahill
	26	Nottingham Forest	3-3	Nethercott, Cahill, Harris
May	4	COVENTRY CITY	2-0	Craig, Cahill

League Cup

Round	Date	Opposition	Score	Scorers
1	Sept 10	Rushden & Diamonds	0-0*	
				*a.e.t Millwall lost on penalties

FA Cup

Round	Date	Opposition	Score	Scorers
3	Jan 4	Cambridge United	1-1	Claridge
3R	14	CAMBRIDGE UNITED	3-2	Claridge (pen), Robinson, Ifil
4	25	Southampton	1-1	Claridge
4R	Feb 5	SOUTHAMPTON	1-2	Reid

2002/03   Football League Division One

	P	W	D	L	F	A	Pts
Portsmouth	46	29	11	6	97	45	98
Leicester City	46	26	14	6	73	40	92
Sheffield United	46	23	11	12	72	52	80
Reading	46	25	4	17	61	46	79
Wolverhampton Wanderers	46	20	16	10	81	44	76
Nottingham Forest	46	20	14	12	82	50	74
Ipswich Town	46	19	13	14	80	64	70
Norwich City	46	19	12	15	60	49	69
MILLWALL	46	19	9	18	59	69	66
Wimbledon	46	18	11	17	76	73	65
Gillingham	46	16	14	16	56	65	62
Preston North End	46	16	13	17	68	70	61
Watford	46	17	9	20	54	70	60
Crystal Palace	46	14	17	15	59	52	59
Rotherham United	46	15	14	17	62	62	59
Burnley	46	15	10	21	65	89	55
Walsall	46	15	9	22	57	69	54
Derby County	46	15	7	24	55	74	52
Bradford City	46	14	10	22	51	73	52
Coventry City	46	12	14	20	46	62	50
Stoke City	46	12	14	20	45	69	50
Sheffield Wednesday	46	10	16	20	56	73	46
Brighton & Hove Albion	46	11	12	23	49	67	45
Grimsby Town	46	9	12	25	48	85	39

Choosing Wisely
2003/04

Having looked at the problems that had besieged the club the previous season on the pitch, in the stands and financially, all of which where inseparably linked, the club needed to revisit the plans put into operation and see if they could be retuned. All of them could be and were.

The membership scheme, which had no doubt played its part in forcing the hooligan element from the club – there had been a dramatic fall in arrests at The Den – had also, for a variety of other reasons, seen the attendance at matches fall. To combat this the need for membership was scrapped for all but four home games and the purchase of tickets for all away matches. The teamcard scheme was still used for these games and, with a view to rewarding loyalty for attendance, used to record the games that season ticket holders and members had seen. The away fans ban was also scrapped and the walkway, finally available for the first time in January and used for the Sunderland game after being tested in the match against Norwich in December, helped in bringing away fans to the ground without any outside interference. There were teething problems with the walkway but the patience of the fans, especially the home ones, while sorting them out, helped to make it a success.

To help the club's finances another share issue was made and because of the rebranding of 24seven, a new shirt sponsor, Rymans, was seen on the new shirts. These were to be blue with white sleeves and were reminiscent of the old Captain Morgan strip. They had been chosen by a fans' vote.

The injury problems that had plagued the club the previous year had highlighted the need to strengthen the squad but initially there were only players leaving. Apart from those mentioned at the end of the previous chapter, Steven Reid moved to Blackburn Rovers and Steve Claridge took over as manager of Weymouth.

There were also changes behind the scenes, with Joe McLaughlin and Steve Gritt leaving. Ray Harford died after losing a long fight against cancer. They were to be replaced by Archie Knox, who it was hoped would take the players to the level needed to reach the Premiership. The fans also said a fond goodbye to Millwall legend Keith 'Rhino' Stevens who, with his family, emigrated to Australia.

The squad strengthening needed seemed a long way off as the pre-season games, all against non-League opposition with the exception of Leyton Orient, Bristol City and Southampton, took place with only Arsenal's left-sided defender/midfield player, Juan, arriving, initially on a three-month loan. Those pre-season games boded well except that David Livermore injured himself and missed the start of the season; the jinx of last season had not yet gone away.

There was a lot of talk about the need for promotion this season and with fourteen players coming to the end of their contracts by the season's close, plus that of McGhee himself, it was perhaps a pressure that they could do without. Obviously some players and possibly the management were playing for new contracts, although McGhee was very open in saying that the decision would be his, taken purely on playing and not financial reasons.

The fixtures computer certainly did not do the club any favours, with two matches against relegated clubs, two against promoted clubs and five local derby games in the first twelve matches. The first of these was on 9 August against the runaway winners of the Second Division, Wigan Athletic. Anxious that the debacle that was the previous season's opening match was not repeated the Lions were understandably nervy at times but they comfortably won 2-0 with goals from Wise, tucking home the rebound from a Harris penalty, and Tim Cahill, carrying on from where he left off at the end of last season. Juan made his debut in this game to be replaced by another debutant, Noel Whelan, the striker having arrived from Middlesbrough on a free transfer in midweek. The only downside to the match was an injury to Paul Ifill that kept him out of the next three matches.

Whelan started the next match, a home Carling Cup game against Division Three Oxford United. A blatant penalty when Harris was pulled to the ground that was not given, a thunderbolt from Roberts, which hit the post, and a glaring miss from Juan, made it seem as if entry to the next round was just a formality. But Oxford scored with their only direct shot of the night and the Lions were out of the competition.

Off to Wearside and the game against Sunderland, with the added attraction of playing a side managed by Mick McCarthy. Whelan's early strike was enough to condemn the Black Cats to yet another defeat and a satisfied McGhee said, 'It was a fantastic result for us. I don't care about the results they've been having, this is a difficult place for anyone to come.'

Paul Ifill was the first of the fourteen to re-sign for the club and more players were coming to The Den. Flying French left-sided winger, Aboubacar Fofana, arrived from Juventus, although an Italian Bank Holiday and a training injury held up his debut, and the 6ft 5in Belgian striker Bob Peeters signed from Vitesse Arnhem and made his debut in the next match, at home to promoted Crewe Alexandra. The Lions never got into their stride, yet the few opportunities Crewe created never turned into goals until a schoolboy error by Warner – he rushed from his area to clear with two defenders better placed and smashed the ball into Darren Ward – allowed Dean Ashton to put the ball into an empty net from a narrow angle. With no sign of an equaliser, Juan replaced the tiring Peeters and McGhee gambled by taking off both full-backs and replacing them with Hearn and the welcome return of Richard Sadlier. Would this be third time lucky for the young Irishman, who had been plagued for the last eighteen months with a hip injury? He certainly livened up the attack for the last fifteen minutes and with just seconds left Whelan headed home Cahill's cross for his second goal for the club to earn them a 1-1 draw and their 2,500th home point in the Football League.

Still unbeaten, the Lions travelled to the Potteries to face table-topping Stoke. McGhee was trying to find the best way of getting something from the side, especially the forward line, and for this game he left out Lawrence and Ryan, moving Roberts to full-back, bringing in Tony Craig at full-back and Charlie Hearn in midfield and dropping Harris to the bench, starting with Peeters and Whelan as his first-choice strike force. This time Warner performed like the goalkeeper he had showed himself to be the previous season. His gutsy display helped the Lions earn a 0-0 draw.

Perhaps the biggest roar that Lions fans had was when the Stoke manager, Tony Pulis, was sent from the dugout although McGhee could easily have joined him. 'It was a bit of handbags with Tony,' said McGhee. 'I'll apologise to him and I'm sure he'll do the same.' Then with a smile on his face he added, 'It was only Tony who got sent off and I don't know why that was as we were both equally abusive. He must be better at it than me.' Again Sadlier put in a fifteen-minute appearance when he joined Harris who had also left the bench. Sadly it was to be his last appearance in a Millwall shirt.

Crystal Palace, who were now topping the table, were next at The Den. This time Harris started, with Peeters taking his place on the bench alongside a returning Dave Livermore. Making his debut for Millwall was full-back Kevin Muscat, who had signed from Glasgow Rangers the previous day. The Palace defence were run ragged by a returning Ifill and their goal lived a charmed life. Goalkeeper Cedric Berthelin will probably never play a better game in his life and when Tommy Black was sent off for his second bookable offence it looked like only a matter of time before the Lions took all three points.

However, after Ben Watson had put Palace in front from a free-kick the ten men continued to defend their lead well, although they still needed a fair amount of good fortune. McGhee eventually sent on Peeters, again forsaking a full-back, this time Tony Craig, and once more the gamble paid off as Peeters scored his first Millwall goal in added-on time to make the score 1-1.

Next came the away match at Gillingham but before the team left for Priestfield Ronnie Bull went on loan to Yeovil and Ben May to Brentford. There was also the news that Richard Sadlier had retired from the game because of his hip injury. Sadlier said, 'I was told eighteen months ago it was possible I wouldn't play again. At the time I refused to take that seriously. I was convinced I would.' McGhee added, 'This is desperate for Richard. He is the best young centre forward I've seen as a manager. He could've gone right to the top.'

Perhaps the way Sadlier felt was best summed up by room mate Robbie Ryan, who said, 'Richard sent me a text message today. It said, "I've retired. Don't want to talk to anybody."' Then Ryan dedicated the Gillingham match to his friend, adding, 'These things always seem to happen to the nicest guys.' The twenty-four-year-old had appeared for Millwall in 103 League matches and scored 34 times in a six-year career.

Sadlier may have approved of the forward play at Priestfield but certainly not the defending of his former colleagues, who were wearing their new green and white striped shirts, also chosen by the fans, for the first time. The match again saw Harris on the bench and the long-awaited debut of Fofana, while Lawrence was back in defence for Muscat, who was away on international duty. Having taken the lead through Ifill on eleven minutes, better finishing would have seen them further ahead yet Millwall were to go in at the break 2-1 down. Bringing Harris and Fofana into the game just after the restart changed the pattern of the match yet again, when a brace from Peeters put the Lions in front. They would have stayed there but for some awful defending that allowed Gillingham to score twice in the last ten minutes to win the game.

'I don't want to change the way I play,' said a defiant Kevin Muscat before the first of five games against clubs whose name began with the letter W. After the game, away at Watford, many wished he would. Having gone behind early in the game, Millwall had levelled through Ifill and were looking comfortably in control of the match when on the stroke of half-time Muscat inexplicably stamped on Watford striker Danny Webber. It earned him a red card, gave away a penalty and cost the Lions the game. McGhee changed the shape of the side in the second half to try to combat the problem, bringing on Robinson for Craig, Harris for Fofana, and a returning Livermore for Roberts. It did not help as Watford won 3-1 with a goal in the dying seconds. Talking about the Muscat incident, skipper Dennis Wise said after the match, 'I asked him why he did it and he said he didn't know.' McGhee was furious. 'He's let me down badly,' he said, adding, 'Normally we'll stick up for each other but nobody seemed to want to stick up for him.'

The incident brought a severe reprimand from the club, who told Muscat that any further on-field event like it within the next twelve months would result in his immediate dismissal from the club. 'We have told Muscat such behaviour will not be tolerated by this football club,' said chief executive Ken Brown, who added, 'He has also been fined in excess of the contractual maximum of two weeks' wages.'

McGhee kept him in the side though when they faced Wimbledon at The Den. The game came after the announcement that the club had made losses of £4.7 million the previous season. However, such financial problems were now not uncommon throughout the Football League.

It might have taken a Harris penalty just before half-time, given for a rash challenge on Ifill by Wimbledon goalkeeper Steve Banks, and a Whelan goal in injury time to seal the 2-0 win but the Lions played better, if only in patches. The win gave them a much-needed confidence boost for the coming home game against Walsall. There were more whistles blown by referee Phil Prosser in this match than in the whole collection of Thomas the Tank Engine and Ivor the Engine books put together. His fussiness saw a multitude of free-kicks retaken and nine players booked. Visitors Walsall also had a player sent off in the tunnel after the match, which the Lions won 2-1 through a Ward header and a Harris penalty. He did have to take it twice though, but secured the points. Wasteful finishing, a post and some stout defending stopped the game from being a rout but it was another three points on the board before the trip to Upton Park.

It may have been a way to psych up the players but before the game McGhee told them that only those good enough would be given new contracts. Brazilian wing-back Juan, who made only two starts for the Lions, returned to Arsenal, with his loan ending a month early.

The match started with the Lions roaring against their east London opponents. Ten years is a long time to wait for this fixture, and they should have been ahead but found themselves a goal behind at half-time. Millwall dominated the second half as McGhee changed the personnel and shape of the side. However, they only had Tim Cahill's goal to show for their hard work and but for some international-class saves from David James, including a fingertip save that put a shot from Ifill against the crossbar, they would have had all three points.

So both the players and the fans had to settle for just one point but it was worth the long queue for tickets and the seemingly eternal wait to be let out of the ground after the match. After all the hype only two fans were arrested and they were both West Ham supporters. Two days later the Lions came back down to earth at The Hawthorns. West Bromwich Albion were two goals to the good inside the first twenty-five minutes and although Stuart Nethercott gave the Lions a fighting chance with a goal just before half-time this time they could not turn their now-normal second-half dominance into goals. The Lions came to the end of September eighth in the table, with statistics reading: P11, W4, D4, L3, F15, A13, Pts16.

Only two things of note happened in the first half of the home game against Coventry. Sky Blues player/manager Gary McAllister hit a post when it was easier to score and Noel Whelan and Tim Cahill fought with each other. The second saw the Lions once again put on their second-half act. Ifill put the Lions in front but they were pegged back after referee Phil Joslin was impressed by Steve Staunton's falling-tree impression. He emphatically put away the resulting penalty himself. Cue Harris and Fofana being released from the bench. Harris duly cracked home the winner. The only downside was Cahill being sent off in injury time for his second yellow card.

Whelan publicly apologised for his spat with Cahill and said he was looking for a contract at the end of the season. Matt Lawrence, however, Player of the Year in 2001, was not getting one as McGhee told him he could leave the club if someone wanted him, as was 2003 Junior Lions Player of the Year Robbie Ryan, who had been replaced at left-back by Tony Craig. Paul Ifill, on the other hand, was looking forward to the rest of the season. 'It won't be long before we hand a thrashing to somebody,' he said confidently.

It would not be Rotherham, who played out a goal-less draw at Millmoor, a point earned by the monumental presence of Tony Warner, so could it be in the home match with Preston? McGhee again changed the shape and personnel of the side starting with a 3-5-2 format, changing to a 3-4-3 and ending 3-3-4 but it was all to no avail as Preston won a poor game 1-0. There were boos at half-time, more at the end and a few cries of 'McGhee out', but that did not faze him as he told a press conference immediately after the match, 'I will go home disappointed by the result, I will wake up disappointed with the result. But in between I will sleep. I gave players the chance to show what they can do. I feel let down by them.'

At eight o'clock the following morning both McGhee and Knox had 'left the club by mutual consent' and before the day was over Dennis Wise had been appointed as caretaker manager, with Ray Wilkins as his assistant, for the next four weeks. Their first match was at home to table topping Sheffield United and Wise brought back the 4-4-2 formation, along with Ryan at full-back and Roberts and Livermore in midfield. He dropped himself to the bench with Peeters and Harris up front, while appointing Muscat as captain.

The team were unrecognisable from the side that had taken the field in recent weeks and tore United apart, although it took a Harris penalty and a deflected Ifill shot to secure all three points in a 2-0 win. The only downside to the match was the sending off of Livermore for two yellow cards and a straight red for Wise, later rescinded on appeal, who came on to shore up

The 2003/04 squad.

the midfield. His presence on the pitch lasted just three minutes and twenty seconds but he had certainly done something for the spirit of the team while off it. 'I don't want the job permanently,' said Wise, but who could tell how he would feel after the trip to Burnley the following week?

Wise decided to keep the same side at Turf Moor, except for the enforced change of Sweeney for Fofana, who was on international duty, and, along with Harris, he caused the Burnley defence no end of trouble. An ankle injury to Harris in the twenty-sixth minute saw Whelan brought into the fray and he put the Lions in front ten minutes into the second half. Unfortunately Burnley equalised ten minutes later and the club shared the points, although a combination of poor finishing, the woodwork and some excellent goalkeeping by the bulky Burnley stopper, Brian Jensen, kept Millwall from the victory that their play deserved.

Before the next game came the cheering news that both Joe Dolan and Mark McCammon were starting on the road to recovery although it was tempered by Mark Phillips having surgery that would keep him out of contention for the rest of the season. Wise certainly was not getting his four-match caretaker tenure easy as the next visitors to The Den were Nottingham Forest. As well as the missing Harris, Paul Ifill was out with a training injury although Fofana was back from the Ivory Coast to take his place. Harris' replacement, Noel Whelan, was injured just before half-time, bringing Kevin Braniff into the match and three minutes later the twenty-year old scored his first league goal – the only goal of the game – having made his first-team debut three years earlier. Having seen the side take seven from a possible nine points Ray Wilkins let it be known that he had 'verbally applied' to become the new manager but there was still one match to go before the announcement on McGhee's replacement. It was away at Norwich.

Before the match Wise spoke about a meeting he was due to have with Paphitis the following Monday. 'If he were to offer the job to me I'd take it,' said Wise, but the match itself did not go the way he planned as the Lions found themselves three goals down by the half-hour mark and by the end had only Ward's scrambled last-gasp goal to show for their efforts. Not that the Lions played badly; it was just that Norwich took their opportunities well, with Darren Huckerby wrecking havoc against his old teammates. At the other end Millwall could not take the chances they created, although that was to be expected with only one recognised striker in the side. Apart from the 3-1 defeat, the game also saw Paul Robinson stretchered off with cruciate knee ligament damage, his season ended.

Losing the game did not do Wise any harm as he was offered the manager's job on a permanent basis with Wilkins as his assistant. On the same day they heard that Harris would be out far longer than at first thought. The new management pairing agreed to take their relative positions until the end of season 2005.

The first job Wise did, having taken the manager's job permanently, was to sort out the problem of players who would be out of contract at the end of the season. 'He has told me what his priorities are, so we will act accordingly,' said Paphitis, adding that a deal had been struck that would see all but one or two players offered new contracts. Although the players would be relieved to know that contracts were soon to be sorted out that was not the case for Stuart Nethercott, who was on the bench for the match at Reading. The man who had captained the side to play-off appearances in 2000 and 2002, the Auto Windscreen Shield final at Wembley in 1999 and the Division Two championship in 2001 was told that he could leave. He also reached 100 consecutive appearances before he was injured in January 2003.

For David Livermore it was a different story as he was given a contract until 2006. 'I am very pleased to have it sorted out,' he said, 'and now the other players are going to get new contracts too it has made it that much easier to make the decision to re-sign.' How many, and who, of the other players that would turn out to be we all needed to wait and see.

The match at Reading was won by the home side 0-1, although Salako's twenty-third minute goal owed more to the deflection it took off Muscat than the shot itself. Things could have been worse had Warner not saved Hughes' eighth-minute penalty. The Lions' lack of striking power – all four main strikers were now out injured – showed on the slippery surface as they created more than enough chances to win the match.

Using his wide circle of friends, Wise brought in Gianluca Vialli and Roberto Di Matteo to assist with coaching the squad when they could. But no amount of coaching would have changed the 0-0 scoreline in the match at home to Derby County. The matchday programme said about County goalkeeper Lee Grant, 'an outstanding prospect who has won rave reviews for his performances', and everyone present could see why as he single-handedly kept the Lions from scoring, although he needed the assistance of the crossbar on one occasion and an incredible goal-line clearance from Mawene on another. Meanwhile, Bob Peeters' return from injury lasted just five minutes.

Desperate to find a solution to his strike force injury problems Wise brought in Nick Chadwick on loan from Everton, and the twenty-one-year-old scored on his debut away at Bradford, putting the Lions two goals ahead after Cahill had opened the scoring. It looked all over at half-time but Bradford had other ideas and the game ended 3-2 in their favour. To add to their woes the Lions had seen Robbie Ryan injured after ten minutes and he would be out for another four weeks. Paul Ifill was also missing from the side with a hernia operation putting him on the sidelines until the end of the year.

It is not often that a 0-0 draw can be called exciting but the home game with Norwich certainly was. After an even first half it was almost one-way traffic in the second as the Lions took control of the game but once more found a goalkeeper, Robert Green, in excellent form. The game erupted in the last ten minutes when Kevin Muscat was controversially sent off for a second bookable offence and both Cahill and Chadwick saw yellow cards. The ten-man Lions fully deserved their point. It could easily have been all three.

Another week, another home game against a side from East Anglia, another 0-0 draw and another red card, although this time it was Ipswich's George Santos who took an early bath for two yellow cards. There was another injury, this time to Fofana, who was replaced by Wise, and the woodwork again stopped Millwall from taking the three points that their play deserved when Sweeney's shot hit the post. Young debutant Mark Quigley almost won the match in the closing seconds but his shot hit Ipswich defender Fabian Wilnis in the face and was scrambled clear. Before the match it was announced that another of the fourteen out-of-contract players, Mark Phillips, along with youngsters Marvin Elliott, Barry Cogan and Jason Rose, had all been given new contracts.

With the televised game against Cardiff came the news that Noel Whelan had had his contract cancelled by mutual consent – he had problems living away from his family – and that another of the original fourteen, Ronnie Bull, would not be given a new contract. Whelan went to sort out his future and ended up on loan at Derby County, Bull went to Brentford to try and sort out his. Nick Chadwick was however staying, at least for another month.

The match at Ninian Park saw a few surprises in the Millwall starting line-up. Harris was back from injury and lasted an hour. He was given the captaincy in place of the suspended Muscat for his 200th League appearance for the club. Wise also started for the first time since taking over as manager and Marvin Elliott started a game for the first time, winning the Man of the Match award in the process. Goals from Roberts, Cahill and Sweeney gave the Lions a comfortable 3-1 win and Trevor Robinson, another youngster, was given his debut a few minutes from the end. It came as no surprise that Wise kept the same side for the Boxing Day game at Selhurst Park. The fact that a few of the players were suffering from food poisoning might have gone some way to explain their performance.

The game had been fairly even when Harris put the Lions in front but, from then on, Crystal Palace dictated the game. Fortunately, Warner had not succumbed to the food poison problem and made a string of extraordinary saves, including one from Andy Johnson from the penalty spot. Along with the woodwork on three occasions, he ensured that the Millwall faithful left happy with the 1-0 win and hoping to see if the six-year Gillingham hoodoo could be broken at The Den two days later. The answer was no. Although Chadwick equalised Hessenthaler's deflected shot, a wonder goal from Kevin James, struck from twenty-five yards with just ten seconds left, sealed the Lions' fate once more. Just how the Gillingham goal survived a second-half onslaught is anyone's guess. It must be that gypsy curse. The year ended with Millwall tenth in the division:

	P	W	D	L	F	A	Pts
MILLWALL	26	9	9	8	29	26	36

It was an unusual start to a new year with no matches being played on New Year's Day so the first game of 2004 was at home to Walsall in the third round of the FA Cup. Stuart Nethercott went on loan to Wycombe Wanderers and the unfortunate Chadwick returned to Everton to have a hernia operation.

The match was won 2-1, with the Lions coming from behind to win with goals from Braniff and Cahill. Although Walsall had Leitao sent off for the second of a series of fouls against Wise that the referee saw fit to book him for, and Walker in the dying seconds for pushing Wise in the face, a trip to giant-killers Telford was easily secured. Before then were league matches against Wigan and Sunderland: the first at the JJB Stadium was a 0-0 draw, the second at The Den a completely different kettle of fish.

Lawrence and Dolan had both signed new contracts and Danny Dichio arrived on loan from West Bromwich Albion, making his debut against one of his old clubs. With the Lions behind on the half hour, Dichio headed home once in each half, the first goal also being the 400th competitive one scored at the new ground, to give the Lions a deserved 2-1 win. How referee George Cain allowed Wise and McAteer to remain on the pitch after their running battle throughout the game was a mystery. All this came on a day when the programme remembered former Lions' legend and manager J.R. (Reg) Smith, a player in the Millwall side that lost to Sunderland (2-1) in the FA Cup semi-final in 1937, who had died aged ninety-one. It was also Tony Warner's 99th consecutive game for the club, his 128th consecutive league match and sadly his last.

With the FA Cup game at Telford postponed due to a waterlogged pitch, there had not been a game completed there since 13 December. Crewe Alexandra became the next team to find themselves used as goal fodder for Dichio, who again scored a brace in the 2-1 away win. There were two debutants in the game as well; Andy Marshall, who was brought in on loan from Ipswich due to an injury to Warner, who was just one game short of 100 consecutive games, and striker John Sutton arrived from Raith Rovers for an undisclosed fee.

After another wasted trip to Telford's Bucks Head ground, it was back to The Den and a 1-1 draw with Stoke City. Dichio ended his one-month loan spell with his fifth goal in three matches. Sadly, West Brom refused to extend his loan period, wanting Millwall to pay £700,000 for his signature, and that for a player seventh in line for a place in their starting line-up. The Lions did sign Brazilian goalkeeper Adriano Basso from Atletico Paranaense on a non-contract basis.

Having refused Millwall's offer to play their cup match at The Den, Telford used forty tons of sand, tarpaulins and finally balloon covers lent to them by Wolverhampton Wanderers to get the match on, and the game ultimately took place on Wednesday 11 February. The pitch was declared fit although it was barely playable in parts. That did not stop the Lions, even though there were a few surprises in the squad. Willy Gueret started a match for the first time since 26 January 2002 (coincidently a fourth round FA Cup game), Mark McCammon found himself on the bench (his first outing since his injury against Coventry in the final game of the previous season) and the biggest surprise of all was Danny Dichio taking his place in the starting line-up as the 600th player the club had used in FA Cup matches.

Hard work behind the scenes by club chairman Theo Paphitis had secured a permanent move for the popular striker for what could reach a £675,000 when appearances and performances were taken into account, albeit for this game he was still at the club on loan. Although not scoring on this occasion he inspired a 2-0 win with the goals coming from Paul Ifill, the 450th FA Cup goal in the club's history, and Dennis Wise. Three days later Burnley were at The Den to play the fifth round tie and it was that man Dichio again with the only goal of the match in the sixty-ninth minute that earned the Lions a home tie against Tranmere Rovers in the quarter-finals. The Clarets had substitute Paul Weller sent off three minutes later but they already had goalkeeper Brian Jensen, and the woodwork, to thank for keeping the score down, although they nearly stole a draw right at the end.

A trip to Deepdale has never been easy but goals from Ifill and Cahill secured a well-earned 2-1 win against a Preston side that had only lost once at home all season and a

Jubilant celebrations as Millwall beat Tranmere Rovers 2-1 and reach the FA Cup semi-final.

Tim Cahill scores the winner over Sunderland in the FA Cup semi-final.

home win by the same score against Rotherham moved the Lions into sixth place. The scoreline does not tell the tale, however, as Millwall had been comfortably winning after Harris had given them the lead but a last-minute penalty looked to have given Rotherham a point they never deserved. However, the never-say-die spirit of this team had came to the fore and Cahill headed home the winner almost from the restart, securing the club's 5,000th League point.

Three more priceless points came from the 2-0 home win over Burnley, thanks to goals from Ifill and Sweeney, and Ifill was scoring again at Bramall Lane. It was his fifth consecutive goal against the Blades, although Sheffield United won the match 2-1 to push the Lions out of the play-off positions. It should have been easy to predict the winner as Dennis Wise had just won the Manager of the Month award. Who said it was not cursed?

The last time the Lions played at the quarter-final stage of the FA Cup was in season 1977/78 when they lost 6-1 to Ipswich. Although the 0-0 score against Tranmere was disappointing, Millwall had dominated the game from start to finish. More than a little luck and an outstanding performance from Tranmere's Dutch goalkeeper John Achterberg – he even saved a Muscat penalty – meant a replay at Prenton Park and the prospect of a semi-final at Old Trafford against Sunderland. The winner was assured European football the following season irrespective of the result in the final.

The day was not all gloomy though, as the play-off spot was regained courtesy of Norwich beating Ipswich, and it was the Tractor Boys who would provide the Lions' next league opponents. Winning at Portman Road in recent years had been more than difficult and when McCammon, making his first start of the season, was knocked unconscious on the half-hour mark it looked likely to stay that way. But his replacement, Neil Harris, had other ideas, scoring twice and making another for Darren Ward, enabling the Lions to run out comfortable 3-1 winners.

In the FA Cup replay Harris did it again, scoring a wonder goal to add to Tim Cahill's opener. Although Tranmere reduced the deficit before half-time the Lions defended well to win the game 2-1.

With West Ham coming to The Den the following Sunday the players were in buoyant mood, boosted by the return from Everton of Nick Chadwick, to complete his loan move after injury. The game itself had all the hallmarks of a media godsend, over 1,000 police on hand in case of trouble and talk of all sorts of things liable to happen.

It could easily have been the story of three penalties, Harris and Cahill missing two for Millwall and Harewood scoring for the Hammers. However, the Lions will never have had an easier win; the 4-1 scoreline was courtesy of Cahill (2), Chadwick and an own goal from Dailly. The behaviour of the Millwall fans once again caught the media attention but this time for all the right reasons as they refused to be drawn into trouble by goading West Ham fans and booed them when they ripped out the hoardings and seats and damaged two of the toilets in the North Stand after goalkeeper Stephen Bywater was sent off for a foul on Harris. The unbeaten run continued with a 1-0 away win over Wimbledon, Cahill scoring again, and with the news that Andy Marshall had signed until the end of the season they overcame some atrocious refereeing to draw 1-1 against Walsall at the Bescot Stadium.

The week was now set up nicely for the FA Cup semi-final. The future of the club was put into the hands of David Tuttle, who took over as chief scout and head of the youth academy after the retirement of Bob Pearson. With international friendly matches being played during the week, the build-up to the game was fraught with worry over injuries that key players might sustain. It had been sixty-seven years since the Lions' previous appearance in an FA Cup semi-final, where they lost 2-1 against Sunderland, and they were in no mood to lose to them at this stage again. When Cahill scored what turned out to be the only goal of the game in the twenty-sixth minute the fans went wild. Sunderland supporters may have outnumbered them but you would not have known it, so vociferous were they. The game was full of incident and the fingers of most Lions supporters were chewed to the bone by the end of the game.

First they saw a free-kick from Sunderland's John Oster hit the bar and Harris have a goal disallowed from a marginal offside decision before Cahill's goal. Then they watched as first Ifill and then Muscat were stretchered from the pitch and we were still only in the first half. Muscat's injury was initially perpetrated by Jason McAteer for which he was only booked, and then minutes after returning to the pitch after treatment had been completed, by George McCartney, who again was only booked. Muscat's season was now brought to a premature end.

Perhaps justice was done with poor Sunderland finishing, resolute Millwall defending and the sending off of McAteer, who was booked again for a foul on Harris when he had burst clear. The sight of Dennis Wise, who hobbled through the last twenty minutes having climbed off a stretcher after yet another cynical tackle, smiling, ecstatic players taking photographs of the fans at the final whistle and the thought of Theo Paphitis keeping his promise to streak naked through the streets of London, sent the fans home delirious. It was still hard to believe they would soon be taking a trip to the Millennium Stadium to play Manchester United in the FA Cup final.

They were brought down to earth with a bang the following Wednesday with a 0-0 home draw with Cardiff, where some poor refereeing throughout the game culminated with the sending off of semi-final hero Cahill for his second bookable offence with just fifteen seconds of the game remaining. There followed a 4-0 away defeat by Coventry three days later. Maybe three games in seven days were a bit too much but Ray Wilkins was not allowing that to be an excuse. 'Tiredness is an impossibility,' he said. 'These are fit young men who should be on the crest of a wave. I won't tolerate tiredness.'

Two days later high-flying West Bromwich Albion came to The Den and the 1-1 draw owed more to some diabolical refereeing decisions by Scott Mathieson than it did the football itself. Perhaps Mr Mathieson's worst decision came at the end of the game with the scores level, Dichio the scorer, and Albion down to ten men, Koumas being sent off in the first half. Dichio was fouled yet again, this time in the penalty area and this time it could not be ignored. Albion's Thomas Gaardsoe still had a handful of his shirt, so the referee pointed to the spot and while

Millwall fans outside Cardiff's Millennium Stadium.

the Millwall players were deciding who should take the spot kick sent Gaardsoe off. Protests followed, the referee decided to give a free-kick outside the box instead of a penalty, booked Albion players for not retreating ten yards, moved the ball forward six inches instead of the required ten yards and blew the final whistle as the free-kick came to nothing.

However Dichio was himself sent off in the following game away at Nottingham Forest and missed the cup final because of it. The game ended 2-2 with the goals coming from Livermore and Chadwick. Not having taken three points in any of the games since the cup semi-final, Millwall found themselves outside of the play-off places in seventh spot. Winning their game in hand was now crucial to the Lions' promotion ambitions and having gone a goal to the good at home to Watford, courtesy of Dichio, some more strange refereeing decisions and a lack of midfield commitment saw them lose the game 1-2, although Barry Cogan will remember the game as his first-team debut.

Reading came to The Den and went home with a 1-0 win although the woodwork stopped both Ifill and Sweeney from scoring. The promotion dream was effectively over. The fans, if not the players, were glad to see April come to an end. The Lions had not won a game since the semi-final and although the conspiracy theorists will point to some very poor refereeing, and they certainly had a point, the fear of missing out at the Millennium Stadium through either injury or suspension played a large part.

The 0-2 defeat by Derby at Pride Park – more strange refereeing decisions including a penalty that Andy Marshall saved – ended any faint promotion hopes and saw Nick Chadwick play his final part in Millwall's season. He returned to Everton, his loan period ended. Andy Roberts signed on for another season, but Robbie Ryan announced that he would be looking for another club. Moses Ashikodi also left, having been suspended by the club due to a training ground incident earlier in the season.

The final league match of the season ended with a 1-0 win at home to relegated Bradford City, Harris scoring from the penalty spot and equalling Sheringham's club record of 54 Football League goals at home. The match was memorable only for more poor refereeing decisions and the return of Joe Dolan to competitive football after eighteen months out injured when he replaced Matt Lawrence. Incidentally Bradford were the opponents when Dolan had initially injured his leg. It also saw the debut of Curtis Weston, soon to make football history, in what was the 5,000th game in all competitions in Millwall's existence. The League season ended with the Lions in tenth position:

	P	W	D	L	F	A	Pts
MILLWALL	46	18	15	13	55	48	69

But there was still the FA Cup final to play.

With 14,000 fewer fans than Manchester United at Cardiff, Millwall supporters were nonetheless going to enjoy the day. Although disappointed to lose 3-0 – Ronaldo netted just before half-time and van Nistelrooy scoring the other two (one an iffy penalty, the other a good yard offside) – they sang their hearts out and their throats dry supporting their team throughout this history-making match, which included Curtis Weston becoming the youngest ever player in the final at 17 years and 119 days when he replaced Wise. The Lions had two good penalty appeals turned down, both on Ifill, and Harris was given offside when clean through, although television replays showed him to have been onside. However it would be churlish not to say the better side won. Hopefully this young Millwall team enjoyed the experience and learned a lot from it.

For the record the teams were:

Manchester United: Tim Howard (Roy Carroll), Gary Neville, Wes Brown, Mikael Silvestre, John O'Shea, Darren Fletcher (Nicky Butt), Roy Keane, Christiano Ronaldo (Ole Gunnar Solskjaer), Ryan Giggs, Paul Scholes, Ruud van Nistelrooy. Subs not used: Eric Djemba-Djemba, Phil Neville.

Millwall: Andy Marshall, Marvin Elliott, Matt Lawrence, Darren Ward, Robbie Ryan (Barry Cogan), Paul Ifill, Dennis Wise (Curtis Weston), David Livermore, Peter Sweeney, Tim Cahill, Neil Harris (Mark McCammon). Subs not used: Willie Gueret, Alan Dunne.

'Compared to what I wanted to achieve when I took over I've failed,' said Wise, looking back on missing out on the play-off positions and possible promotion to the Premiership. The fans, in the main, felt differently about this historic season and now looked forward to playing in the UEFA Cup and having another tilt at promotion.

2003/04   Football League Division One

Date		Opposition	Score	Scorers
Aug	9	WIGAN ATHLETIC	2-0	Wise, Cahill
	16	Sunderland	1-0	Whelan
	23	CREWE ALEXANDRA	1-1	Whelan
	26	Stoke City	0-0	
	30	CRYSTAL PALACE	1-1	Peeters
Sept	6	Gillingham	3-4	Peeters (2), Ifill
	13	Watford	1-3	Ifill
	16	WIMBLEDON	2-0	Harris (pen), Whelan
	20	WALSALL	2-1	Ward, Harris (pen)
	28	West Ham United	1-1	Cahill
	30	West Bromwich Albion	1-2	Nethercott
Oct	4	COVENTRY CITY	2-1	Ifill, Harris
	11	Rotherham United	0-0	
	14	PRESTON NORTH END	0-1	
	18	SHEFFIELD UNITED	2-0	Harris (pen), Ifill
	25	Burnley	1-1	Whelan
Nov	1	NOTTINGHAM FOREST	1-0	Braniff
	8	Norwich City	1-3	Ward
	15	Reading	0-1	
	22	DERBY COUNTY	0-0	
	29	Bradford City	2-3	Cahill, Chadwick
Dec	6	NORWICH CITY	0-0	
	13	IPSWICH TOWN	0-0	
	20	Cardiff City	3-1	Roberts, Cahill, Sweeney
	26	Crystal Palace	1-0	Harris
	28	GILLINGHAM	1-2	Chadwick
	10	Wigan Athletic	0-0	
	17	SUNDERLAND	2-1	Dichio (2)
	31	Crewe Alexandra	2-1	Dichio (2)
Feb	7	STOKE CITY	1-1	Dichio
	21	Preston North End	2-1	Ifill, Cahill
	24	ROTHERHAM UNITED	2-1	Harris, Cahill
	28	BURNLEY	2-1	Ifill, Sweeney
Mar	2	Sheffield United	1-2	Ifill
	13	Ipswich Town	3-1	Harris (2), Ward
	21	WEST HAM UNITED	4-1	Cahill (2), Chadwick, Opp OG
	24	Wimbledon	1-0	Cahill
	27	Walsall	1-1	Ifill
Apr	7	CARDIFF CITY	0-0	
	10	Coventry City	0-4	
	12	WEST BROMWICH ALBION	1-1	Dichio
	17	Nottingham Forest	2-2	Livermore, Chadwick
	20	WATFORD	1-2	Dichio
	24	READING	0-1	
May	1	Derby County	0-2	
	9	BRADFORD CITY	1-0	Harris (pen)

League Cup

Round	Date	Opposition	Score	Scorers
1	Aug 12	OXFORD UNITED	0-1	

FA Cup

Round	Date	Opposition	Score	Scorers
3	Jan 3	WALSALL	2-1	Braniff, Cahill
4	Feb 11	Telford United	2-0	Ifill, Wise
5	Feb 14	BURNLEY	1-0	Dichio
6	Mar 7	TRANMERE ROVERS	0-0	
6R	Mar 16	Tranmere Rovers	2-1	Cahill, Harris
SF	Apr 4	Sunderland	1-0	Cahill
F	May 22	Manchester United	0-3	

2003/04   Football League Division One

	P	W	D	L	F	A	Pts
Norwich	46	28	10	8	79	39	94
West Bromwich Albion	46	25	11	10	64	42	86
Sunderland	46	22	13	11	62	45	79
West Ham United	46	19	17	10	67	45	74
Ipswich Town	46	21	10	15	84	72	73
Crystal Palace	46	21	10	15	72	61	73
Wigan Athletic	46	18	17	11	60	45	71
Sheffield United	46	20	11	15	65	56	71
Reading	46	20	10	16	55	57	70
MILLWALL	46	18	15	13	55	48	69
Stoke City	46	18	12	16	58	55	66
Coventry City	46	17	14	15	67	54	65
Cardiff City	46	17	14	15	68	58	65
Nottingham Forest	46	15	15	16	61	58	60
Preston North End	46	15	14	17	69	71	59
Watford	46	15	12	19	54	68	57
Rotherham United	46	13	15	18	53	61	54
Crewe Alexandra	46	14	11	21	57	66	53
Burnley	46	13	14	19	60	77	53
Derby County	46	13	13	20	53	67	52
Gillingham	46	14	9	23	48	67	51
Walsall	46	13	12	21	45	65	51
Bradford City	46	10	6	30	38	70	36
Wimbledon	46	8	5	33	42	89	29

Shot in the Foot
2004/05

The prospect of seeing Millwall playing in European football certainly sparked the imagination of the fans, with over 7,000 season tickets being sold before the start of the season. It was an unprecedented number and the Family Enclosure was sold out.

Strangely the size of the pitch had to be altered to accommodate European football; it was shrunk three metres in length. The club announced that its membership scheme would continue and that only members could buy tickets for European games.

There were other changes to be taken on board as well. New league sponsors were found to replace Nationwide and the division became known as the Coca-Cola Football League Championship, with Divisions One and Two becoming League One and League Two. There were a few new FA rules, perhaps the most significant being that players who were sent off or were banned under the cumulative yellow card rule would serve their suspension from the next game rather than waiting for two weeks under new FIFA directives. And the club also had a change in sponsorship when the name BEKO, an electrical goods manufacturer with outlets all over Europe, found its way onto the new blue shirts that were matched with blue shorts and socks for the home strip, replaced by an amber/gold shirt when colours clashed away from home.

Inevitably there were changes in personnel. Having told of his intention to leave the club, Robbie Ryan found new employment with Bristol Rovers and both goalkeepers left as well, Tony Warner to Cardiff and Willy Gueret to Swansea. All three players went on Bosman ruling moves, while Stuart Nethercott signed permanently for Wycombe Wanderers. John Sutton was loaned to Dundee for the season, Kevin Braniff went on a three-month loan to Rushton & Diamonds and Ben May on an initial two-month loan to Colchester United that was then extended to the end of November. Aboubacar Fofana returned to Juventus but the big, although inevitable, sale was Tim Cahill's £1.5 million move to Everton. It could have been worse; he nearly went to Crystal Palace. Andy Roberts was out all season due to the knee injury sustained the season before and the suspended Moses Ashikodi went to West Ham.

The big name coming into the side was midfield player Jody Morris, who was a free transfer from Leeds. Joining him were goalkeeper Graham Stack on a season's loan from Arsenal, striker Stefan Moore on a three-month loan from Aston Villa and Josh Simpson, a left-sided wing-back discovered on the club's pre-season tour of Canada. Andy Marshall signed a new two-year deal and Darren Ward an extension to his contract keeping him at the club until 2007. Wise though spoke of his frustration at not being able to bring in more players to boost his squad before the season started.

Listing the players he had pursued and failed to sign Wise said, 'It's been disappointing, because we've not got the experienced players in we need to push on as a team.' Then, speaking about himself and Ray Wilkins, he added, 'We'll give it our best shot and make sure the players do too – the fans can rest assured about that. But those fans have got to be patient.'

After a good pre-season the real thing started on 7 August with an away match against the previous season's Division Two champions, Plymouth Argyle. Moore, Morris, Simpson and Stack all made their debuts in the 0-0 draw, which was a game with few chances, high temperatures and where defenders were on top. Although Moore (twice) and Dichio could have won the match in the last ten minutes the result was about right, even if the early injury to Ifill curtailed Millwall somewhat. The fans looked forward to Tuesday evening and the visit of Wigan Athletic to The Den.

However, they were not happy when they left, taking all three points with them in a 2-0 win. The Lions looked toothless until a triple substitution of Wise, McCammon and Harris, for Elliott, Moore, and Simpson looked to provide more urgency in the team, although once more chances went begging. Suitably unimpressed, some fans started calling for Paphitis' head, demanding that money be spent on the side. His response was to say that money was available for the right player at the right time and that he would be relinquishing the position of chairman at the end of the season, although he wanted to stay on as a director and called on the fans not to panic.

As the only team in the Championship not to have scored a goal, prospects looked bleak with the arrival of most people's favourites for promotion, Leicester City. Wise made a few positional changes to the side, moving Elliott to right-back, switching the roles of Simpson and Livermore, keeping himself in the starting line up along with McCammon and giving a debut to a £5,000 buy from Toronto Lynx, Adrian Serioux, a midfield player also discovered on the club's pre-season tour.

A minute's silence was held before the start of the game as a mark of respect to Private Lee O'Callaghan, a supporter of the club, who had tragically been killed in Iraq, and for others such as Keith 'The Albatross' Pegg and Carl Prosser, both heavily involved in two of the club's fanzines who had also passed away during the summer break. The noise level soon rose though as Serioux demonstrated his midfield skills. These and his phenomenally long throw were both instrumental in the Lions' 2-0 win. Jody Morris opened the scoring, latching onto a fifty-yard throw from Serioux, and Dichio made it safe long before Makin was sent for an early bath after a foul on substitute Moore, who had raced clear of the Leicester defence. In fact the Foxes were lucky only to have had one player sent off in a very physical game. Commenting on Serioux's throw, Ray Wilkins said, 'We saw him throw it across the whole pitch when we were in Canada and he plays football in the right way... to win.' Replying to questions about his first game in England, Serioux said, 'It was a big difference to what I'm used to. I don't know how my throws are so long; it's just practice. Now I can throw further than some can kick.'

Along with fellow countryman Josh Simpson, he certainly travelled further that week – 12,000 miles to be exact – as they made the return trip to play for Canada in a World Cup qualifying match, but Wise started with the same side against Coventry at Highfield Road the following Saturday. The reward was a 1-0 win with a late Dichio goal and he did it again to secure victory at home over Reading the following Saturday. This time it needed some inspired goalkeeping by Stack to keep it that way after Mark McCammon had a goal ruled out for a dubious offside decision.

A break for some World Cup qualifying matches meant the Lions did not play again for two weeks, which allowed them to make a few adjustments to the squad. Joe Dolan and Tim Clancy both went on a one-month loan to Waltham & Hersham, with Dolan moving on to Crawley Town until January when the first loan finished and then on to Stockport County for another month, and finally on loan at Brighton until the season ended. Clancy had his contract cancelled at the same time and later joined Fisher Athletic. Meanwhile promising goalkeeper Terry Masterson went on loan with Weymouth. Bob Peeters, out of action since the previous December, needed an operation on a broken foot that would keep him out of action for most of the season. The break also allowed the fans to get used to the idea of playing Hungarian champions Ferencváros in the UEFA Cup and to get their ballot papers in if they wanted a chance to visit Hungary for the second leg.

There was also the news that Barry Hayles had signed from Sheffield United for £75,000 and he made his debut at Portman Road. It was short-lived however, as he left the field with broken ribs just on the hour mark. The Lions certainly looked to have done enough to take at least a point, even after having an obvious penalty appeal turned down, but two goals in the last six minutes, the first coming after Ward was pushed over by goalscorer Bent, gave Ipswich a win they could not have expected.

And so to Millwall's first ever match in European competition, and Wise sprang a surprise with his team selection by starting all three substitutes used in the Ipswich game, Moore, Harris and the returning Muscat, making his first start since the FA Cup semi-final. The 11,667 attendance was disappointing, as was the fact that only small satellite station, Bravo, were brave enough to transmit the game live. But none would be disappointed in the way the Lions played.

A disallowed goal denied Elliott his first for the club the day after his twentieth birthday when he had signed a new two-and-a-half-year deal. A turned down penalty appeal for a foul on Harris, some missed chances and some incredible saves from Szucs in the Ferencváros goal did not dampen anyone's spirits and it was Wise who scored Millwall's first European goal from a free-kick after Moore was cynically chopped down. Unfortunately Stack's first real job of the night was to pick the ball out of the net with just twelve minutes left. The late introduction of Ifill, back from injury, could not produce a winner and the players left the field without the victory their play deserved. The teams for Millwall's first every European match were:

Millwall: Stack, Muscat, Lawrence, Ward, Simpson, Wise, Elliott, Livermore, Morris (Cogan), Moore (Ifill), Harris (Dichio). Subs not used: Marshall, Sweeney, McCammon, Serioux.

Ferencváros: Szucs, Vukmir, Gyepes, Botis, Balog (Zavadsky), Kapic, Rosa, Tozser, Lipcsei, Vagner (Penska), Bajevski (Sowumni). Subs not used: Udvaracz, Kiss, Leandro, Zovath.

Wise changed the side again for the visit of Watford three days later and although they had another disallowed goal, this time from Dichio, to contend with, they never really got going, although some contentious refereeing contributed to that fact. Watford took the lead with a goal that looked more than suspiciously offside and after Dichio was sent off for his second caution of the game the result was never in doubt. Perhaps Watford's 2-0 win was a fair reflection of the game overall.

Lonestar Partners LP, an American company based in Texas, invested a reported £500,000 in the club, giving them a 10.9 per cent stake. Perhaps that helped encourage everyone in the next game at home to Derby County. An impeccably held one-minute silence marking the death of Brian Clough (once a manager at Derby), preceded the game but the Lions wasted no time when the match started when Wise put them in front after just two minutes. The start of the second half saw a goal twelve seconds faster than that in the first when Simpson put the Lions further ahead with his first goal for the club and, although Derby pulled one back almost immediately the game was well won before Derby's Vincent was sent off. Ifill wrapped up the 3-1 win in the dying seconds.

A 1-1 draw away at Rotherham, Ifill again the scorer, was not the best preparation for the return leg against Ferencváros, nor the news that Dichio needed a hernia operation or that McCammon had asked for a transfer. All this however was tempered by the arrival of Norwegian striker Jo Tessem on a one-month loan from Southampton.

The 1,200 fans who made the trip to Hungary enjoyed the sights of the city through the day and were looking forward to enjoying a result in the evening. However being 3-0 down to what initially appeared to be, and was later shown to be, two offside goals and another that had taken a wicked deflection did not dampen their spirits especially when Wise pulled a goal back just before half-time. It was virtual one-way traffic in the second half and although McCammon and Sweeney both hit the woodwork Millwall failed to turn things round.

It was after the match that news filtered through that four Millwall fans had been hospitalised, two with serious knife wounds, after being attacked in the street. Supporters of the club at the game had also been physically and verbally assaulted, although it must be noted that Millwall's fans were impeccably behaved throughout, and the players had been racially abused and spat at during the match. Millwall chairman Paphitis said after describing an attack where objects including food and coins had been thrown at him and other club officials, 'Even as a kid I cannot remember it being as bad as that. It was like going back into the dismal time of football

The banner says it all. The UEFA Cup tie in Hungary.

that we are all trying to forget. I'm proud of our fans.' Dennis Wise added, 'I don't mind a bit of tackling but spitting in someone's face is appalling.' A UEFA investigation into the match resulted in a £26,600 fine for the home club.

Jo Tessem was ineligible for the game in Hungary and made his debut in the home game against Nottingham Forest. David Livermore scored the only goal of the game, and the 1,000th goal of the season so far in Coca-Cola's £1 million goal chase, from a free-kick, in his 200th game for the club. Just how it stayed that way, especially after Alan Dunne had been sent off for his second bookable offence with fifteen minutes left, can only be put down to some woeful finishing by Forest and some spectacular goalkeeping from Graham Stack. The game was also notable for the return to first-team action for Mark Phillips after almost two years out with injury.

A two-week break due to World Cup qualifying games being played allowed the Lions to recuperate, especially with Dichio having undergone surgery for a problem with torn abdominal muscles and Serioux recovering from a dislocated shoulder.

Visiting the Stadium of Light is normally a daunting task yet this time the man with the easiest job for the whole of the afternoon was Graham Stack. It was ironic then that he should be the one to pick the ball from the net after Kevin Muscat had sliced the ball past him while attempting to clear it. How different it could have been if Sunderland goalkeeper Mart Poom had not decided this was to be a Man of the Match-winning performance, as Sunderland held onto a 1-0 win.

At least the return to action of Barry Hayles after injury as a late substitute gave the fans something to be cheerful about and he found the net for the first time in Millwall colours when he opened the scoring against Gillingham on his home debut. Alan Dunne also scored his first senior goal. However the match was not without incident as Andy Marshall replaced Graham Stack, who needed five stitches across his nose, and Matt Lawrence had four to close a cut right eye that meant constant changes of a blood-covered shirt. However the Lions held on to win 2-1 and break the Gillingham hoodoo that had lasted eleven games.

Meanwhile Tony Craig went on a three-month loan to Wycombe Wanderers.

Neil Harris had been finding goals hard to come by. He had not scored since the last game of the previous season, which had also been lacking goals by his standard. Playing out of position, a change of playing style and a lack of first-team starts had not helped his cause and he was not in the starting line-up when Millwall played their 1,700th League match, when Cardiff visited

The Den. Yet when he came on at the start of the second half with the Lions trailing by a goal to nil after dominating the first half he transformed the game.

Within seconds he had supplied the pass for Tessem's first Millwall goal and having seen Cardiff take the lead again after a terrible decision by referee Howard Webb, allowing Alan Lee to climb all over Stack before scoring, he levelled the match. In doing so he equalled Teddy Sheringham's League goalscoring record of 93 goals, in his 231st League match. 'I was so chuffed for him because he has been having a hard time recently,' commented Dennis Wise after the game. 'I asked him to play tucked in on the left and to roam and I was very pleased with his excellent performance.' Ray Wilkins added, 'He probably won't score a finer header in his career.'

Losing at home 3-0 to Liverpool in the Carling Cup did not really give an indication of how well the Lions played, and it took two late goals from the Golden Boot winner of Euro 2004, Czech international Milan Baros, to end Millwall's valiant attempt to beat them. Yet it was off the pitch activities that saw newspaper headlines. Whatever the reason, riot police were needed to quieten Liverpool fans who broke seventy seats and tried hard to get at the Millwall fans in the West Stand, who bafflingly were blamed for the trouble. Theo Paphitis later welcomed an FA probe into the violence that resulted.

Taking their new-found vigour to the Potteries, the Lions battered Stoke but only had Dunne's post-rattling shot to show for their efforts and some glaring misses and an obvious penalty turned down led to them losing 1-0 when Stoke scored with just five minutes left. So Wise changed the format when the team went to Loftus Road the following Tuesday, bringing in Mark Phillips and playing with three at the back and five in the middle.

Although playing well, the Lions fans found more enjoyment in singing songs to ex-Lion Marc Bircham than in what was happening on the pitch. The loss of Jody Morris through injury in the first half also changed the style slightly. The noise rose to an even higher level when Hayles put Millwall in front but again some glaring misses and the sending off of Adrian Serioux when he threw the ball at QPR winger Lee Cook, who had been jumping up and down in front of him when he was taking one of his long throws throughout the match, again changed the complexion of the game. Although the Lions should have been easy winners, they ended up with a 1-1 draw. After the game both Wise and Wilkins signed extended contracts for an additional year, although Wise's was a non-playing one, and Tessem extended his loan to 1 January 2005.

There was a firework display in Southwark Park and others were seen high in the sky the following Friday when television viewers were able to watch the Lions continue with their new rampaging style against Sunderland. There were certainly fireworks on the pitch with six bookings (two for Millwall) and goals from Wise (a penalty) and Livermore. It was, however, a more comprehensive result than the 2-0 scoreline suggests with Phillips hitting the post and Myhre making some useful saves in the Sunderland goal. As well as the win the fans were pleased to see the return from injury of Danny Dichio, when he came on as a late substitute. A fitting way to end the 300th game played at The New Den.

With Stefan Moore having returned to Aston Villa (his loan spell not being very successful) the number eleven shirt was filled swiftly as Wise moved into the transfer market, bringing in Scottish international striker Scott Dobie from West Bromwich Albion for £500,000 (rising to £750,000 if the Lions won promotion) from under the noses of Preston North End. As always with the vagaries of the Football League fixture computer he made his Millwall debut at Deepdale. Once more the Lions did more than enough to win, having been behind after fifteen minutes, but had to settle for a 1-1 draw, Hayles the scorer this time after Ifill, returning from injury as a late substitution, had hit the bar. However the fans were stunned to hear of the death of former Den favourite Keith Weller before the game, which muted their joy at a great comeback.

West Ham fans once again brought the wrong kind of publicity to The Den when they threw coins at Dennis Wise during the game but a goal from substitute Danny Dichio gave the Lions a 1-0 victory against the Hammers, who ended the match with ten men after Marlon Harewood received two yellow cards, his second for diving in the box. Just how Tomas Repka did not precede him after he pushed referee Peter Walton when he took umbrage to a decision given against him is anyone's guess but the end result was satisfactory. It gave Millwall their 4,000th Football League point, even though more chances went begging.

It was now catch-up time with the team about to play the two games in hand they had over the other sides in the division. In order to help the squad it was decided to stay in the North of the country for the Burnley and Crewe games. The match at Turf Moor saw the Lions lose 1-0 to a hotly disputed penalty and picking the ball from the net was the only thing Stack had to do all afternoon.

A goal down after just twelve seconds did not help the cause at Gresty Road and, although Millwall equalised through substitute Ifill, they lost again 1-2. With so many chances going begging in both games it prompted an unhappy Wise to say it was time to ring the changes adding, 'We are not finishing teams off.' The answer was to send four players, none of whom who had been involved in much of the season, out on loan. Ben May went to Brentford for three months, Kevin Braniff to Canvey Island, Charlie Hearn to Northampton, where he stayed for the rest of the season and, most surprisingly, Neil Harris to Cardiff.

However, worse followed. When Kevin Muscat was sent off with Sheffield United goalkeeper Paddy Kenny for a fight in the tunnel at half-time it looked odds on a Millwall win as Sheffield had no goalkeeper on the bench. The Blades put defender Jagielka between the sticks. When Mark Phillips scored his first goal for the club fourteen minutes after the restart it looked like the floodgates were about to open. However, inexplicably, Wise withdrew all his strikers and having been given the initiative, Sheffield went on to win the game 1-2. A trip to Wolverhampton did not look promising but a change of playing style brought a 2-1 victory with Dobie scoring his first goal for the club and Dichio the winner after another dubious penalty had given Wolves an equaliser.

With Jo Tessem returning to Southampton before the end of his loan period, Wise kept an unchanged side for the visit of Brighton to The Den and Mark McGhee's side, which included Steve Claridge, were beaten 2-0 with goals from Dobie, the 3,000th League home goal for the Lions, and Ifill. Marshall saved a penalty, but once more Millwall had failed to kill off their opponents. Brighton left and took Mark McCammon with them on loan for two months, after which he signed on a permanent basis.

There had been a furious reaction a few days before the game to a charge of racism, the first brought against any club, during the Carling Cup match against Liverpool. A report in the *Sun* newspaper after the game against Brighton, in which reporter Raymond Enisuoh claimed to have heard racist abuse and Nazi chants, added fuel to the fire. However letters from fans of both teams complaining about the inaccuracy of the article brought an investigation from the Press Complaints Commission. In fact the 'Sieg Heil' chants he reportedly heard were in fact chants of 'Seagulls' from the Brighton supporters.

It was a dream come true for Jody Morris when he equalised from the penalty spot late in the game the following Sunday afternoon at Elland Road. The Leeds fans had been taunting him all through the game and the 1-1 draw was about right on the balance of play. The shock came two days later. It was not the two-month loan of Paul Robinson to Torquay but the sale of Neil Harris to Nottingham Forest for an undisclosed fee. He had scored 98 times in 268 appearances for the club.

If pantomimes start on Boxing Day then there was certainly one at The Den when Millwall took on league leaders Ipswich. The first half was all one-way traffic, Millwall had not even found a way of getting the ball into the Ipswich penalty area and had seen both Ifill and Ward leave the pitch, both injured, when with two minutes of the half left, the ball, having bounced around the area for the first time, broke to Hayles, Ifill's replacement, who mishit home. Six minutes into the second half and the Ipswich defence ran away from a Livermore cross, leaving three Millwall players in acres of space and Dichio added a second.

The referee then decided to join in the fun and awarded a free-kick against Lawrence, Ward's replacement, for kicking fresh air and the ball eventually found its way into the net off of Kuqi's heel. The class act then came onstage and Dobie took a twenty-five-yard pass from Elliott, ran on and scored with ease. A classic 3-1 smash and grab win.

Pride Park two days later was no easier but a Hayles hat-trick, the first since Paul Ifill's in April 2001, gave the Lions a 3-0 win and took them back to sixth in the table as the year ended.

	P	W	D	L	F	A	Pts
MILLWALL	26	12	6	8	31	23	42

Yet if the old year ended well the new one started atrociously. After a minute's silence for the victims of the Indian Ocean tsunami, Millwall found themselves down to ten men when Dichio was sent off for the second time against Watford. Although both Dunn and Simpson hit the woodwork the Hornets won 1-0.

Basement club Rotherham were at The Den two days later and, although short of strikers, – Braniff was recalled from his loan at Canvey Island to answer the problem – Dunne's goal looked to be the first of a landslide. Yet somehow the team contrived to lose the game 1-2 and the infamous post-Christmas slide down the table looked to have started.

The third round of the FA Cup took the Lions to Molineux but a combination of injuries, illness and suspensions meant Wise had to field a weakened side, giving a first-team debut to Anton Robinson and having a bench with less than forty-five minutes' first team experience between all five of them. At two goals down within the first twelve minutes they did well to end up losing only 0-2.

Four defeats in a row would be unthinkable and, before the trip to Nottingham Forest, Dave Bassett, Wise's first boss at Wimbledon, was added to the coaching staff until the end of the season. The Lions were grateful that the ex-striker curse did not have a chance to strike. Neil Harris only played for the last three minutes of the game, and goals from Hayles and Dunne sealed a 2-1 win, although poor finishing from the home side certainly played its part in the Lions taking all three points.

The player analysis system, Prozone, was installed at The Den and it would find itself used to the full after the league match against Wolves. Finding themselves a goal down at half-time, the Lions drew level with a Wise penalty and, but for some fantastic goalkeeping from Michael Oakes, and the crossbar, which prevented Dunne from scoring, and more wasteful finishing, they would have been in front. Yet once again they managed to throw the points away in the final seconds, losing the game 1-2. The only plus was the return from injury of Paul Ifill for the last thirty-five minutes but even that came to nothing as he broke down again later in the week and was out of action for almost the rest of the season. Coupled with Graham Stack tearing a cartilage and Andy Marshall suffering from viral meningitis it was not a good week.

At least the players were able to get some rest with no game the following week due to their early FA Cup exit, so everyone was looking forward to a better display when Queens Park Rangers arrived at The Den. It did not happen. In fact the Lions were lucky to escape a very plausible penalty appeal in the last minute and some crucial saves from Marshall, now back in goal, helped them to a 0-0 draw in a game where Millwall did not have a single shot on target.

The midweek news that Jeff Burnige would take over as full-time chairman of the club at the end of the season, with both Reg Burr and Peter Meade standing down as directors, did not leave Dennis Wise a happy man. He constantly argued that he was now being stopped from bringing in the players he wanted, giving various reasons as to why. Burnige, however, was more than pleased to be taking over. 'Every Millwall fan will know how I'm feeling now,' he said after the announcement was made. 'I'm a very lucky man and I hope I can bring the club luck too. Millwall is my life and I hope the fans will see me as one of their own.'

He did not bring much luck to the team at Priestfield in a game that, in atrocious conditions, produced another scoreless draw, this time against relegation-contenders Gillingham. The players were booed from the pitch and a few chants for Wise to be removed as manager were heard. An early goal was enough to give Stoke all three points when they came to The Den and increased the fans' discontent, so the 1-0 win over Cardiff at Ninian Park courtesy of a Dichio penalty brought some relief. It came though with another shot in the foot; both Dunne and Livermore were sent off in the last minute along with Cardiff's James Collins.

Young striker Joe Healy joined Crawley on loan before the Stoke match but it was the transfer of Scott Dobie for £525,000 to Nottingham Forest before the game at the Withdean Stadium against Brighton that shook the fans. Ben May was recalled to the squad from his loan at Brentford and a boring game looked set for another goal-less draw until Brighton scored in the last minute, and then Phillips received his second yellow card. It was another foot-shooting exercise. It could have been worse had the referee taken stronger action over a bout of wrestling in the rain between McCammon and Elliott.

Two days later the death of ex-chairman Alan Thorne was announced and then came the announcement that the club was over £1.5 million in debt, an amount that would have been doubled but for the pre-season sale of Tim Cahill and was perhaps the reason for the sale of Dobie.

With Dunne (six games), Livermore (three games) and Phillips (one game) all suspended and a long injury list, options were getting limited for Wise. Paul Robinson was recalled from his loan at Torquay and he found himself playing and scoring in the 1-1 home game against Leeds. The Lions' play was vastly improved from that seen over the previous weeks and the match also saw the return of Bob Peeters, albeit for just two minutes, after his injury in December 2003.

Richard Sadlier left his position in the club's academy to return to Ireland and pursue other interests including work in the media, a decision not taken lightly. Andy Impey joined the club on loan from Nottingham Forest before Millwall made the trip to Championship leaders Wigan, and he made his debut coming on as a substitute. The Lions were beaten 0-2, although had a penalty claim for an obvious handball been given before Wigan took the lead through a penalty of their own, things might have been different. This result saw the Lions drop out of the top ten in the division.

Perhaps the behind-the-scenes problems were starting to affect the players as members of the management team started to argue among themselves, as did chairmen, past, present and future. Both groups also started to blame each other for the predicament the club found itself in.

However, things looked to have turned a corner when a Morris penalty put the Lions ahead against Coventry the following Tuesday night, only for the most bizarre goal ever seen at The Den, and possibly any other ground, to stop them in their tracks. With just two minutes to go until the end of the game, Coventry substitute Claus Jorgensen burst into the Millwall penalty area, barged over Tony Craig and both players fell to the floor. Everybody in the ground heard referee Clive Penton blow his whistle, the players stopped and Jorgensen, still lying on the floor, kicked the ball into the net.

Nobody bothered as he got up and ran towards the Coventry fans, presumably thinking he had won a penalty. Neither Millwall's fans nor the Millwall players were concerned as Mr Penton signalled a free-kick to Millwall, taking up a position on the edge of the box. Two Coventry players protested and then leapt upon their colleague as Mr Penton inexplicably awarded a goal. It was now the turn of the Millwall players to argue but the referee would not change his mind again and the match ended in a 1-1 draw.

Later, after looking at replays of the incident Mr Penton apologised, saying that he had made a mistake but then as if to extract himself from the position he found himself in, he declared that he should have awarded a penalty. Although his initial actions showed otherwise and whatever decision he should have made, the one he did make cost Millwall two points. Although an FA inquiry into what happened was promised, they eventually decided to take no action against the referee and anyway nothing would change the outcome of the game.

The Den was buzzing five days later when goals from Sweeney, Hayles and Dichio, the 400th Millwall league goal at the new stadium in their 2,500th home game in all competitions, gave the Lions an easy 3-0 win over Plymouth Argyle, Hayles' goal being the first scored by a striker in open play since he scored in the 2-1 defeat of Nottingham Forest in January, ten games

The 2004/05 squad.

previously. In truth it should have been a much bigger margin for although Plymouth looked good going forward defensively they were poor and Millwall again missed many chances.

World Cup qualifying matches meant a week's break during which some senior players joined in the arguments tearing at the club, and it showed in the half-hearted display some gave in the 1-3 defeat at Leicester, Dichio scoring to level the game. Again chances went begging but it looked like some of the older players in particular had already given up on the season. Dichio scored again at the Madejski Stadium, but Reading scored two late goals to win 1-2, keeping their play-off hopes alive, and virtually ended those of Millwall, who once again had thrown away the chance to win.

A 4-3 scoreline should tell the tale of a thrilling game. The home match against Crewe Alexandra was not. In fact it was rather boring until Hayles opened the scoring on twenty-five minutes. A Sweeney shot and a post hit by Crewe's Varney were the only other highlights of the first half. Yet three minutes after the break things changed. Marvin Elliott increased the lead with his first senior goal and a minute later Morris added a third. That should have been game over but when referee Andre Mariner, a replacement for appointed referee Paul Armstrong, pointed to the spot when Varney's theatrical fall was adjudged a foul, Lunt converted the spot kick. Five minutes later Jones added a second and with five minutes left Varney levelled the score.

It looked like there would only be one winner, especially with Millwall's end-of-game record, but when the referee again pointed to the spot, this time for a similarly dubious foul on Wise, playing as a substitute since his injury in February, Ben May, himself a late replacement for Dichio who had injured himself in the pre match warm-up, thumped home the winner.

The 1-1 draw away against West Ham, Hayles scoring, saw the return of Muscat and Ifill after long injuries and the 2,500 fans at the game, plus the 1,600 at The Den watching the live broadcast, enjoyed putting a dent into the Hammers' play-off hopes, and they put one into the aspirations of another play-off hopeful, Preston North End, who came to The Den a week later for a televised game. The 2-1 win came courtesy of goals from Sweeney, almost a carbon copy of that scored against Crewe, and Hayles. An injury to Andy Marshall, which knocked him unconscious for eight minutes and ended his season, put a damper on proceedings.

Then, perhaps to prove a point, they went to Sheffield United, still clinging to an outside chance of a play-off place, and won again. This time the 1-0 victory came through an early Morris goal. So dominant were the Lions that Stack's first save of note came in the final minute of the game.

The final game of the season, Burnley at home, was a 0-0 draw. The team took the opportunity to wear the new season's kit – all blue with white trim – that included the addition of shirt sponsors DAS AIR CARGO on the back as well as BEKO on the front, as the club took advantage of new sponsorship rules.

By coincidence the match was played on the sixtieth anniversary of VE (Victory in Europe) Day, 8 May. As people all over the country were remembering the heroics of many members of the armed forces, fans at The Den were saying their goodbyes; firstly to Theo Paphitis who was standing down as chairman after an eventful eight years, secondly to Kevin Muscat who was returning home to Australia to play for Melbourne Victoria, thirdly to Graham Stack, (who saved an early Burnley penalty), who was returning to Arsenal after his season-long loan and finally to Reg Burr, whose last game as a director of the club proved to be his last ever as he sadly died a few weeks later. It was also the final match for Dennis Wise, whose playing contract had come to an end and who after the game resigned as manager of the club. Two days later, after a meeting with Burnige, Ray Wilkins also decided to leave although promising to stay until a new manager had been appointed and to discuss the playing staff with him.

Maybe injuries and suspensions to key players at key times did not help. The Lions ended the season in tenth place:

	P	W	D	L	F	A	Pts
MILLWALL	46	18	12	16	51	45	66

A season that had promised so much ended with a groan and perhaps, looking back, too many late goals conceded had contributed to the team's downfall. A new beginning, with a new chairman and a new management team, beckoned and hopefully the Lions would start roaring again.

2004/05   **Football League Championship**

Date		Opposition	Score	Scorers
Aug	7	Plymouth Argyle	0-0	
	10	WIGAN ATHLETIC	0-2	
	14	LEICESTER CITY	2-0	Morris, Dichio
	21	Coventry City	1-0	Dichio
	28	READING	1-0	Dichio
Sept	12	Ipswich Town	0-2	
	19	WATFORD	0-2	
	22	DERBY COUNTY	3-1	Wise, Simpson, Ifill
	25	Rotherham United	1-1	Ifill
Oct	3	NOTTINGHAM FOREST	1-0	Livermore
	16	Sunderland	1-0	
	19	GILLINGHAM	2-1	Hayles, Dunne
	23	CARDIFF CITY	2-2	Tessem, Harris
	30	Stoke City	0-1	
Nov	2	Queen's Park Rangers	1-1	Hayles
	5	SUNDERLAND	2-0	Wise, Livermore
	13	Preston North End	1-1	Hayles
	21	WEST HAM UNITED	1-0	Dichio
	27	Burnley	0-1	
	30	Crewe Alexandra	1-2	Ifill
Dec	4	SHEFFIELD UNITED	1-2	Phillips
	7	Wolverhampton Wanderers	2-1	Dobie, Dichio
	11	BRIGHTON & HOVE ALBION	2-0	Dobie, Ifill
	19	Leeds United	1-1	Morris
	26	IPSWICH TOWN	3-1	Hayles, Dichio, Dobie
	28	Derby County	3-0	Hayles (3)
Jan	1	Watford	0-1	
	3	ROTHERHAM UNITED	1-2	Dunne
	15	Nottingham Forest	2-1	Hayles, Dunne
	22	WOLVERHAMPTON WANDERERS	1-2	Wise
Feb	5	QUEEN'S PARK RANGERS	0-0	
	12	Gillingham	0-0	
	19	STOKE CITY	0-1	
	22	Cardiff City	1-0	Dichio
	26	Brighton & Hove Albion	0-1	
Mar	6	LEEDS UNITED	1-1	Robinson P. M.
	12	Wigan Athletic	0-2	
	15	COVENTRY CITY	1-1	Morris
	20	PLYMOUTH ARGYLE	3-0	Sweeney, Hayles, Dichio
Apr	2	Leicester City	1-3	Dichio
	5	Reading	1-2	Dichio
	9	CREWE ALEXANDRA	4-3	Hayles, Elliott, Morris, May
	16	West Ham United	1-1	Hayles
	24	PRESTON NORTH END	2-1	Sweeney, Hayles
	30	Sheffield United	1-0	Morris
May	8	BURNLEY	0-0	

League Cup

Round	Date		Opposition	Score	Scorers
3	Oct	26	LIVERPOOL	0-3	

FA Cup

Round	Date		Opposition	Score	Scorers
3	Jan	8	Wolverhampton Wanderers	0-2	

UEFA Cup

Round	Date		Opposition	Score	Scorers
1/1	Sept	16	FERENCVÁROS	1-1	Wise
1/2	Sept	30	Ferencváros	1-3	Wise

2004/05   Football League Championship

	P	W	D	L	F	A	Pts
Sunderland	46	29	7	10	76	41	94
Wigan Athletic	46	25	12	9	79	35	87
Ipswich Town	46	24	13	9	85	56	85
Derby County	46	22	10	14	71	60	76
Preston North End	46	21	12	13	67	58	75
West Ham United	46	21	10	15	66	56	73
Reading	46	19	13	14	51	44	70
Sheffield United	46	18	13	15	57	56	67
Wolverhampton Wanderers	46	15	21	10	72	59	66
MILLWALL	46	18	12	16	51	45	66
Queen's Park Rangers	46	17	11	18	54	58	62
Stoke City	46	17	10	19	36	38	61
Burnley	46	15	15	16	38	39	60
Leeds United	46	14	18	14	49	52	60
Leicester City	46	12	21	13	49	46	57
Cardiff City	46	13	15	18	48	51	54
Plymouth Argyle	46	14	11	21	52	64	53
Watford	46	12	16	18	52	59	52
Coventry City	46	13	13	20	61	73	52
Brighton & Hove Albion	46	13	12	21	40	65	51
Crewe Alexandra	46	12	14	20	66	86	50
Gillingham	46	12	14	20	45	66	50
Nottingham Forest	46	9	17	20	42	66	44
Rotherham United	46	5	14	27	35	69	29

Milestones

Season 1987/88

Debuts
S. Anthrobus	away *v.* Plymouth	20 October
A. Cascarino	away *v.* Middlesbrough	15 August
R. Cooke	home *v.* Manchester City	12 December
G. Lawrence	away *v.* Middlesbrough	15 August
S. Sparham	away *v.* Middlesbrough	15 August
D. Thompson	away *v.* Barnsley	19 December
S. Wood	home *v.* Barnsley	22 August

Goals
A. Cascarino	Hat-trick	14 November *v.* Leeds United
E. Sheringham	Hat-trick	26 December *v.* West Bromwich
E. Sheringham	30 Football League	26 December *v.* West Bromwich Albion
E. Sheringham	30 All Competitions	28 November *v.* Hull City
A. Cascarino	6,500th club goal	14 November *v.* Leeds United
E. Sheringham	40 All Competitions	12 March *v.* Crystal Palace
E. Sheringham	40 Football League	7 May *v.* Blackburn Rovers

Appearances
A. McLeary	200 All Competitions	19 April *v.* Bournemouth
K. Stevens	200 All Competitions	15 August *v.* Middlesbrough
L. Briley	150 All Competitions	14 November *v.* Leeds United
A. McLeary	150 Football League	13 February *v.* Reading
E. Sheringham	100 Football League	27 February *v.* Swindon Town
N. Coleman	100 All Competitions	30 April *v.* Stoke City
E. Sheringham	100 All Competitions	10 November *v.* West Ham United

Season 1988/89

Debuts
I. Dawes	away *v.* Aston Villa	27 August
W. Reid	away *v.* Southampton	13 May
P. Stephenson	away *v.* Liverpool	12 November
D. Treacy	away *v.* Nottingham Forest	3 May

Goals

E. Sheringham	50 Football League	6 May *v.* Newcastle United
E. Sheringham	50 All Competitions	11 October *v.* Gillingham
A. Cascarino	30 Football League	19 November *v.* Newcastle United
E. Sheringham	60 All Competitions	6 May *v.* Newcastle United

Appearances

K. Stevens	250 All Competitions	5 November *v.* Luton Town
A. McLeary	200 Football League	13 May *v.* Southampton
K. Stevens	200 Football League	15 October *v.* Coventry City
L. Briley	200 All Competitions	26 December *v.* Wimbledon
L. Briley	150 Football League	27 August *v.* Aston Villa
E. Sheringham	150 All Competitions	17 December *v.* Sheffield Wed
B. Horne	100 Football League	25 February *v.* Coventry City
D. Salmon	100 All Competitions	1 April *v.* Sheffield Wednesday

Season 1989/90

Debuts

M. Allen	home *v.* Everton	21 March
K. Branagan	away *v.* Swindon Town	13 December
K. Cunningham	away *v.* Norwich City	17 March
P. Goddard	home *v.* Derby County	1 January
M. McCarthy	away *v.* Luton Town	24 March
S. Torpey	away *v.* Wimbledon	29 August
G. Waddock	away *v.* Stoke City	19 September

Goals

E. Sheringham	70 All Competitions	15 January *v.* Manchester City
E. Sheringham	60 Football League	17 March *v.* Norwich City
A. Cascarino	40 All Competitions	29 August *v.* Wimbledon
A. Cascarino	40 Football League	26 December *v.* Tottenham Hotspur

Appearances

K. Stevens	300 All Competitions	7 April *v.* Manchester United
A. McLeary	250 All Competitions	19 August *v.* Southampton
L. Briley	200 Football League	21 March *v.* Everton
E. Sheringham	200 All Competitions	31 March *v.* Crystal Palace
E. Sheringham	150 Football League	23 September *v.* Sheffield Wed
B. Horne	150 All Competitions	28 October *v.* Luton Town
A. Cascarino	100 Football League	20 January *v.* Wimbledon
T. Hurlock	100 Football League	31 March *v.* Crystal Palace
J. Carter	100 All Competitions	21 April *v.* Aston Villa

Season 1990/91

Debuts

A. Dowson	home v. Watford	15 December
M. Fillery	away v. West Bromwich Albion	23 March
J. Goodman	home v. Leicester City	26 December
P. Kerr	away v. Leicester City	30 March
J. McGinlay	away v. Hull City	16 April
J. McGlashan	away v. Charlton Athletic	22 September
A. Rae	away v. Watford	25 August

Goals

E. Sheringham	4 (plus 1 o.g.)	16 February v. Plymouth Argyle
E. Sheringham	Hat-trick	6 October v. West Bromwich Albion
E. Sheringham	Hat-trick	10 April v. Charlton Athletic
E. Sheringham	Hat-trick	27 April v. Bristol City
E. Sheringham	110 All Competitions	4 May v. Sheffield Wednesday
E. Sheringham	100 All Competitions	23 March v. West Bromwich Albion
E. Sheringham	90 Football League	27 April v. Bristol City
E. Sheringham	80 Football League	16 February v. Portsmouth
E. Sheringham	70 Football League	1 December v. Bristol Rovers

Appearances

K. Stevens	350 All Competitions	16 April v. Hull City
A. McLeary	300 All Competitions	20 October v. Notts County
A. McLeary	250 Football League	1 December v. Bristol Rovers
K. Stevens	250 Football League	15 September v. Ipswich Town
L. Briley	250 All Competitions	25 August v. Watford
E. Sheringham	250 All Competitions	23 March v. West Bromwich Albion
E. Sheringham	200 Football League	19 January v. Newcastle United
B. Horne	150 Football League	1 December v. Bristol Rovers
J. Carter	100 Football League	3 November v. Blackburn Rovers
I. Dawes	100 Football League	3 April v. Wolverhampton Wanderers
S. Wood	100 Football League	29 December v. Oldham Athletic
I. Dawes	100 All Competitions	19 December v. Norwich City
K. O'Callaghan	100 All Competitions	3 November v. Blackburn Rovers
S. Wood	100 All Competitions	22 September v. Charlton Athletic

Season 1991/92

Debuts

C. Armstrong	home v. Middlesbrough	17 August
P. Barber	home v. Middlesbrough	17 August
I. Bogie	home v. Middlesbrough	17 August
J. Colquhoun	home v. Middlesbrough	17 August
C. Cooper	home v. Middlesbrough	17 August
A. Davison	home v. Middlesbrough	17 August
M. Falco	home v. Middlesbrough	17 August
K. Keller	home v. Southend United	2 May
A. Roberts	away v. Cambridge United	4 April
E. Verveer	away v. Brighton & Hove Albion	21 December

Millwall FC Since 1987

Appearances

A. McLeary	350 All Competitions	16 November *v.* Wolverhampton Wanderers
A. McLeary	300 Football League	21 March *v.* Port Vale
K. Stevens	300 Football League	8 February *v.* Derby County
I. Dawes	150 All Competitions	1 January *v.* Swindon Town
P. Stephenson	100 All Competitions	1 February *v.* Ipswich Town
D. Thompson	100 All Competitions	1 February *v.* Ipswich Town

Season 1992/93

Debuts

J. Byrne	away *v.* Bristol Rovers	31 October
T. Dolby	home *v.* Charlton Athletic	2 September
T. Gaynor	away *v.* West Ham United	28 March
P. Holsgrove	home *v.* Swindon Town	5 September
M. Kennedy	home *v.* Charlton Athletic	24 April
J. Kerr	away *v.* Luton Town	24 March
P. Manning	away *v.* Portsmouth	29 September
A. May	away *v.* Watford	15 August
A. McCarthy	home *v.* Peterborough United	27 January
G. Maguire	away *v.* West Ham United	28 March
J. Moralee	away *v.* Portsmouth	29 September
R. Sion	away *v.* Portsmouth	29 September
D. Wallace	home *v.* Portsmouth	3 April

Goals

| A. Rae | 30 All Competitions | 17 January *v.* Brentford |

Appearances

K. Stevens	400 All Competitions	15 November *v.* West Ham United
I. Dawes	150 Football League	15 September *v.* Peterborough United
A. Rae	100 Football League	13 March *v.* Derby County
A. Rae	100 All Competitions	18 October *v.* Charlton Athletic

Season 1993/94

Debuts

C. Allen	away v. Watford	26 March
M. Beard	home v. Watford	2 October
G. Berry	away v. Watford	26 March
T. Carter	home v. Bolton Wanderers	15 January
C. Emberson	away v. Crystal Palace	14 September
N. Emblen	home v. Tranmere Rovers	20 November
R. Huxford	home v. Southend United	22 August
L. Luscombe	away v. Wolverhampton Wanderers	25 August
D. Mitchell	away v. Bolton Wanderers	16 October
B. Murray	away v. Stoke City	14 August
W. Patmore	home v. Notts County	20 October
B. Thatcher	away v. Leicester City	28 August
P. Van Den Hauwe	away v. Charlton Athletic	11 September

Goals

J. Goodman	Hat-trick (1st at New Den)	2 October v. Watford
A. Rae	Hat-trick	11 December v. Notts County
A. Rae	40 Football League	15 March v. Charlton Athletic
A. Rae	40 All Competitions	19 December v. Stoke City
A. Rae	30 Football League	20 October v. Notts County

Appearances

K. Stevens	450 All Competitions	27 December v. Portsmouth
K. Stevens	350 Football League	11 September v. Charlton Athletic
I. Dawes	200 Football League	2 March v. Southend United
A. Rae	150 All Competitions	15 January v. Bolton Wanderers
P. Barber	100 Football League	22 January v. West Bromwich Albion
K. Cunningham	100 Football League	20 November v. Tranmere Rovers
P. Barber	100 All Competitions	6 November v. Oxford United
K. Cunningham	100 All Competitions	21 September v. Watford
J. Goodman	100 All Competitions	31 October v. Birmingham City
K. Keller	100 All Competitions	30 April v. Bristol City
A. Roberts	100 All Competitions	30 March v. Luton Town

Millwall FC Since 1987

Season 1994/95

Debuts

J. Beckford	away v. Southend United	17 December
R. Cadette	home v. Stoke City	15 October
D. Chapman	away v. Bolton Wanderers	31 August
J. Conner	home v. Stoke City	15 October
K. Dixon	home v. Tranmere Rovers	25 March
A. Edwards	away v. Sheffield United	14 January
S. Forbes	home v. Bristol City	7 May
R. Joseph	away v. Luton Town	4 March
A. Kelly	away v. Grimsby Town	12 November
L. McRobert	away v. Barnsley	21 February
D. Oldfield	home v. Middlesbrough	26 February
D. Savage	home v. Southend United	13 August
S. Taylor	home v. Port Vale	5 April
J. Van Blerk	away v. Tranmere Rovers	17 September
D. Webber	home v. Barnsley	19 November
A. Witter	home v. Stoke City	15 October

Goals

J. Kerr	Hat-trick (first by a sub)	27 August v. Derby County
A. Rae	50 Football League	11 March v. Derby County
A. Rae	50 All Competitions	27 December v. Watford
J. Goodman	30 Football League	10 September v. West Bromwich Albion
J. Van Blerk	7,000th club goal	1 March v. Swindon Town

Appearances

K. Stevens	400 Football League	27 December v. Watford
I. Dawes	250 All Competitions	25 October v. Mansfield Town
A. Rae	200 All Competitions	18 January v. Arsenal
A. Rae	150 Football League	14 September v. Burnley
K. Cunningham	150 All Competitions	25 October v. Mansfield Town
K. Keller	150 All Competitions	5 April v. Port Vale
A. Roberts	150 All Competitions	15 March v. Portsmouth
J. Goodman	100 Football League	10 September v. West Bromwich Albion
K. Keller	100 Football League	1 October v. Middlesbrough
A. Roberts	100 Football League	10 September v. West Bromwich Albion

Season 1995/96

Debuts

M. Bennett	home *v.* Grimsby Town	12 August
K. Black	away *v.* Derby County	1 October
R. Bowry	away *v.* Port Vale	19 August
M. Doyle	home *v.* Grimsby Town	12 August
U. Fuchs	home *v.* Southend United	26 August
D. Gordon	away *v.* Leicester City	23 March
S. Iouran	home *v.* Port Vale	13 January
D. Keown	away *v.* Oxford United	16 January
V. Kulkov	home *v.* Port Vale	13 January
G. Lavin	away *v.* Stoke City	25 November
C. Malkin	home *v.* Grimsby Town	12 August
L. Neill	away *v.* Luton Town	17 February
R. Newman	away *v.* Port Vale	19 August
A. Rogan	away *v.* Port Vale	19 August
M. Weir	home *v.* Crystal Palace	30 March

Goals

R. Bowry	100th goal at New Den	24 February *v.* Norwich City
A. Rae	70 All Competitions	27 April *v.* Stoke City
A. Rae	60 Football League	23 March *v.* Leicester City
A. Rae	60 All Competitions	7 October *v.* Watford

Appearances

K. Stevens	500 All Competitions	19 August *v.* Port Vale
A. Rae	250 All Competitions	16 March *v.* Sheffield United
A. Rae	200 Football League	5 December *v.* Charlton Athletic
K. Keller	200 All Competitions	20 April *v.* Oldham Athletic
K. Keller	150 Football League	11 November *v.* Ipswich Town
B. Thatcher	100 All Competitions	6 April *v.* West Bromwich Albion

Season 1996/97

Debuts

S. Aris	away *v.* Hereford United	7 December
M. Bircham	home *v.* Preston North End	11 January
M. Bright	away *v.* Hereford United	7 December
D. Canoville	home *v.* Watford	22 March
S. Crawford	home *v.* Wrexham	17 August
J. Dair	home *v.* Wrexham	17 August
S. Fitzgerald	home *v.* Chesterfield	12 October
M. Harle	away *v.* Watford	24 August
P. Hartley	home *v.* Wrexham	17 August
D. Hockton	home *v.* Stockport County	2 October
D. Huckerby	home *v.* Bristol Rovers	7 September
A. Iga	home *v.* Peterborough United	26 December
G. Robertson	away *v.* Plymouth Argyle	5 October
S. Roche	home *v.* Preston North End	11 January
R. Sadlier	home *v.* Bristol City	1 February
D. Sinclair	home *v.* Wrexham	17 August
R. Wilkins	home *v.* Colchester United	7 January

Goals

D. Huckerby	100th League Goal at New Den	7 September *v.* Bristol Rovers

Appearances

K. Stevens	450 Football League	17 August *v.* Wrexham
D. Savage	100 All Competitions	11 January *v.* Preston North End
T. Witter	100 All Competitions	5 April *v.* Burnley

Season 1997/98

Debuts

P. Allen	home *v.* Brentford	9 August
M. Black	home *v.* Blackpool	4 October
K. Brown	home *v.* Brentford	9 August
T. Cahill	home *v.* AFC Bournemouth	2 May
A. Cook	away *v.* Brentford	10 January
M. Crossley	home *v.* Northampton Town	21 February
K. Grant	home *v.* Brentford	9 August
A. Gray	away *v.* York City	24 January
N. Harris	home *v.* Bristol Rovers	4 April
B. Law	home *v.* Brentford	9 August
S. Nethercott	away *v.* York City	24 January
D. Nurse	home *v.* Wimbledon	1 October
S. Reid	home *v.* AFC Bournemouth	2 May
R. Ryan	away *v.* Southend United	31 January
P. Shaw	away *v.* Wimbledon	16 September
N. Spink	away *v.* Northampton Town	27 September
P. Sturgess	home *v.* Brentford	9 August
G. Tomlinson	away *v.* Chesterfield	28 March
C. Veart	away *v.* Plymouth Argyle	13 December
P. Wilkinson	away *v.* Grimsby Town	20 September

Appearances

K. Stevens	550 All Competitions	28 December *v.* Luton Town
A. McLeary	400 All Competitions	11 October *v.* Oldham Athletic
R. Bowry	100 Football League	17 March *v.* Wrexham
R. Newman	100 Football League	28 December *v.* Luton Town
D. Savage	100 Football League	9 August *v.* Brentford
T. Witter	100 Football League	18 April *v.* Wycombe Wanderers
R. Bowry	100 All Competitions	17 January *v.* Wrexham
R. Newman	100 All Competitions	4 October *v.* Blackpool
D. Savage	150 All Competitions	13 April *v.* Plymouth Argyle

Season 1998/99

Debuts

B. Bubb	home *v.* Colchester United	14 April
R. Bull	home *v.* Colchester United	14 April
J. Dolan	home *v.* Gillingham	16 February
M. Hicks	home *v.* Colchester United	14 April
P. Ifill	away *v.* Lincoln City	13 February
J. McDougald	away *v.* Wigan Athletic	8 August
L. Odunsi	home *v.* Cardiff City	9 December
A. Roberts	home *v.* Macclesfield Town	29 August
B. Roberts	away *v.* Lincoln City	13 February
P. Smith	away *v.* Gillingham	29 December
J. Stuart	away *v.* Wigan Athletic	8 August

Appearances

R. Bowry	150 All Competitions	16 March v. Walsall
R. Newman	150 All Competitions	16 March v. Walsall
L. Neill	100 All Competitions	27 February v. Northampton Town

Season 1999/2000

Debuts

S. Dyche	away v. Luton Town	11 March
M. Gilkes	home v. Swansea City	24 August
C. Kinet	home v. AFC Bournemouth	19 February
M. Lawrence	away v. Wrexham	21 March
D. Livermore	away v. Cardiff City	7 August
P. Moody	away v. Cardiff City	7 August
D. Tuttle	home v. Bristol City	4 March
A. Warner	away v. Cardiff City	7 August

Goals

P. Moody	Hat-trick	16 November v. Reading
N. Harris	Hat-trick	15 April v. Brentford
N. Harris	40 Football League	6 May v. Oxford United
N. Harris	40 All Competitions	15 April v. Brentford
N. Harris	30 Goals Football League	8 January v. Wycombe Wanderers
N. Harris	30 Goals All Competitions	4 December v. Cardiff City
M. Gilkes	200th League Goal at New Den	22 January v. Stoke City

Appearances

R. Newman	150 Football League	29 January v. Chesterfield
L. Neill	100 Football League	25 September v. Colchester United
P. Shaw	100 Football League	4 March v. Bristol City
P. Shaw	100 All Competitions	9 November v. Oldham Athletic

Season 2000/01

Debuts

K. Braniff	away v. Brighton & Hove Albion	22 August
S. Claridge	home v. Stoke City	3 April
L. Constantine	away v. Peterborough United	30 September
T. Cottee	away v. Wycombe Wanderers	27 March
W. Gueret	home v. Northampton Town	5 December
S. Parkin	home v. Oxford United	23 September
T. Tyne	away v. Brighton & Hove Albion	22 August

Goals

N. Harris	Hat-trick	23 September v. Oxford United
N. Harris	Hat-trick	26 December v. Colchester United
N. Harris	Hat-trick	6 January v. Reading
P. Ifill	Hat-trick	17 April v. Cambridge United
C. Kinet	Hat-trick	5 December v. Northampton Town
P. Moody	Hat-trick	13 January v. Wigan Athletic
N. Harris	70 All Competitions	5 May v. Oldham Athletic
N. Harris	60 Football League	6 January v. Reading
N. Harris	60 All Competitions	26 December v. Colchester United
N. Harris	50 Football League	21 October v. Stoke City
N. Harris	50 All Competitions	23 September v. Oxford United
T. Cahill	30 All Competitions	28 April v. Wrexham

Appearances

L. Neill	150 All Competitions	17 October v. Bristol City
T. Cahill	100 Football League	11 November v. Wrexham
N. Harris	100 Football League	16 December v. Walsall
S. Nethercott	100 Football League	2 December v. Rotherham United
R. Ryan	100 Football League	26 December v. Colchester United
R. Sadlier	100 Football League	14 April v. Swindon Town
T. Cahill	100 All Competitions	9 September v. Swansea City
S. Fitzgerald	100 All Competitions	14 October v. Bury
N. Harris	100 All Competitions	16 September v. Brentford
P. Ifill	100 All Competitions	27 March v. Wycombe Wanderers
S. Nethercott	100 All Competitions	16 September v. Brentford
S. Reid	100 All Competitions	14 April v. Swindon Town
R. Ryan	100 All Competitions	24 October v. Swindon Town
R. Sadlier	100 All Competitions	26 December v. Colchester United

Season 2001/02

Debuts

D. Dublin	home v. Stockport County	30 March
A. Dunne	away v. Sheffield United	19 March
R. Green	home v. Nottingham Forest	20 October
C. Hearn	away v. Walsall	29 September
S. McPhail	home v. Sheffield Wednesday	16 March
R. Naylor	away v. Manchester City	30 January
M. Phillips	away v. Preston North End	15 September
G. Savarese	home v. Burnley	25 August
P. Stamp	away v. Crystal Palace	8 September
P. Sweeney	home v. Stockport County	30 March
D. Ward	away v. West Bromwich Albion	11 October

Goals

N. Harris	70 Football League	21 April v. Grimsby Town
T. Cahill	40 Football League	9 February v. Nottingham Forest
T. Cahill	40 All Competitions	29 December v. Crewe Alexandra
R. Sadlier	40 All Competitions	2 February v. Walsall
T. Cahill	30 Football League	18 September v. Barnsley
R. Sadlier	30 Football League	26 December v. Crystal Palace
R. Sadlier	30 All Competitions	3 November v. Coventry City
N. Harris	300th League Goal at New Den	2 February v. Walsall

Appearances

T. Cahill	150 Football League	1 January v. Watford
L. Neill	150 Football League	19 August v. Birmingham City
S. Nethercott	150 Football League	30 January v. Manchester City
R. Ryan	150 Football League	2 March v. Barnsley
T. Cahill	150 All Competitions	15 September v. Preston North End
N. Harris	150 All Competitions	1 January v. Watford
P. Ifill	150 All Competitions	21 April v. Grimsby Town
S. Nethercott	150 All Competitions	11 October v. West Bromwich Albion
R. Ryan	150 All Competitions	1 December v. Bradford City
R. Sadlier	150 All Competitions	30 January v. Manchester City
M. Bircham	100 Football League	30 January v. Manchester City
P. Ifill	100 Football League	15 September v. Preston North End
D. Livermore	100 Football League	20 January v. Norwich City
S. Reid	100 Football League	8 December v. Sheffield Wednesday
T. Warner	100 Football League	1 December v. Bradford City
M. Bircham	100 All Competitions	11 October v. West Bromwich Albion
D. Livermore	100 All Competitions	31 October v. Wolverhampton Wanderers
T. Warner	100 All Competitions	11 September v. Gillingham

Season 2002/03

Debuts

M. Ashikodi	away v. Brighton & Hove Albion	22 February
S. Baltacha	away v. Grimsby Town	18 January
T. Craig	away v. Nottingham Forest	26 April
K. Davies	away v. Portsmouth	14 September
M. Elliott	away v. Nottingham Forest	26 April
G. Johnson	away v. Norwich City	19 October
B. May	away v. Watford	13 August
M. McCammon	away v. Bradford City	5 April
P. Robinson	home v. Preston North End	9 November
D. Wise	away v. Coventry City	28 September

Goals

N. Harris	80 Football League	12 April v. Stoke City
N. Harris	80 All Competitions	26 December v. Gillingham
S. Claridge	30 All Competitions	14 January v. Cambridge United
P. Ifill	30 All Competitions	22 March v. Sheffield Wednesday
P. Ifill	7,500th Club Goal	27 August v. Sheffield United

Appearances

S. Nethercott	200 Football League	26 April v. Nottingham Forest
T. Cahill	200 All Competitions	21 April v. Crystal Palace
N. Harris	200 All Competitions	18 March v. Norwich City
P. Ifill	200 All Competitions	21 April v. Crystal Palace
S. Nethercott	200 All Competitions	21 September v. Walsall
R. Ryan	200 All Competitions	11 January v. Watford
N. Harris	150 Football League	7 September v. Brighton & Hove Albion
P. Ifill	150 Football League	30 October v. Sheffield Wednesday
D. Livermore	150 Football League	12 April v. Stoke City
T. Warner	150 Football League	21 December v. Wolverhampton Wanderers
D. Livermore	150 All Competitions	16 November v. Leicester City
S. Reid	150 All Competitions	26 December v. Gillingham
T. Warner	150 All Competitions	31 August v. Grimsby Town
M. Lawrence	100 Football League	26 December v. Gillingham
S. Claridge	100 All Competitions	26 April v. Nottingham Forest
M. Lawrence	100 All Competitions	17 August v. Gillingham

Season 2003/04

Debuts

N. Chadwick	away v. Bradford City	29 November
B. Cogan	home v. Watford	20 April
D. Dichio	home v. Sunderland	17 January
A. Fofana	away v. Gillingham	6 September
Juan	home v. Wigan Athletic	9 August
A. Marshall	away v. Crewe Alexandra	31 January
K. Muscat	home v. Crystal Palace	30 August
R. Peeters	home v. Crewe Alexandra	23 August
M. Quigley	home v. Ipswich Town	13 December
T. Robinson	away v. Cardiff City	20 December
J. Sutton	away v. Crewe Alexandra	31 January
C. Weston	home v. Bradford City	9 May
N. Whelan	home v. Wigan Athletic	9 August

Goals

N. Harris	90 Football League	13 March v. Ipswich Town
N. Harris	90 All Competitions	4 October v. Coventry City
T. Cahill	50 Football League	24 February v. Rotherham United
T. Cahill	50 All Competitions	20 December v. Cardiff City
P. Ifill	30 Football League	13 September v. Watford
P. Ifill	4,000th Club League Goal	4 October v. Coventry City
P. Ifill	450th Club FA Cup Goal	11 February v. Telford United
D. Dichio	400th Club Goal at New Den	17 January v. Sunderland

Appearances

T. Cahill	250 All Competitions	22 May v. Manchester United
N. Harris	250 All Competitions	20 April v. Watford
R. Ryan	250 All Competitions	12 April v. West Bromwich Albion
T. Cahill	200 Football League	26 December v. Crystal Palace
N. Harris	200 Football League	20 December v. Cardiff City
P. Ifill	200 Football League	21 February v. Preston North End
A. Roberts	200 Football League	24 March v. Wimbledon
R. Ryan	200 Football League	16 September v. Wimbledon
T. Warner	200 Football League	17 January v. Sunderland
D. Livermore	200 All Competitions	31 January v. Crewe Alexandra
A. Roberts	200 All Competitions	26 August v. Stoke City
T. Warner	200 All Competitions	26 August v. Stoke City
M. Lawrence	150 All Competitions	20 December v. Cardiff City
D. Ward	100 All Competitions	7 March v. Tranmere Rovers

Season 2004/05

Debuts

S. Dobie	away v. Preston North End	13 November
B. Hayles	away v. Ipswich Town	12 September
J. Healy	home v. Liverpool	26 October
A. Impey	away v. Wigan Athletic	12 March
S. Moore	away v. Plymouth Argyle	7 August
J. Morris	away v. Plymouth Argyle	7 August
A. Robinson	away v. Wolverhampton Wanderers	8 January
A. Serioux	home v. Leicester City	14 August
J. Simpson	away v. Plymouth Argyle	7 August
G. Stack	away v. Plymouth Argyle	7 August
J. Tessem	home v. Nottingham Forest	3 October

Goals

B Hayles	Hat-trick	28 December v. Derby County
P. Ifill	40 Football League	11 December v. Brighton & Hove Albion
P. Ifill	40 All Competitions	22 September v. Derby County
N. Harris	Equals Football League goals record of 93	22 October v. Cardiff City
N. Harris	Club record of 55 home League goals	22 October v. Cardiff City
N. Harris	Equals 98 All Competition goals of J. Calvey	22 October v. Cardiff City
D. Livermore	6,500th Football League club goal	5 November v. Sunderland
S. Dobie	3,000th Football League home goal	11 December v. Brighton & Hove Albio
D. Dichio	400th Football League goal at New Den	20 March v. Plymouth Argyle

Appearances

P. Ifill	250 All Competitions	21 November v. West Ham United
D. Livermore	250 All Competitions	1 January v. Watford
D. Livermore	200 Football League	2 October v. Nottingham Forest
M. Lawrence	200 All Competitions	27 November v. Burnley
M. Lawrence	150 Football League	7 August v. Plymouth Argyle
D. Ward	150 All Competitions	26 February v. Brighton & Hove Albion
D. Ward	100 Football League	7 August v. Plymouth Argyle

Internationals

The pinnacle of any player's career is to play for his country and there have been many who have worn the Millwall shirt and represented their country over the years. Listed below are the players who have done so during the period covered by this book and who have played for the Millwall first team. It lists the country they represented and at what level(s).

Of course they may have played for their country before arriving or after leaving Millwall or similarly represented them at a different level but these occurrences are not mentioned here and neither are those where a player has not made a Millwall first-team debut but won caps at junior levels.

Player	Country	Level(s)
M. Allen	Wales	Full and 'B'
M. Ashikodi	England	U-16 and U-17
M. Bircham	Canada	Full
K. Braniff	Northern Ireland	U-18, U-20, U-21
J. Byrne	Republic of Ireland	Full
T. Cahill	Australia	Full
A. Cascarino	Republic of Ireland	Full
B. Cogan	Republic of Ireland	U-21
K. Cunningham	Republic of Ireland	Full, 'B' and U-21
J. Dolan	Republic of Ireland	U-18 and U-21
M. Gilkes	Barbados	Full
C. Hearne	England	U-18
B. Horne	England	U-21
T. Hurlock	England	'B'
P. Ifill	Barbados	Full
K. Keller	United States of America	Full and U-23
M. Kennedy	Republic of Ireland	U-18 and -21
J. Kerr	United States of America	Full
M. McCarthy	Republic of Ireland	Full
A. McLeary	England '	B'
D. Mitchell	Australia	Full
D. Morgan	Wales	'B'
K. Muscat	Australia	Full
L. Neill	Australia	Full
M. Quigley	Republic of Ireland	Youth and U-21
A. Rae	Scotland	'B' and U-21
S. Reid	Republic of Ireland	Full and U-21
S. Roche	Republic of Ireland	U-18
A. Rogan	Republic of Ireland	Full
R. Ryan	Republic of Ireland	U-21
R. Sadlier	Republic of Ireland	Full, U-18, U-19, U-20, U-21
D. Savage	Republic of Ireland	Full and U-21

Player	Country	Level(s)
A. Serioux	Canada	Full
E. Sheringham	England	'B'
J. Simpson	Canada	Full
P. Sweeney	Scotland	U-18, U-19, U-20, U-21
B. Thatcher	England	U-18 and U-21
J. Van Blerk	Australia	Full
G. Waddock	Republic of Ireland	Full and 'B'

Jon Goodman, Paul Kerr, Andy Roberts and Ben Thatcher all represented the Football League against Italian Serie 'B' at various times.

The Management

During the period covered by this book there have been eight managers of the club, nine if you count the joint management of Stevens and McLeary as a separate management team. Here is a potted history of each of them and their record with the club. You, dear reader, can make up your own mind just how successful each one was.

John Docherty: June 1986-March 1990 and February 1997-May 1997

Docherty took over when George Graham left to join Arsenal in the summer of 1986. With little cash for players John started with two inexperienced youth-team graduates up front, Teddy Sheringham and Michael Marks. Although both reached double figures the club's tally of 39 league goals was the lowest since the war.

John Docherty.

By Millwall standards the directors let John go on a spending spree with the acquisitions of Terry Hurlock, Jimmy Carter, Tony Cascarino, George Lawrence, Kevin O'Callaghan and Steve Wood. Docherty brought in players who could play his way, getting the ball forward quickly, and focused around the hard-working, skilful midfield duo of Briley and Hurlock, the culmination of which was winning the Second Division championship on a memorable Bank Holiday Monday in Hull in 1988.

His team led the First Division early both the following season and the next, but lack of investment by the board of directors saw the Lions fail to stay in the top flight and Docherty left in spring 1990. He gave outstanding youth-team goalkeeper Brian Horne his debut as well as signing Ian Dawes and Paul Stephenson.

As a player Docherty, who was born in Glasgow, joined Brentford playing as a winger, moving to Sheffield United and then Reading, and he also had further spells with Brentford. He was also manager at Brentford, as well as Cambridge United and Bradford City.

Docherty returned to manage the Lions in February 1997, with the club now in administration, but he resigned prior to the last fixture in the May of that year because of ill health. His first game in charge was the 1-0 win at Reading in August 1986.

Bruce Rioch: April 1990-March 1992

Rioch came to The Den towards the end of the 1989/90 season, with Millwall's relegation from the First Division already confirmed, and he set about the task of rebuilding confidence in a demoralised team. Bringing in Mick McCarthy, who was already on loan from Lyon, and

Bruce Rioch.

selling fans' hero Terry Hurlock to Rangers, he also discovered two young Scots, Alex Rae and John McGlashan.

Rioch settled the side and they got off to a great start in 1990/91 with nine unbeaten games, but by the end of the season the Lions had slipped to fifth place and lost to Brighton in the play-off semi-final. Teddy Sheringham, the fans' goalscoring idol, was sold to Nottingham Forest at the end of Rioch's first full season in charge.

Rioch started his League playing career at Luton Town as a skilful, goal-scoring midfielder, joining Aston Villa in 1969. He then joined Derby in 1974 and later Everton, before returning to Derby. He finished his playing career as player-coach at Torquay. In his career Bruce won 24 Scottish caps, scoring 6 goals.

He became assistant manager and manager at Middlesbrough before moving to Millwall and, after leaving The Den in 1992, during a poor run of form, he managed Bolton, Arsenal, Norwich and Wigan.

Rioch made some other astute signings while at The Den: Jon Goodman from non-League Bromley, Paul Kerr, Colin Cooper and Chris Armstrong. His first game in charge was the 0-1 defeat at Villa Park, April 1990.

Mick McCarthy: March 1992-February 1996

McCarthy took over as caretaker player/manager in March 1992 before getting the job permanently in the April. He organised the midfield into a diamond formation, focused on the hard-working Andy May and Alex Rae, achieving some excellent results.

He introduced some of the youth-team stars, such as Andy Roberts, Tony Dolby, Mark Kennedy, Paul Manning, Ben Thatcher, Mark Beard, Danny Chapman and James Connor, to the first team. He guided the Lions to the play-offs in May 1994.

After months of speculation, which was unsettling for the team and fans, he was appointed manager of the Republic of Ireland, for whom he had won over 50 caps in his playing days.

McCarthy started his league career at his home-town club of Barnsley; he then joined Manchester City and then Celtic, where he won the double in 1988.

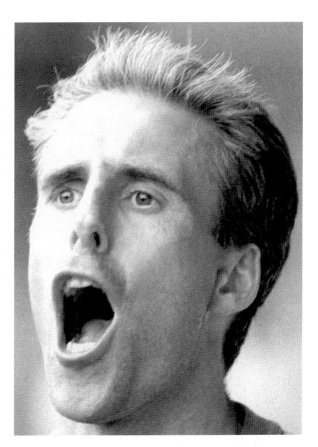

Mick McCarthy.

He then went to France and returned to England in March 1990 to link up with Millwall.

After guiding the national team to the World Cup Finals of 2002, he retired from the international scene but he was back in club management with Sunderland in the spring of 2003. His first game in charge of Millwall was a 1-0 win at home to Port Vale in March 1992.

Jimmy Nicholl: February 1996-February 1997

Nicholl joined Millwall from Raith Rovers following McCarthy's departure, but was unable to stave off relegation to Division Two in May 1996. He signed four Scots at the start of the 1996/97 season and two of them, Steve Crawford, who became top scorer, and Paul Hartley, quickly established themselves as crowd favourites at The Den.

Nicholl was settling into the job when the financial crisis caused by relegation forced the club into administration. The administrators immediately started cost-cutting measures and Nicholl was fired. He then played for Bath City before returning to Scotland to manage Raith Rovers again and then Dunfermline.

His footballing career started with the youth sides at Old Trafford, playing for Manchester United before joining Sunderland in 1982, West Bromwich Albion in 1984, Rangers in 1986 and Dunfermline in 1989 before turning to management with Raith Rovers. He was capped over 70 times in his long, distinguished international career with Northern Ireland.

While at Millwall, Nicholl gave debuts to outstanding young prospects Lucas Neill, Marc Bircham and Richard Sadlier. His first game in charge was a 0-2 defeat to Sheffield United in February 1996.

Jimmy Nicholl.

Billy Bonds: May 1997-May 1998

Bonds only had one season in charge as manager, leaving in May 1998 to concentrate on media work. After an illustrious career with Charlton Athletic and West Ham United, he became West Ham manager in 1990, then coached at Queens Park Rangers and Reading.

He brought in a number of experienced players and, although not hitting the high spots, he stabilised the club, which had just come out of administration. Later in the season he gave debuts to some of the young players who would soon form the backbone of the first team, including Robbie Ryan, Neil Harris, Tim Cahill and Steven Reid. His first game in charge was a 3-0 home win over Brentford in August 1997.

Billy Bonds.

Keith Stevens: May 1998-April 1999
Keith Stevens & Alan McLeary: April 1999-September 2000

Stevens became player-manager in May 1998 after an extremely successful playing career with the Lions, which had started as a sixteen-year-old in October 1981. He soon made the right-back position his own, later moving into the centre-back slot. A serious knee injury finished his long playing career, in which he had won a Second Division championship in 1988 and the Football League Trophy in 1983.

'Rhino' became the second Lion to pass the 500 appearances mark for the club and completed 557 games in all competitions, including appearances as a substitute. This makes him number two on the Lions' all-time appearances chart.

Outstanding youth team players introduced to the first team by 'Rhino' were Paul Ifill, Joe Dolan, Ronnie Bull, Tommy Tyne and Kevin Braniff. He managed as he played, instilling in his players the passion and the need to give over 100 per cent in every game.

His teammate and also former youth team player, Alan McLeary, was given equal status with him in 1999, helping him guide the Lions to Wembley in April 1999 for the Auto Windscreen Shield final where Millwall sadly lost to a very late Wigan goal.

'Macca' also played in the Football League Trophy final, scoring once in a 3-2 victory over Lincoln City. After winning a Second Division Championship medal in 1988 he earned 2 England 'B' international caps. He left the Lions in 1993, joining Charlton Athletic. He then moved to Bristol City before returning to The Den in 1997.

McLeary's appearances total in his two spells at The Den was 353, starting off in midfield and later moving to centre-back. He is now coaching successful youth sides with the Lions.

Both men were relieved of the manager's job by the chairman, Theo Paphitis, in September 2000. Together they had brought in Tony Warner, Dave Livermore, Paul Moody, Christophe Kinnet, Sean Dyche and Matt Lawrence to bolster a promotion challenge that ended with a play-off defeat in 2000 against Wigan. Stevens' first game in charge was a 1-0 win at Wigan in August 1998.

Keith Stevens and Alan McLeary.

Mark McGhee: September 2000-October 2003

When McGhee took over the Lions they had slipped down to mid-table but he soon galvanised the club into a championship-winning side. The title was gained with a 5-0 win over Oldham Athletic on the last day of his first season in charge and by the following May he had guided the Lions into a play-off place in Division One. Unfortunately the aftermath of the home leg coupled with the collapse of the ITV Digital sport channel meant there was no money for new players to cover the serious injuries to Joe Dolan, Tim Cahill, Richard Sadlier and illness to Neil Harris. It did mean that the prolific conveyor belt of young talent was stretched to the limit by further injuries.

Introduced by him to the first team were Mark Phillips, Charlie Hearn, Alan Dunne, Peter Sweeney, Ben May, Paul Robinson, Tony Craig, Marvin Elliott and Moses Ashikodi, who became the youngest player (15 years 241 days) to play in the Football League for the club when he came on as substitute against Brighton on 22 February 2003 (the youngest known player for the club is William Jones at 15 years 169 days).

McGhee started his footballing life as an apprentice at Bristol City but found success in his native Scotland with Aberdeen and Celtic, winning 4 Scottish caps. After his second spell with Newcastle United he became player-manager at Reading, then manager of Leicester City and Wolverhampton Wanderers. Then, after a couple of years in the media, he returned to football management with the Lions.

His best transfer deal was getting the evergreen Steve Claridge to sign on loan before the transfer deadline in March 2001 and then persuade him to sign a permanent deal, but he also bolstered the squad with the signings of Noel Whelan, Bob Peeters and Kevin Muscat as well as Dennis Wise but, although the 2003/04 season started with a 2-0 victory over Wigan Athletic and with the side in eighth place in the table after fifteen games, he was relieved of the manager's job. By the end of the season he was back in the same division, having guided Brighton to promotion via the play-offs. His first game in charge of the team was a 4-1 win at Peterborough in September 2000 and not, as generally supposed, the Worthington Cup defeat at Ipswich Town a few days earlier.

Mark McGhee.

Dennis Wise: October 2003-May 2005

Wise became player-manager in November after a short spell as caretaker, appointing Ray Wilkins as coach. The duo made an immediate impact on the league form with a 2-0 win over Sheffield United, although they lost his first match after taking the post permanently 1-0 away at Reading.

It was at the beginning of the new year that the Lions really started to roar again, as Wise's infectious enthusiasm spurred the side to Millwall's first ever FA Cup final, in which he had already played four times, winning three of them, and a brief excursion into Europe the following season, scoring twice.

Wise introduced five young players to the first team, four of them, Trevor Robinson, Mark Quigley, Barry Cogan and Curtis Weston from the youth side and John Sutton, bought from Raith Rovers. He also added the experience of Danny Dichio and Andy Marshall, Barry Hayles and Jody Morris.

Wise played for Wimbledon, Chelsea and Leicester City before joining the Lions as a player in the late summer of 2003.

Dennis Wise.

After Wise's tenure as Millwall manager ended he was succeeded briefly by Steve Claridge in the summer of 2005 before Colin Lee took the helm in July for the start of the 2005/06 season.

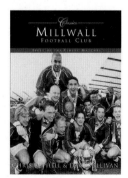

Millwall Football Club Fifty of the Finest Matches
CHRIS BETHELL & DAVE SULLIVAN

This collection of fifty classic matches has been chosen from the myriad of encounters that Millwall Football Club have taken part in. There are reports from the epic FA Cup run of 1900 and the defeat of East End rivals West Ham in 1912. More recently, this volume documents the Lions in the old First Division, along with their other championship and promotion successes. It is essential reading for any fan of the club.
0 7524 2705 9

If you are interested in purchasing other books published by Tempus, or in case you have difficulty finding any Tempus books in your local bookshop, you can also place orders directly through our website
www.tempus-publishing.com